W9-BWP-123

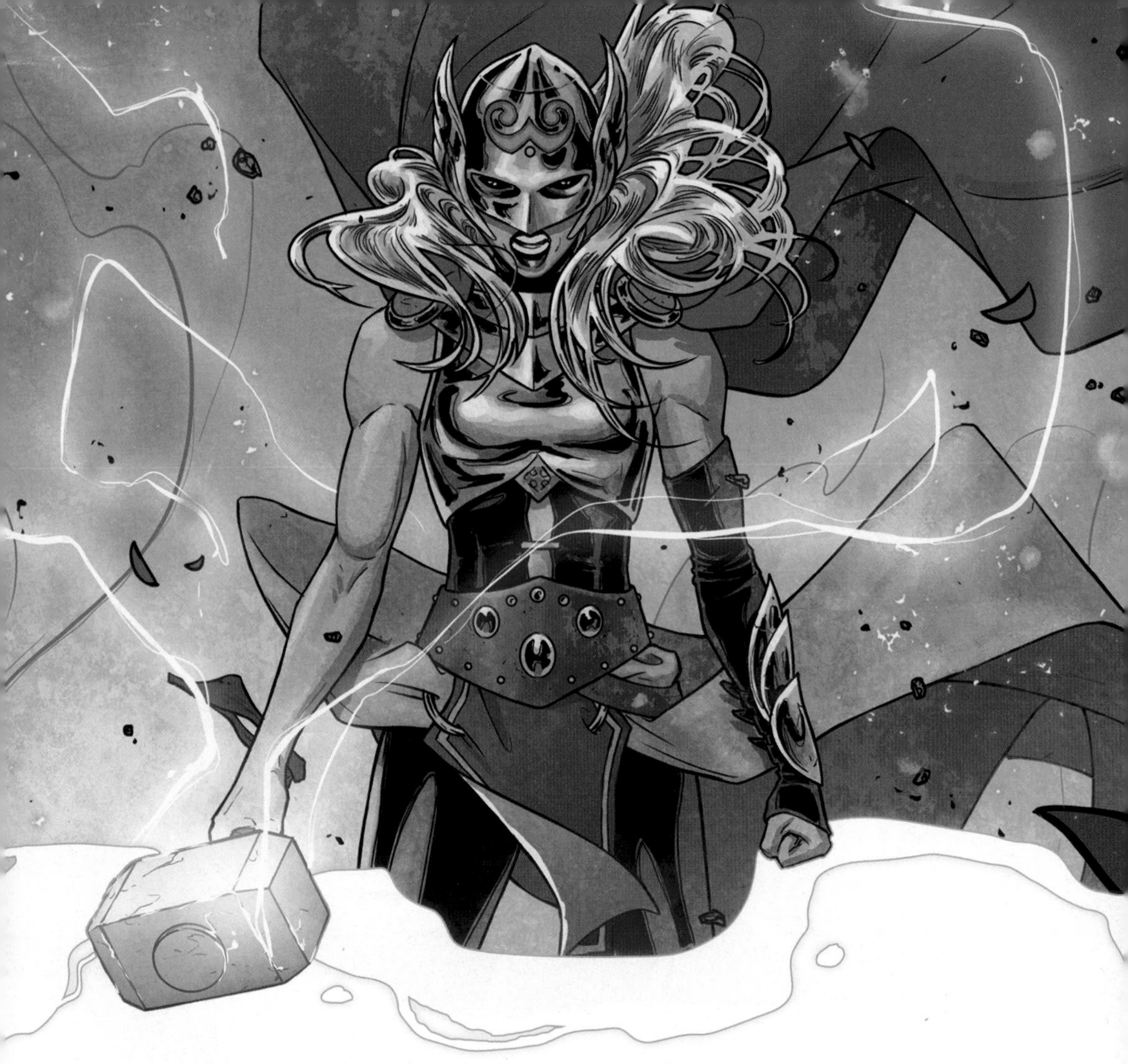

COLLECTION EDITOR: **JENNIFER GRÜNWALD**

ASSOCIATE EDITOR: **SARAH BRUNSTAD**

ASSOCIATE MANAGING EDITOR: **ALEX STARBUCK**

EDITOR, SPECIAL PROJECTS: **MARK D. BEAZLEY**

VP, PRODUCTION & SPECIAL PROJECTS: **JEFF YOUNGQUIST**

SVP PRINT, SALES & MARKETING: **DAVID GABRIEL**

BOOK DESIGNER: **ADAM DEL RE**

EDITOR IN CHIEF: **AXEL ALONSO**

CHIEF CREATIVE OFFICER: **JOE QUESADA**

PUBLISHER: **DAN BUCKLEY**

EXECUTIVE PRODUCER: **ALAN FINE**

THOR CREATED BY **STAN LEE, LARRY LIEBER** & **JACK KIRBY**

MIGHTY THOR VOL. 1: THUNDER IN HER VEINS. Contains material originally published in magazine form as MIGHTY THOR #1-5. First printing 2016. ISBN# 978-0-7851-9522-1. Published by MAR
WORLDWIDE, INC., a subsidiary of MARVEL ENTERTAINMENT, LLC. OFFICE OF PUBLICATION: 135 West 50th Street, New York, NY 10020. Copyright © 2016 MARVEL No similarity between any of
names, characters, persons, and/or institutions in this magazine with those of any living or dead person or institution is intended, and any such similarity which may exist is purely coincidental. **Prin
in the U.S.A.** ALAN FINE, President, Marvel Entertainment; DAN BUCKLEY, President, TV, Publishing & Brand Management; JOE QUESADA, Chief Creative Officer; TOM BREVOORT, SVP of Publish
DAVID BOGART, SVP of Business Affairs & Operations, Publishing & Partnership; C.B. CEBULSKI, VP of Brand Management & Development, Asia; DAVID GABRIEL, SVP of Sales & Marketing, Publish
JEFF YOUNGQUIST, VP of Production & Special Projects; DAN CARR, Executive Director of Publishing Technology; ALEX MORALES, Director of Publishing Operations; SUSAN CRESPI, Production Manag
STAN LEE, Chairman Emeritus. For information regarding advertising in Marvel Comics or on Marvel.com, please contact Vit DeBellis, Integrated Sales Manager, at vdebellis@marvel.com. For Ma
subscription inquiries, please call 888-511-5480. **Manufactured between 3/18/2016 and 5/2/2016 by R.R. DONNELLEY, INC., SALEM, VA, USA.**

10 9 8 7 6 5 4 3 2 1

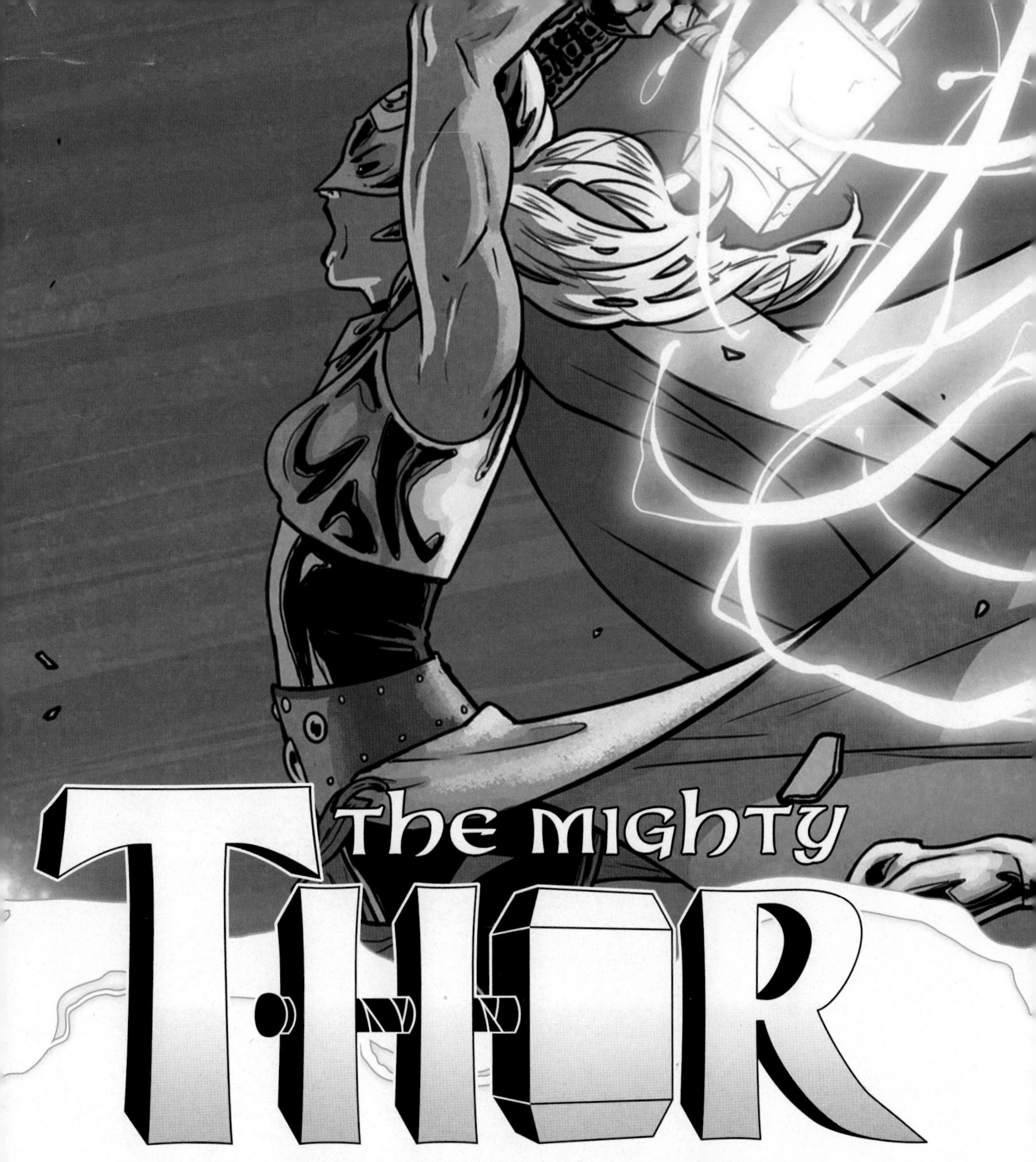
THE MIGHTY
THOR

THUNDER IN HER VEINS

WHEN **DR. JANE FOSTER** LIFTS THE MYSTIC HAMMER MJOLNIR, SHE IS TRANSFORMED INTO
THE GODDESS OF THUNDER, THE MIGHTY THOR!
HER ENEMIES ARE MANY, AS ASGARD DESCENDS FURTHER INTO CHAOS AND WAR THREATENS TO SPREAD THROUGHOUT THE TEN REALMS. YET HER GREATEST BATTLE WILL BE AGAINST A FAR MORE PERSONAL FOE: THE CANCER THAT IS KILLING HER MORTAL FORM…

WRITER
JASON AARON

ARTIST
RUSSELL DAUTERMAN

COLOR ARTIST
MATTHEW WILSON

LETTERER
VC'S JOE SABINO

COVER ART
RUSSELL DAUTERMAN & MATTHEW WILSON

ASSISTANT EDITOR
CHRIS ROBINSON

EDITOR
WIL MOSS

EXECUTIVE EDITOR
TOM BREVOORT

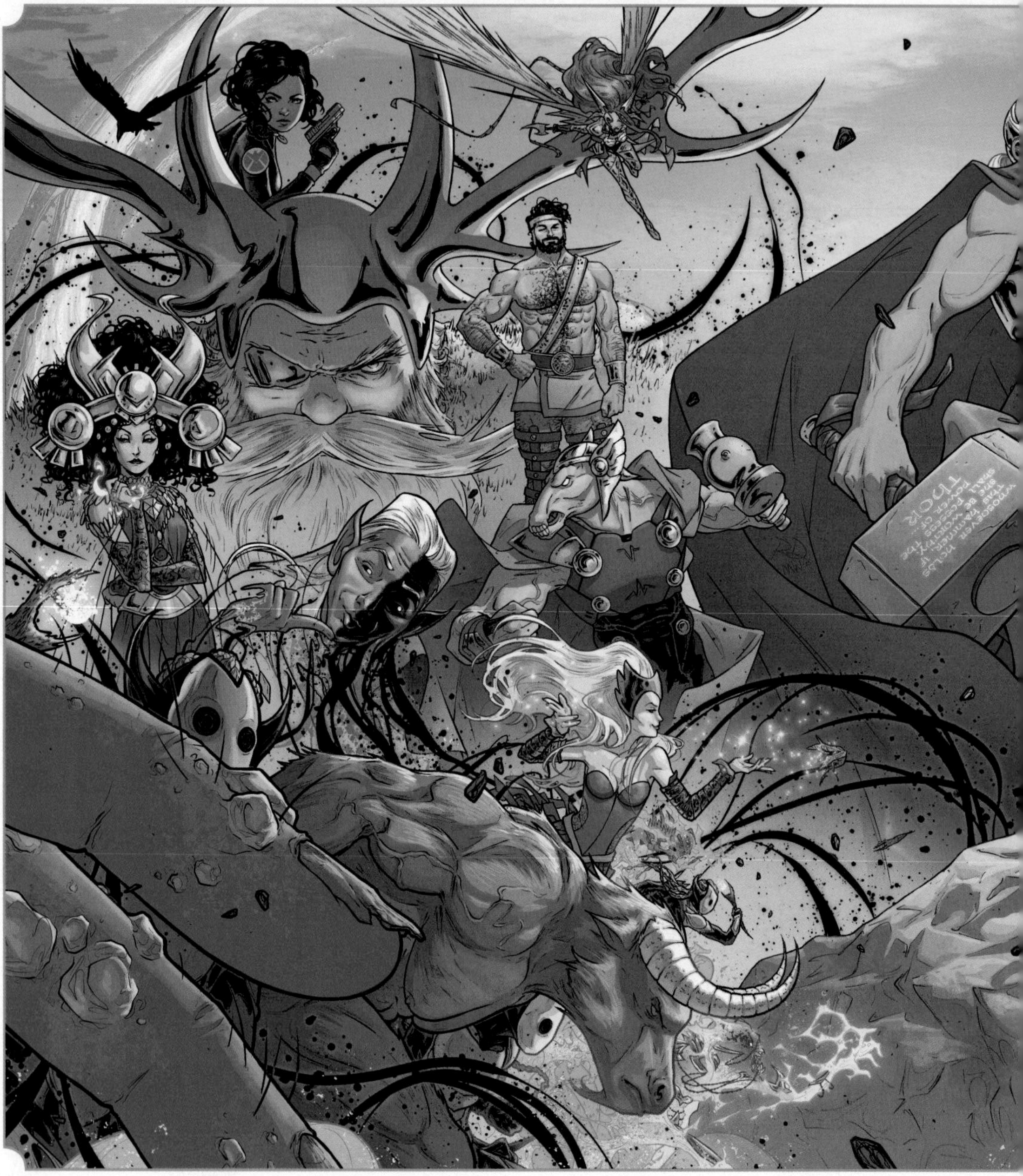

— 1 —

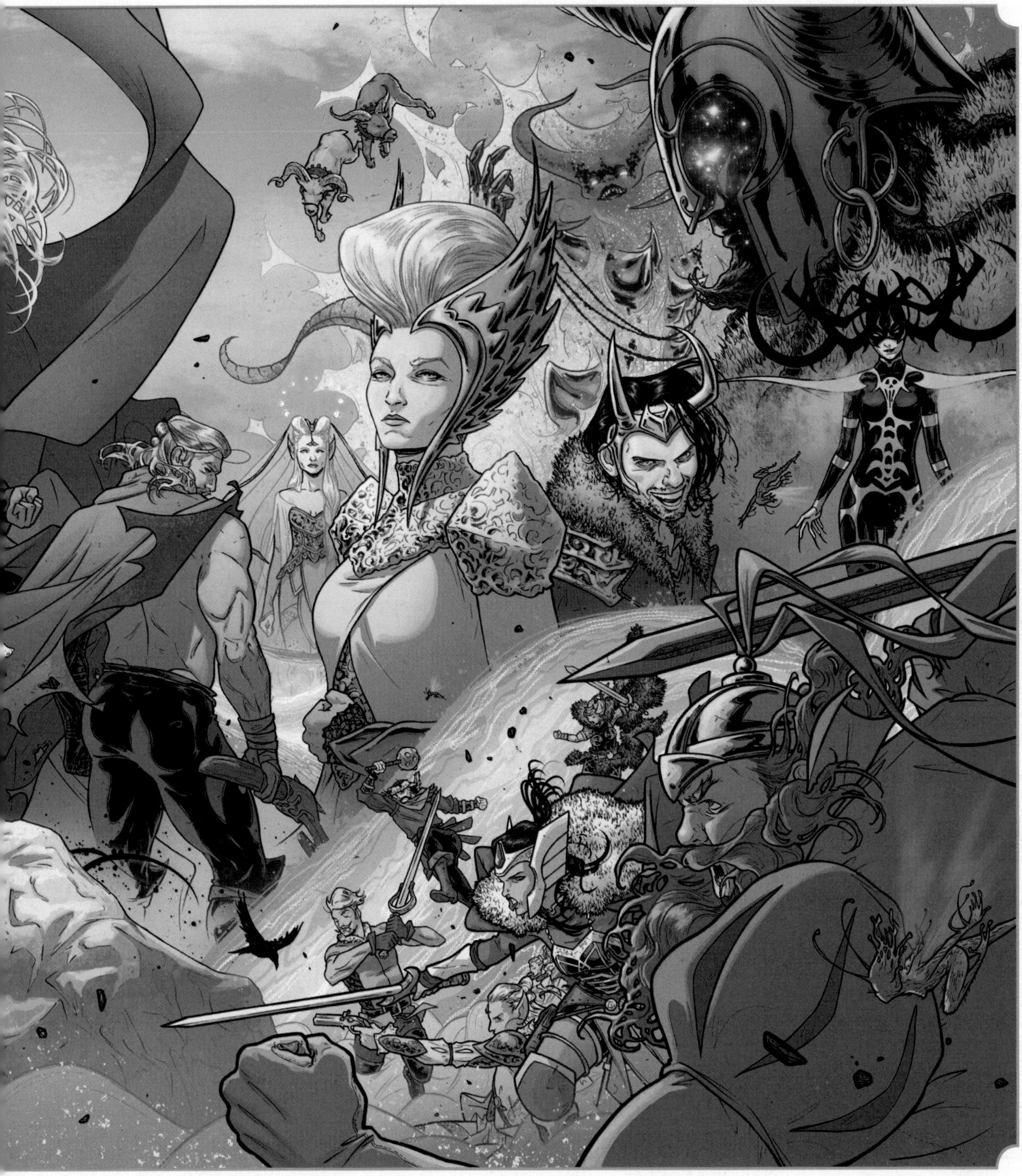

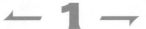

THUNDER IN HER VEINS

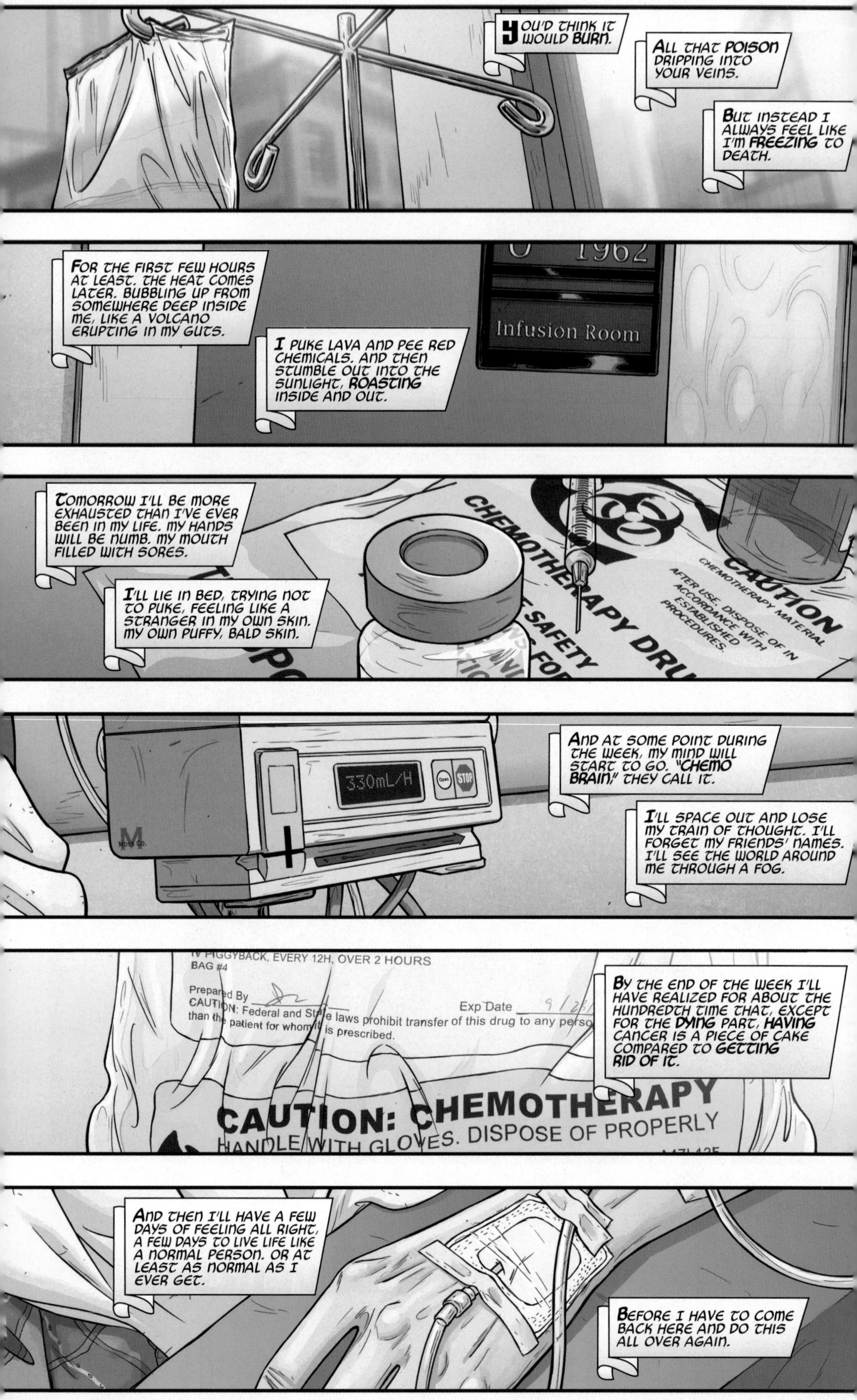
You'd think it would burn.
All that poison dripping into your veins.
But instead I always feel like I'm freezing to death.
1962
Infusion Room
For the first few hours at least. The heat comes later. Bubbling up from somewhere deep inside me, like a volcano erupting in my guts.
I puke lava and pee red chemicals. And then stumble out into the sunlight, roasting inside and out.
Tomorrow I'll be more exhausted than I've ever been in my life. My hands will be numb. My mouth filled with sores.
I'll lie in bed, trying not to puke, feeling like a stranger in my own skin. My own puffy, bald skin.
CHEMOTHERAPY DRU
CAUTION
CHEMOTHERAPY MATERIAL
AFTER USE, DISPOSE OF IN ACCORDANCE WITH ESTABLISHED PROCEDURES.
330mL/H
Open
STOP
And at some point during the week, my mind will start to go. "Chemo brain," they call it.
I'll space out and lose my train of thought. I'll forget my friends' names. I'll see the world around me through a fog.
IV PIGGYBACK, EVERY 12H, OVER 2 HOURS
BAG #4
Prepared By
Exp Date
CAUTION: Federal and State laws prohibit transfer of this drug to any perso
than the patient for whom it is prescribed.
By the end of the week I'll have realized for about the hundredth time that, except for the dying part, having cancer is a piece of cake compared to getting rid of it.
CAUTION: CHEMOTHERAPY
HANDLE WITH GLOVES. DISPOSE OF PROPERLY
And then I'll have a few days of feeling all right, a few days to live life like a normal person. Or at least as normal as I ever get.
Before I have to come back here and do this all over again.

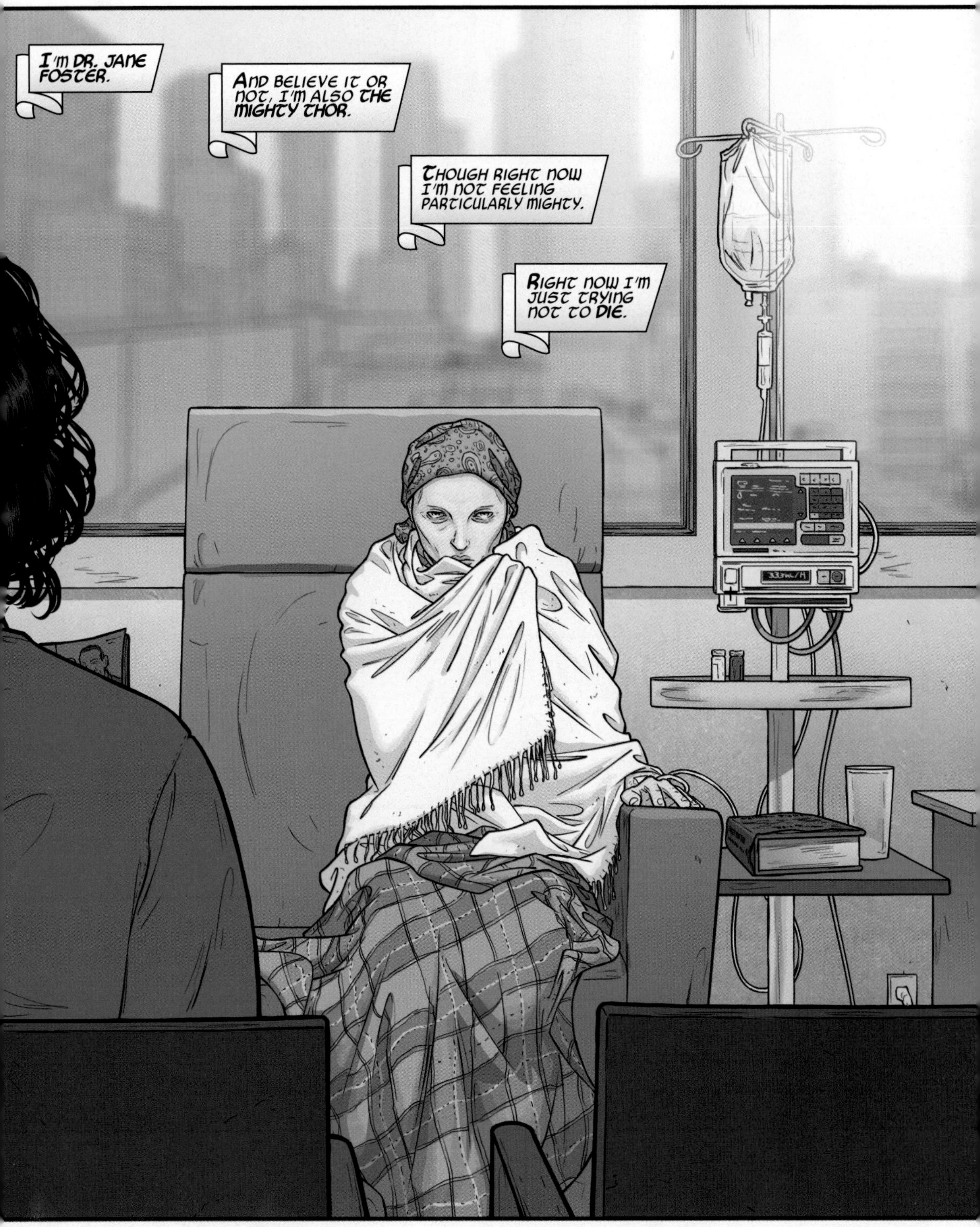
I'M DR. JANE FOSTER.
AND BELIEVE IT OR NOT, I'M ALSO THE MIGHTY THOR.
THOUGH RIGHT NOW I'M NOT FEELING PARTICULARLY MIGHTY.
RIGHT NOW I'M JUST TRYING NOT TO DIE.

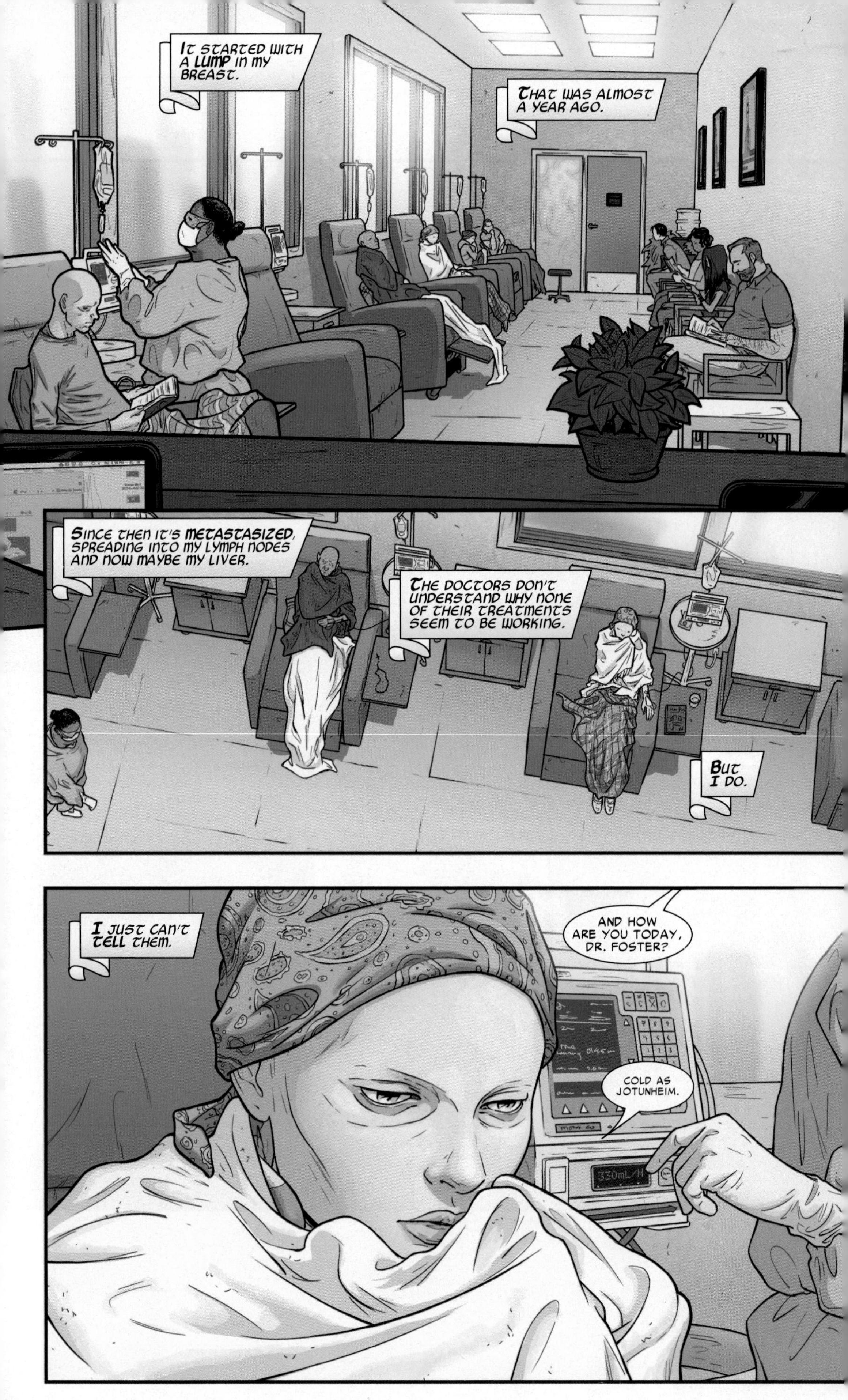

IT STARTED WITH A LUMP IN MY BREAST.
THAT WAS ALMOST A YEAR AGO.
SINCE THEN IT'S METASTASIZED, SPREADING INTO MY LYMPH NODES AND NOW MAYBE MY LIVER.
THE DOCTORS DON'T UNDERSTAND WHY NONE OF THEIR TREATMENTS SEEM TO BE WORKING.
BUT I DO.
I JUST CAN'T TELL THEM.
AND HOW ARE YOU TODAY, DR. FOSTER?
COLD AS JOTUNHEIM.
330mL/H

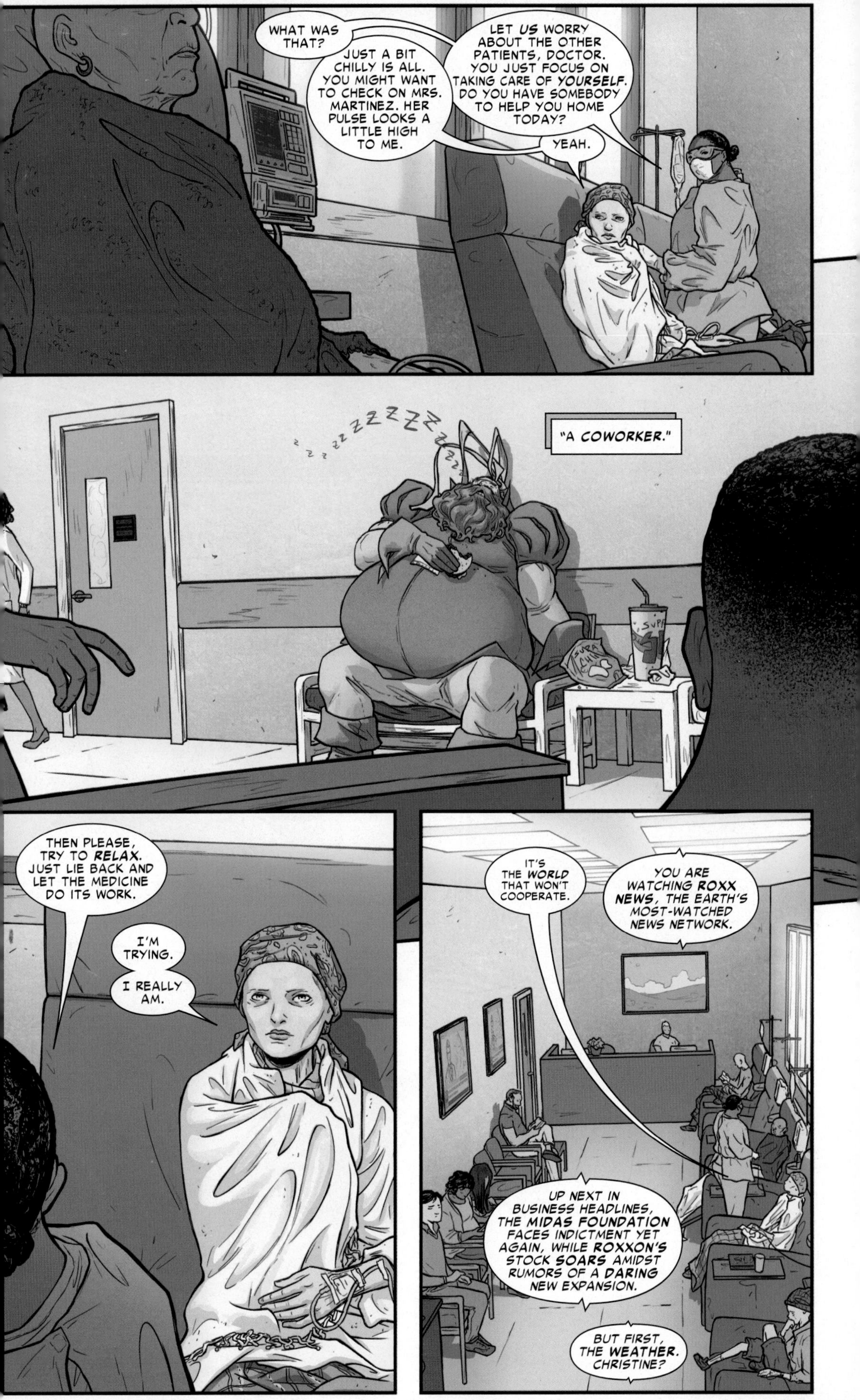
WHAT WAS THAT?
JUST A BIT CHILLY IS ALL. YOU MIGHT WANT TO CHECK ON MRS. MARTINEZ. HER PULSE LOOKS A LITTLE HIGH TO ME.
LET US WORRY ABOUT THE OTHER PATIENTS, DOCTOR. YOU JUST FOCUS ON TAKING CARE OF YOURSELF. DO YOU HAVE SOMEBODY TO HELP YOU HOME TODAY?
YEAH.
ZZZZZZZZZZZZ
"A COWORKER."
THEN PLEASE, TRY TO RELAX. JUST LIE BACK AND LET THE MEDICINE DO ITS WORK.
I'M TRYING.
I REALLY AM.
IT'S THE WORLD THAT WON'T COOPERATE.
YOU ARE WATCHING ROXX NEWS, THE EARTH'S MOST-WATCHED NEWS NETWORK.
UP NEXT IN BUSINESS HEADLINES, THE MIDAS FOUNDATION FACES INDICTMENT YET AGAIN, WHILE ROXXON'S STOCK SOARS AMIDST RUMORS OF A DARING NEW EXPANSION.
BUT FIRST, THE WEATHER. CHRISTINE?

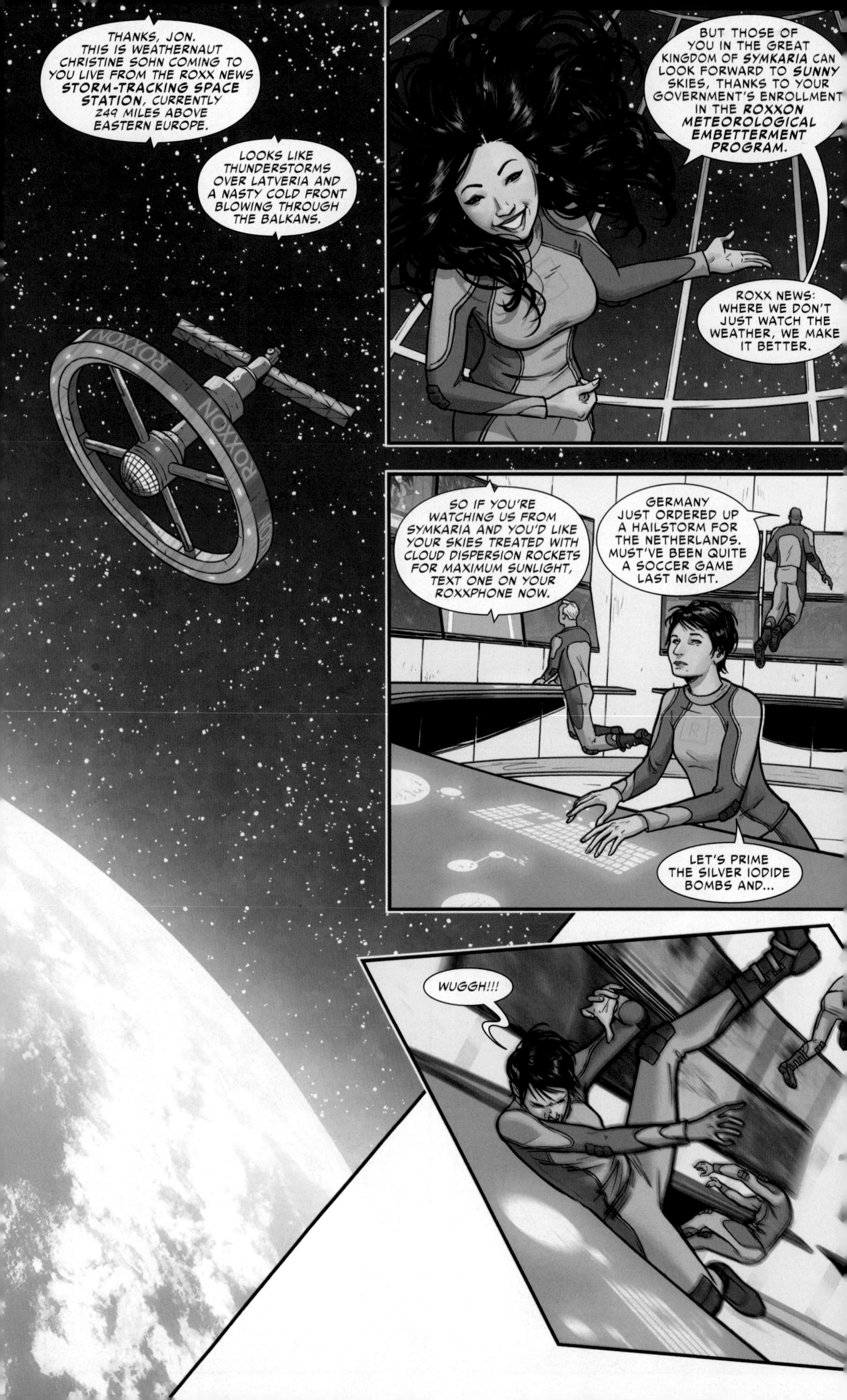
THANKS, JON. THIS IS WEATHERNAUT CHRISTINE SOHN COMING TO YOU LIVE FROM THE ROXX NEWS STORM-TRACKING SPACE STATION, CURRENTLY 249 MILES ABOVE EASTERN EUROPE.
LOOKS LIKE THUNDERSTORMS OVER LATVERIA AND A NASTY COLD FRONT BLOWING THROUGH THE BALKANS.
ROXXON
BUT THOSE OF YOU IN THE GREAT KINGDOM OF SYMKARIA CAN LOOK FORWARD TO SUNNY SKIES, THANKS TO YOUR GOVERNMENT'S ENROLLMENT IN THE ROXXON METEOROLOGICAL EMBETTERMENT PROGRAM.
ROXX NEWS: WHERE WE DON'T JUST WATCH THE WEATHER, WE MAKE IT BETTER.
SO IF YOU'RE WATCHING US FROM SYMKARIA AND YOU'D LIKE YOUR SKIES TREATED WITH CLOUD DISPERSION ROCKETS FOR MAXIMUM SUNLIGHT, TEXT ONE ON YOUR ROXXPHONE NOW.
GERMANY JUST ORDERED UP A HAILSTORM FOR THE NETHERLANDS. MUST'VE BEEN QUITE A SOCCER GAME LAST NIGHT.
LET'S PRIME THE SILVER IODIDE BOMBS AND...
WUGGH!!!

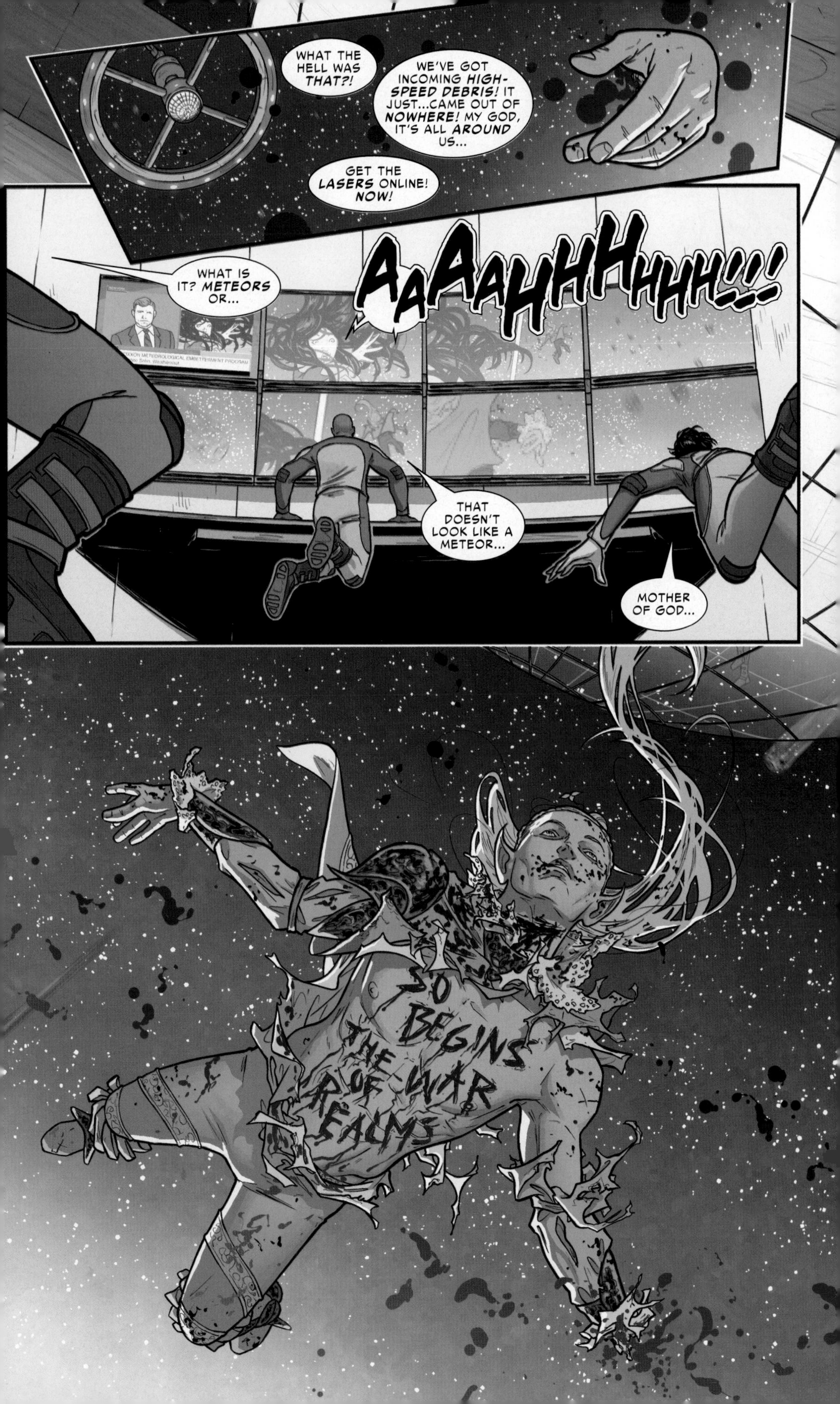

WHAT THE HELL WAS THAT?!
WE'VE GOT INCOMING HIGH-SPEED DEBRIS! IT JUST...CAME OUT OF NOWHERE! MY GOD, IT'S ALL AROUND US...
GET THE LASERS ONLINE! NOW!
WHAT IS IT? METEORS OR...
AAAAHHHHHH!!!
THAT DOESN'T LOOK LIKE A METEOR...
MOTHER OF GOD...
SO BEGINS THE WAR OF REALMS

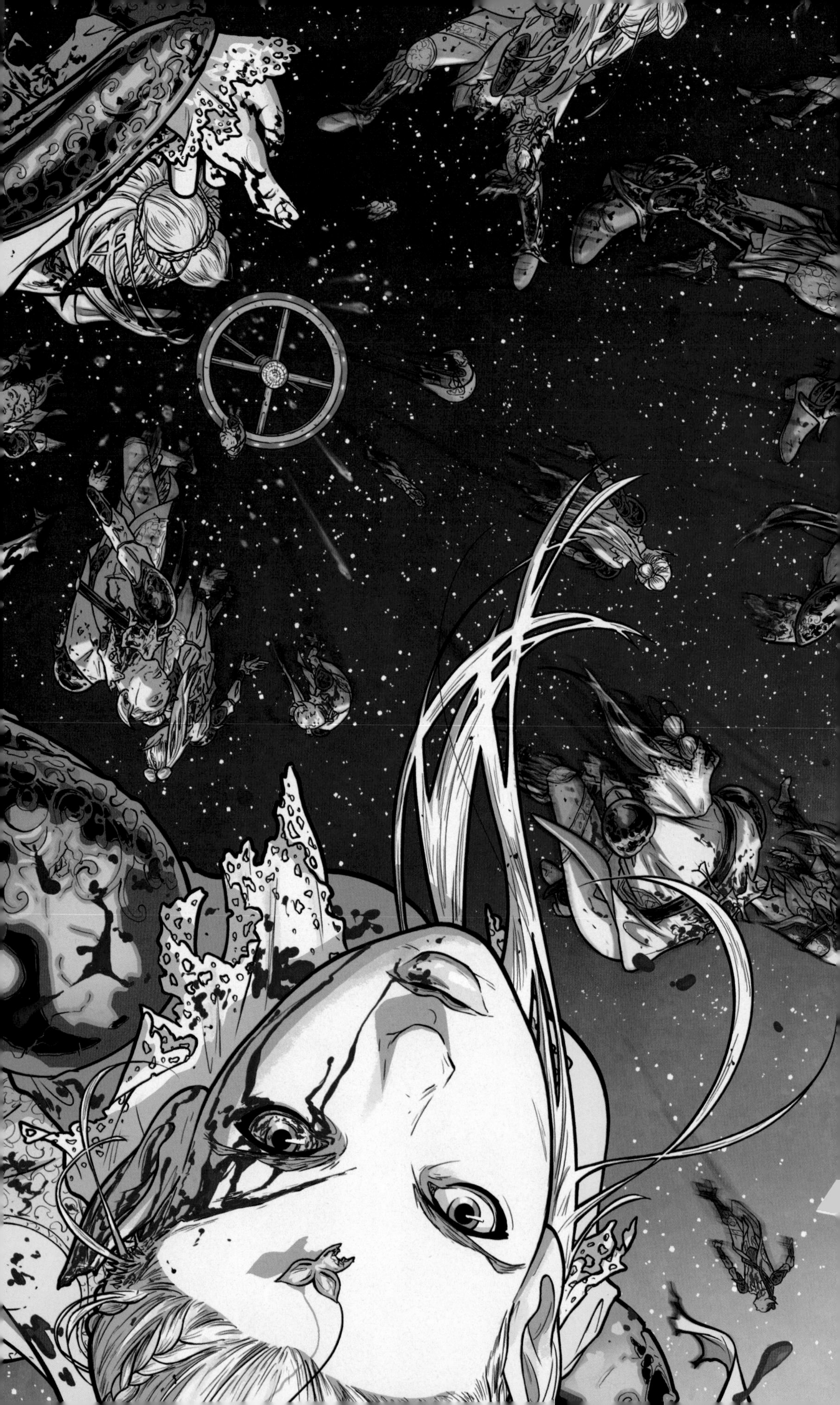

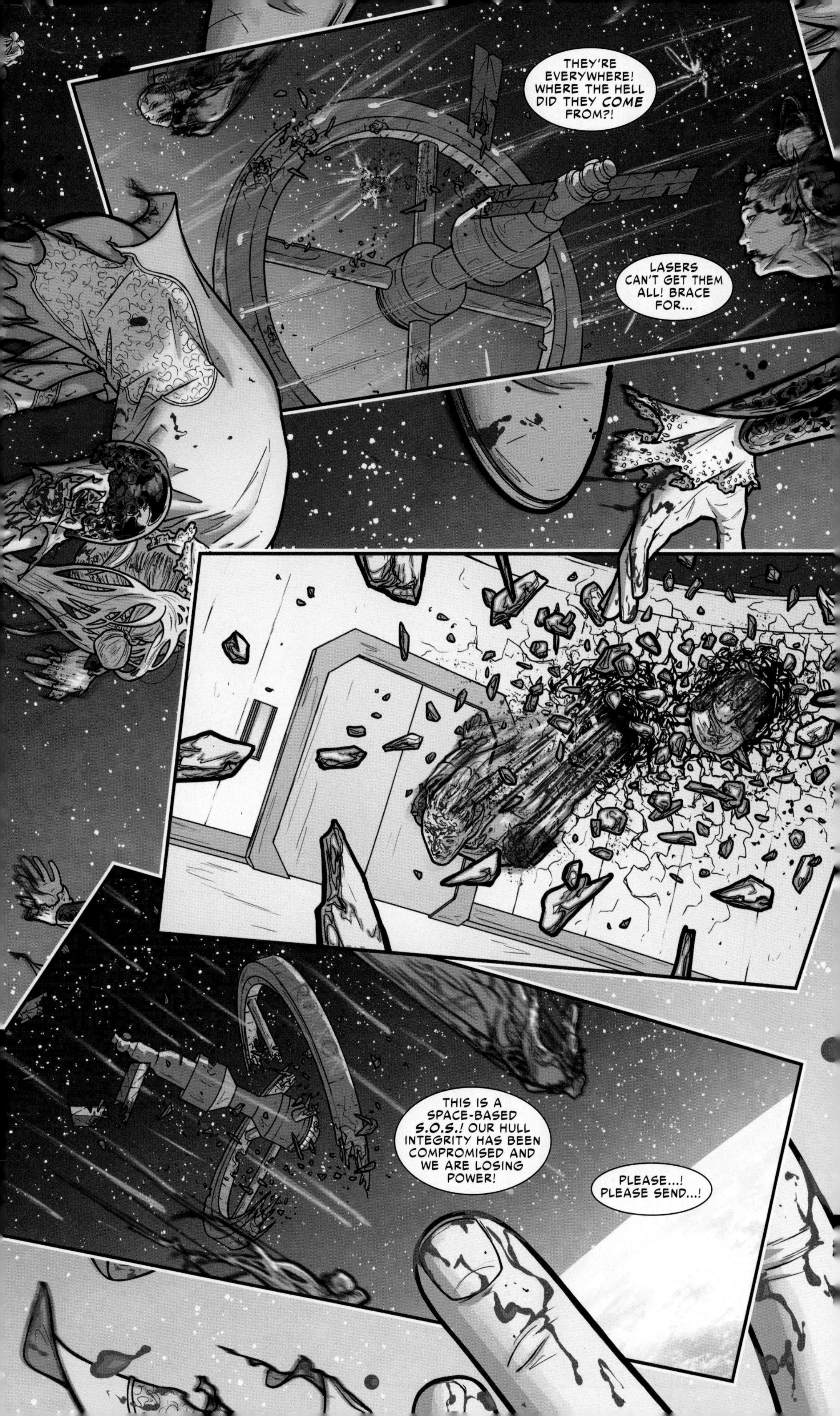

THEY'RE EVERYWHERE! WHERE THE HELL DID THEY COME FROM?!
LASERS CAN'T GET THEM ALL! BRACE FOR...
THIS IS A SPACE-BASED S.O.S.! OUR HULL INTEGRITY HAS BEEN COMPROMISED AND WE ARE LOSING POWER!
PLEASE...! PLEASE SEND...!

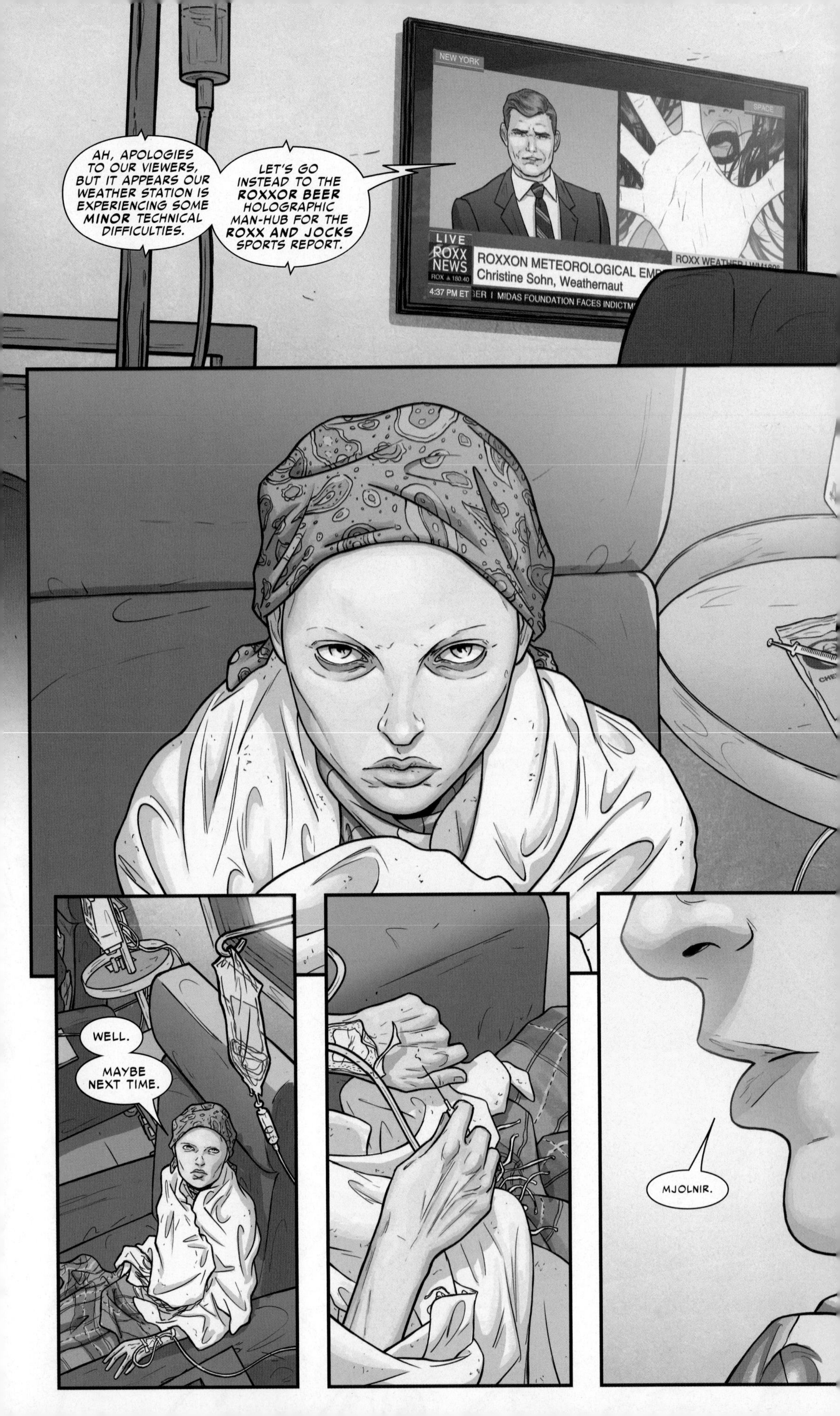
AH, APOLOGIES TO OUR VIEWERS, BUT IT APPEARS OUR WEATHER STATION IS EXPERIENCING SOME MINOR TECHNICAL DIFFICULTIES.
LET'S GO INSTEAD TO THE ROXXOR BEER HOLOGRAPHIC MAN-HUB FOR THE ROXX AND JOCKS SPORTS REPORT.
NEW YORK
SPACE
LIVE
ROXX NEWS
ROXXON METEOROLOGICAL EME
Christine Sohn, Weathernaut
4:37 PM ET
MIDAS FOUNDATION FACES INDICTM
WELL.
MAYBE NEXT TIME.
MJOLNIR.

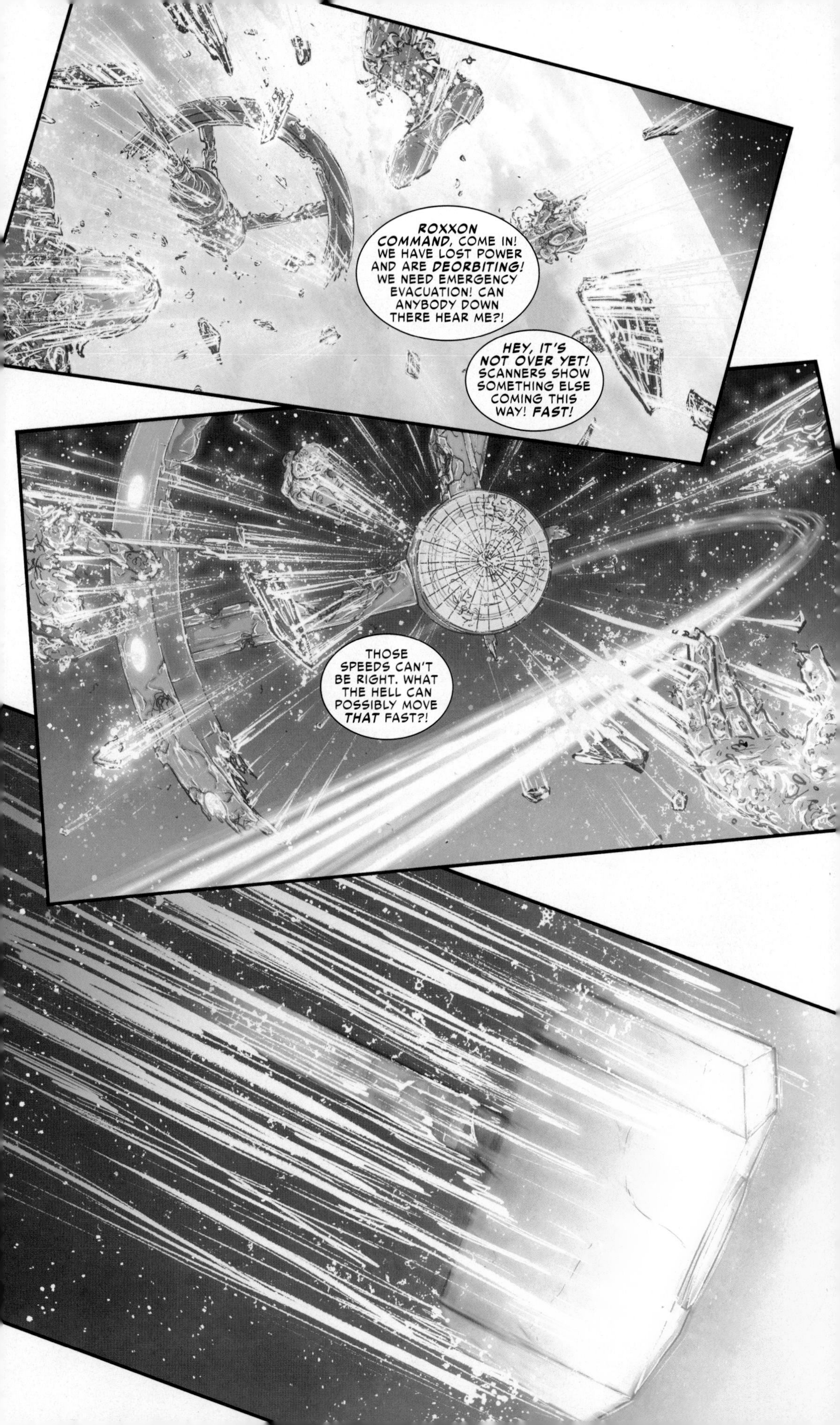
ROXXON COMMAND, COME IN! WE HAVE LOST POWER AND ARE *DEORBITING!* WE NEED EMERGENCY EVACUATION! CAN ANYBODY DOWN THERE HEAR ME?!
HEY, IT'S NOT OVER YET! SCANNERS SHOW SOMETHING ELSE COMING THIS WAY! *FAST!*
THOSE SPEEDS CAN'T BE RIGHT. WHAT THE HELL CAN POSSIBLY MOVE *THAT* FAST?!

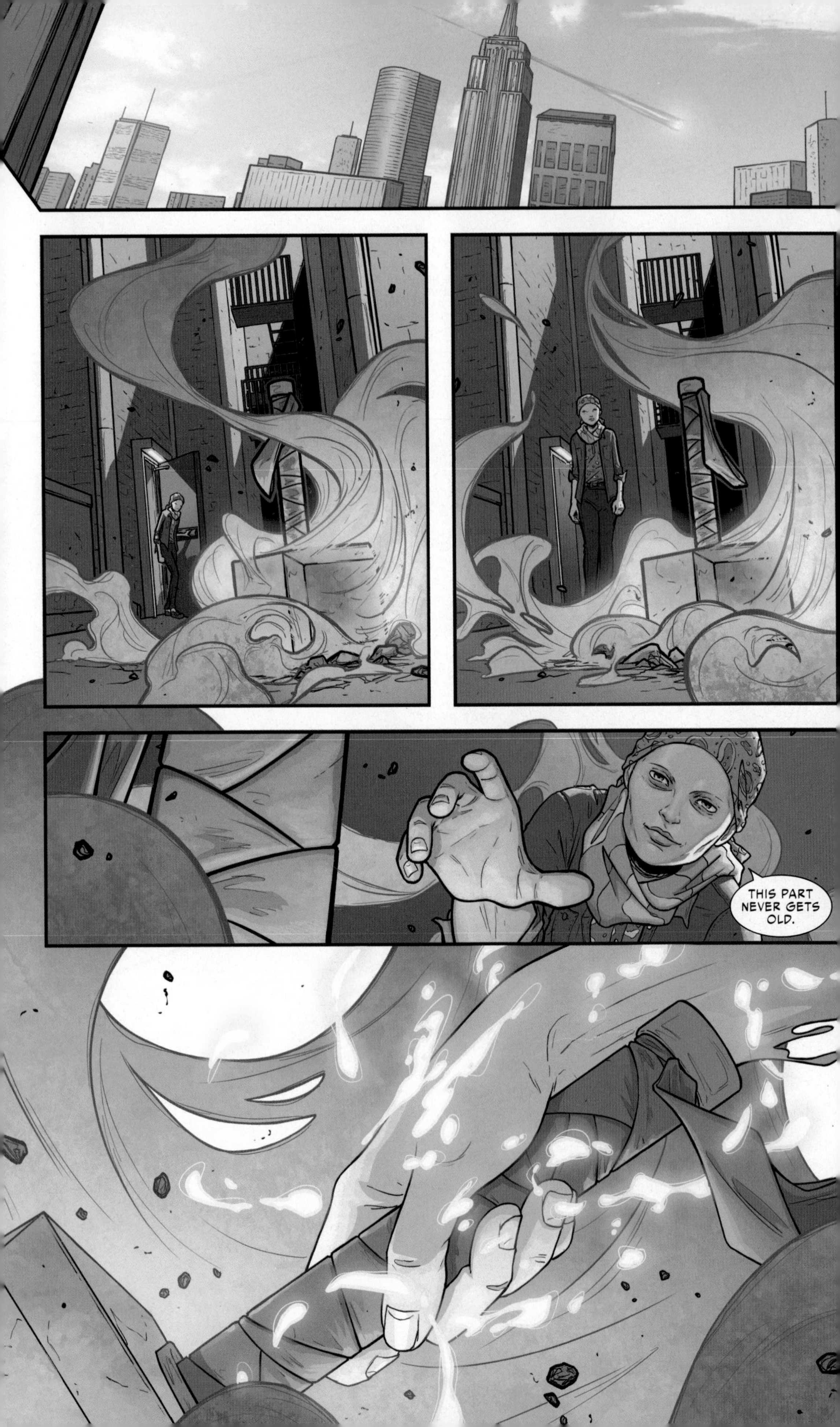
THIS PART NEVER GETS OLD.

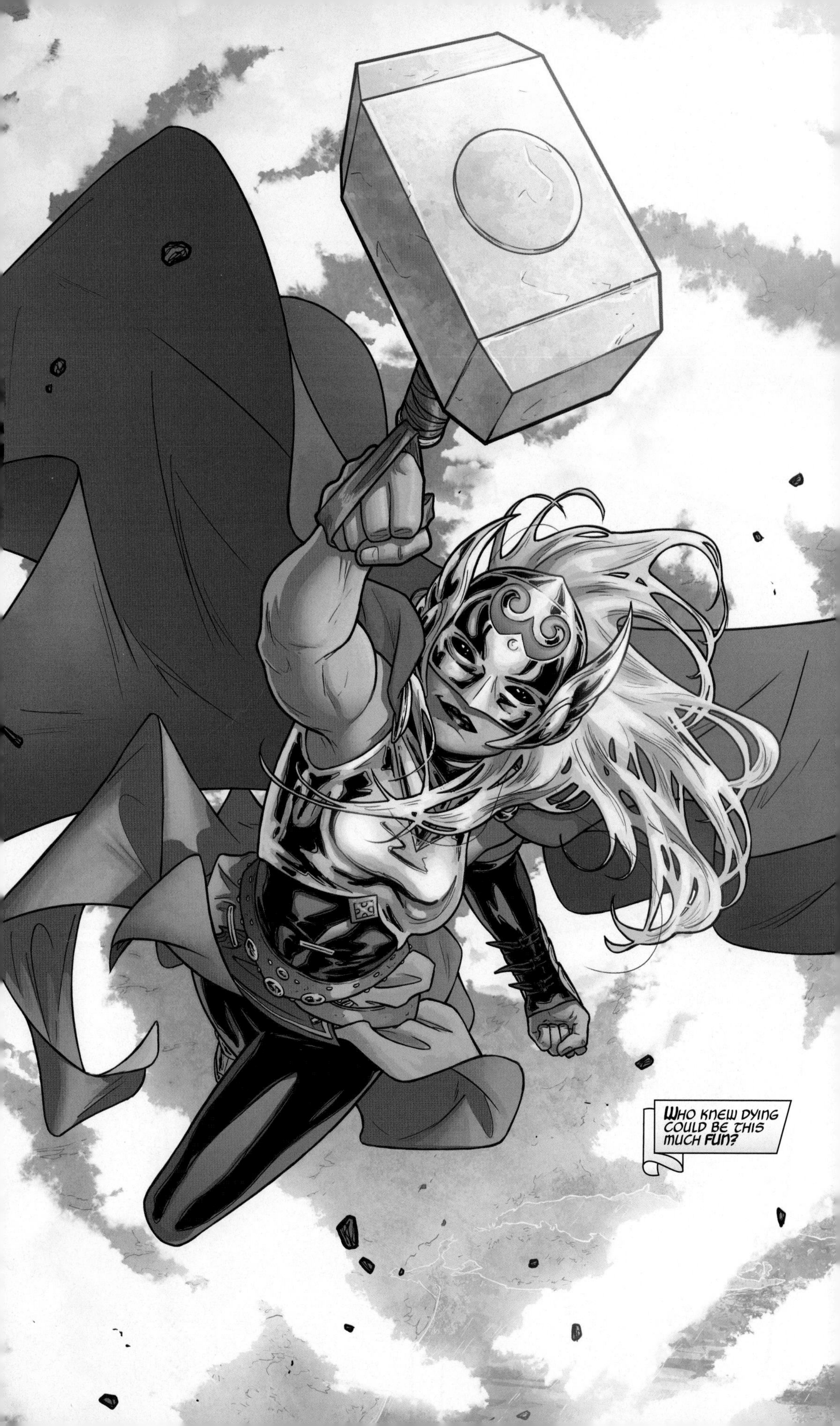
WHO KNEW DYING COULD BE THIS MUCH FUN?

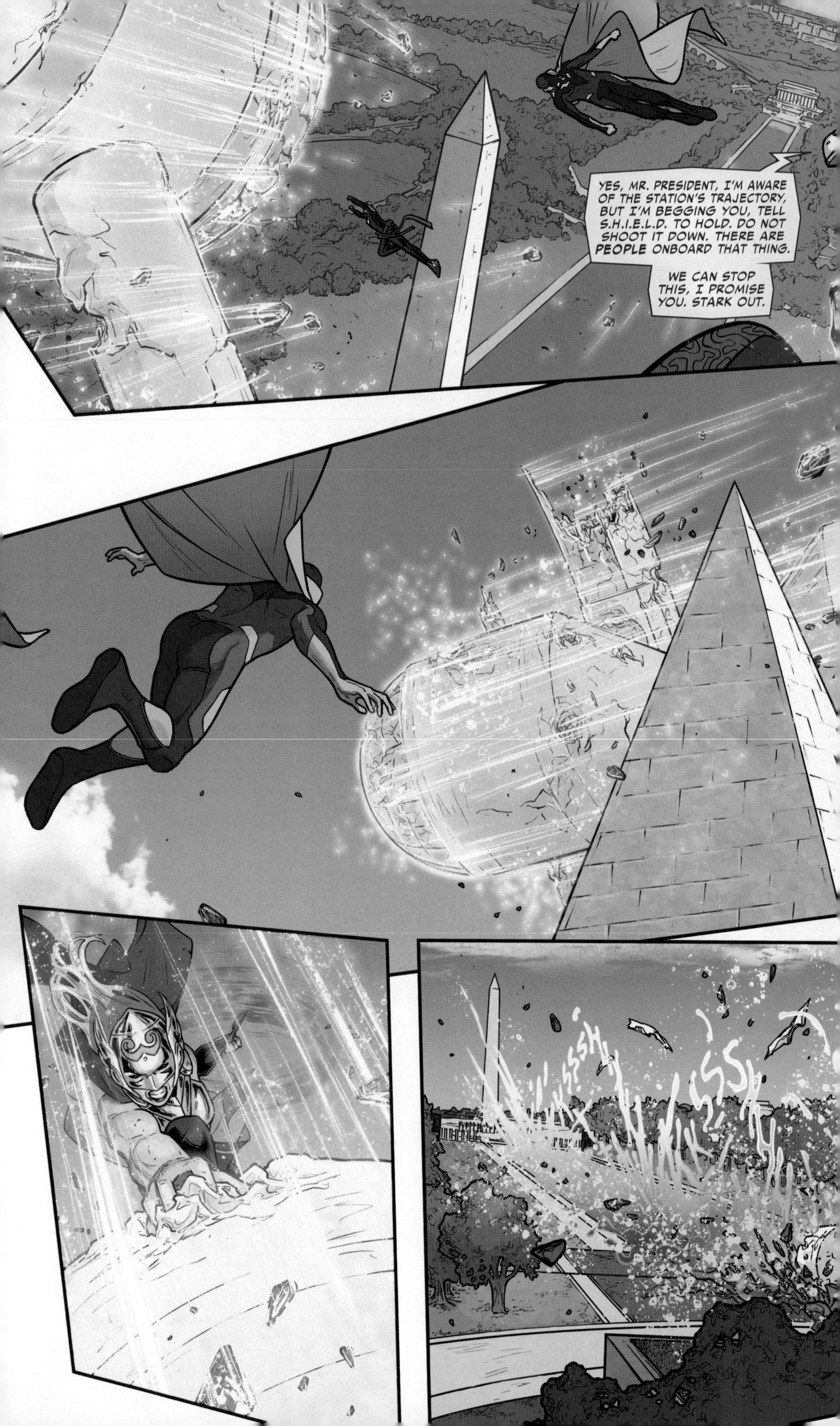
YES, MR. PRESIDENT, I'M AWARE OF THE STATION'S TRAJECTORY, BUT I'M BEGGING YOU, TELL S.H.I.E.L.D. TO HOLD. DO NOT SHOOT IT DOWN. THERE ARE PEOPLE ONBOARD THAT THING.
WE CAN STOP THIS, I PROMISE YOU. STARK OUT.

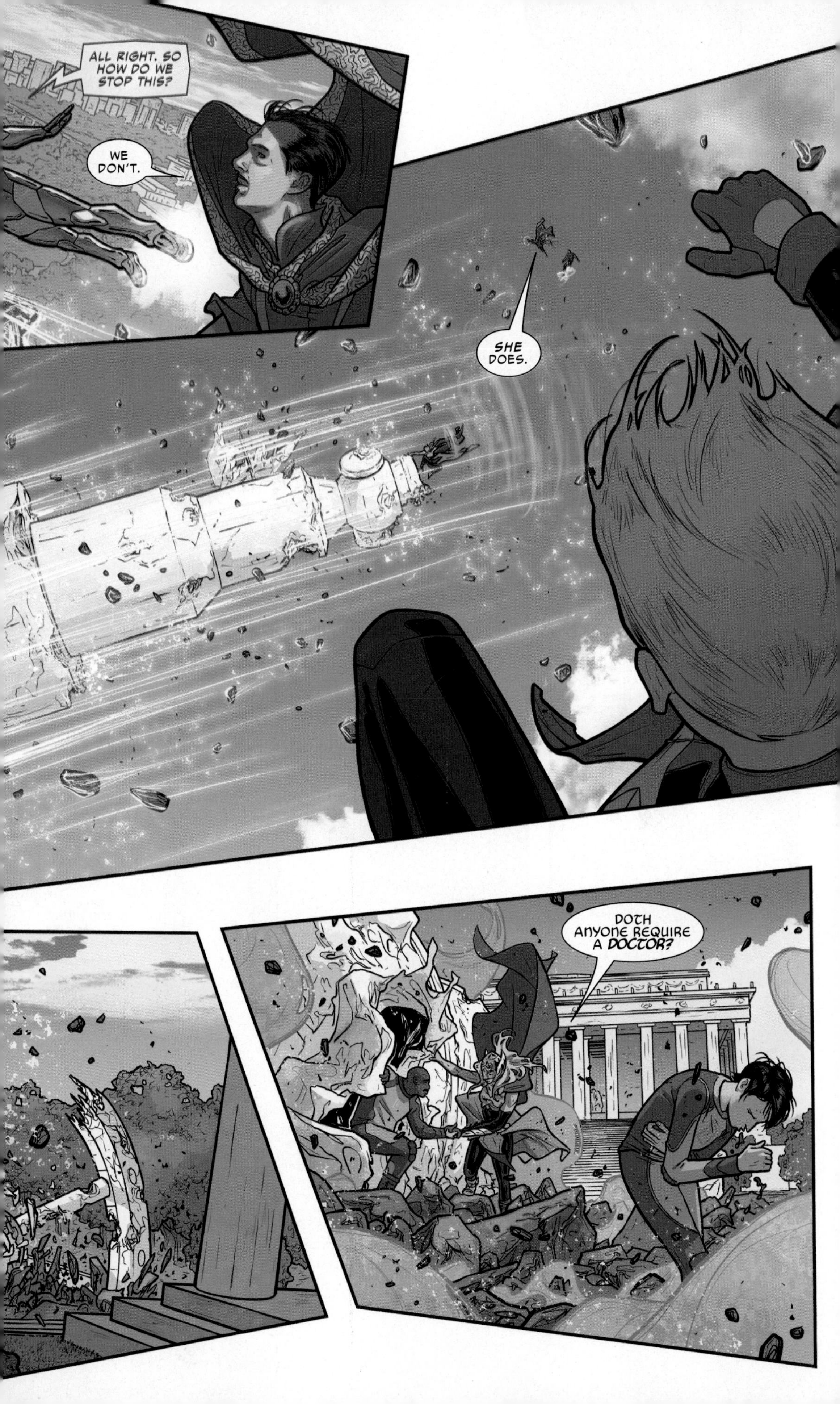
ALL RIGHT. SO HOW DO WE STOP THIS?
WE DON'T.
SHE DOES.
DOTH ANYONE REQUIRE A DOCTOR?

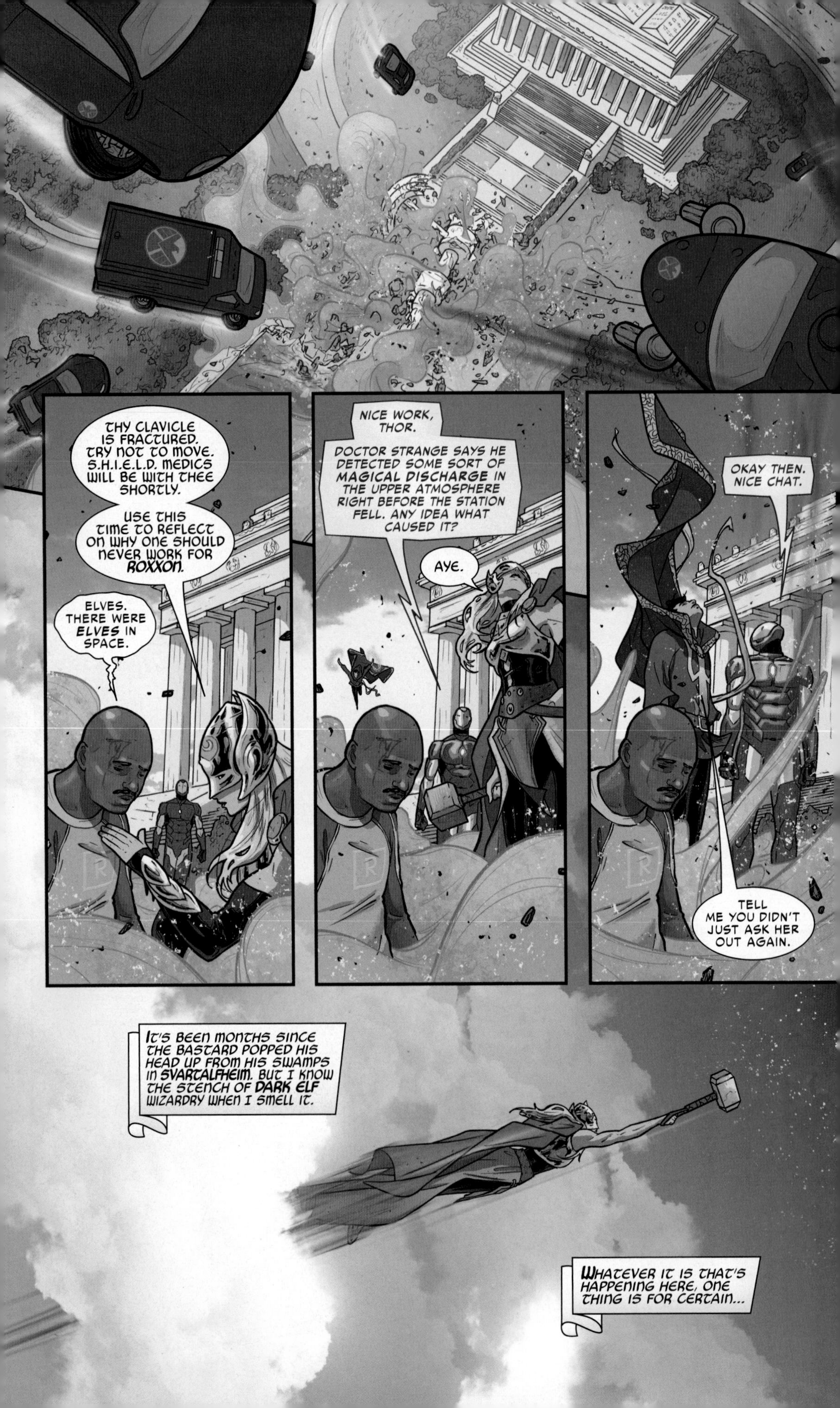
THY CLAVICLE IS FRACTURED. TRY NOT TO MOVE. S.H.I.E.L.D. MEDICS WILL BE WITH THEE SHORTLY.
USE THIS TIME TO REFLECT ON WHY ONE SHOULD NEVER WORK FOR ROXXON.
ELVES. THERE WERE ELVES IN SPACE.
NICE WORK, THOR.
DOCTOR STRANGE SAYS HE DETECTED SOME SORT OF MAGICAL DISCHARGE IN THE UPPER ATMOSPHERE RIGHT BEFORE THE STATION FELL. ANY IDEA WHAT CAUSED IT?
AYE.
OKAY THEN. NICE CHAT.
TELL ME YOU DIDN'T JUST ASK HER OUT AGAIN.
IT'S BEEN MONTHS SINCE THE BASTARD POPPED HIS HEAD UP FROM HIS SWAMPS IN SVARTALFHEIM. BUT I KNOW THE STENCH OF DARK ELF WIZARDRY WHEN I SMELL IT.
WHATEVER IT IS THAT'S HAPPENING HERE, ONE THING IS FOR CERTAIN...

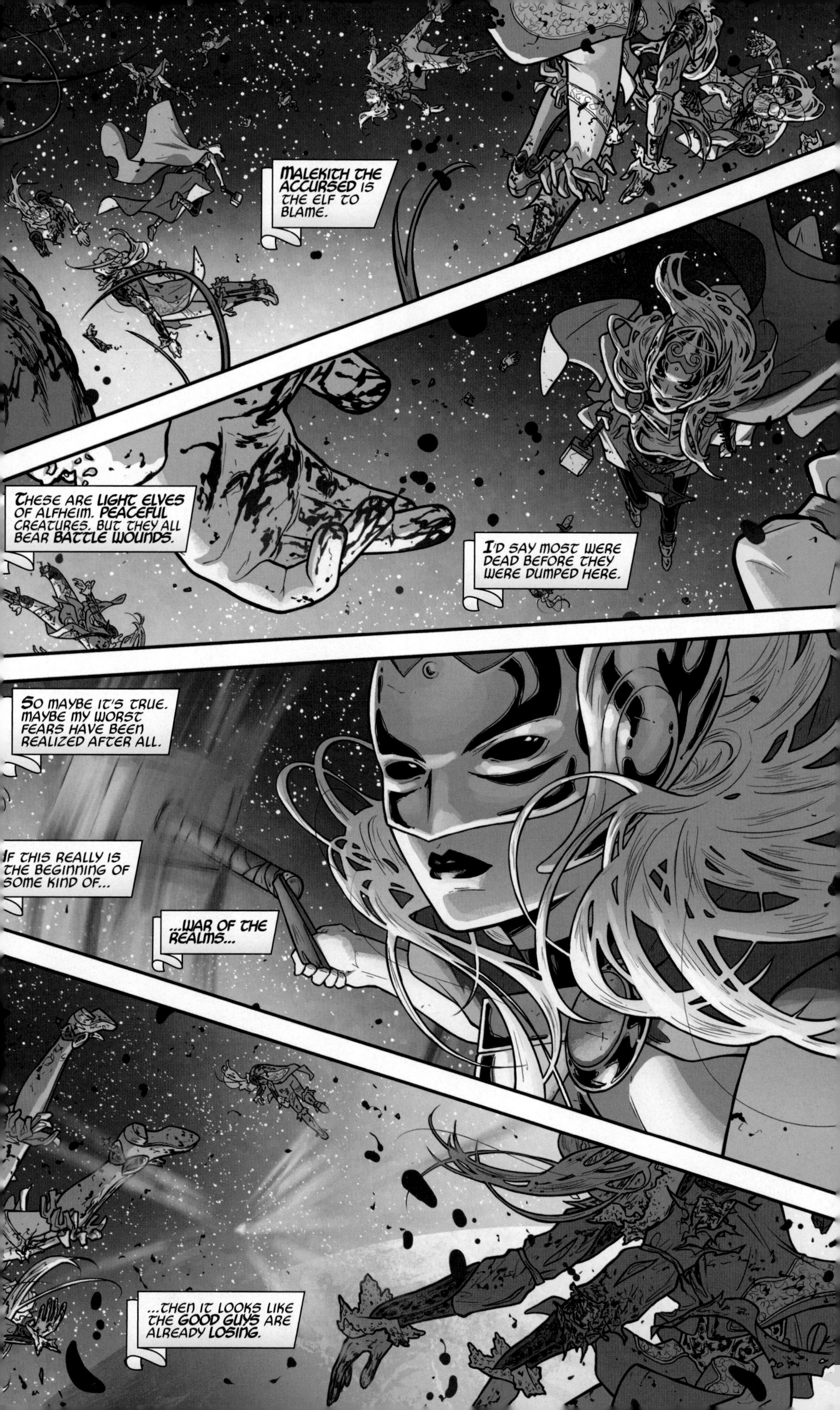
MALEKITH THE ACCURSED IS THE ELF TO BLAME.
THESE ARE LIGHT ELVES OF ALFHEIM. PEACEFUL CREATURES. BUT THEY ALL BEAR BATTLE WOUNDS.
I'D SAY MOST WERE DEAD BEFORE THEY WERE DUMPED HERE.
SO MAYBE IT'S TRUE. MAYBE MY WORST FEARS HAVE BEEN REALIZED AFTER ALL.
IF THIS REALLY IS THE BEGINNING OF SOME KIND OF...
...WAR OF THE REALMS...
...THEN IT LOOKS LIKE THE GOOD GUYS ARE ALREADY LOSING.

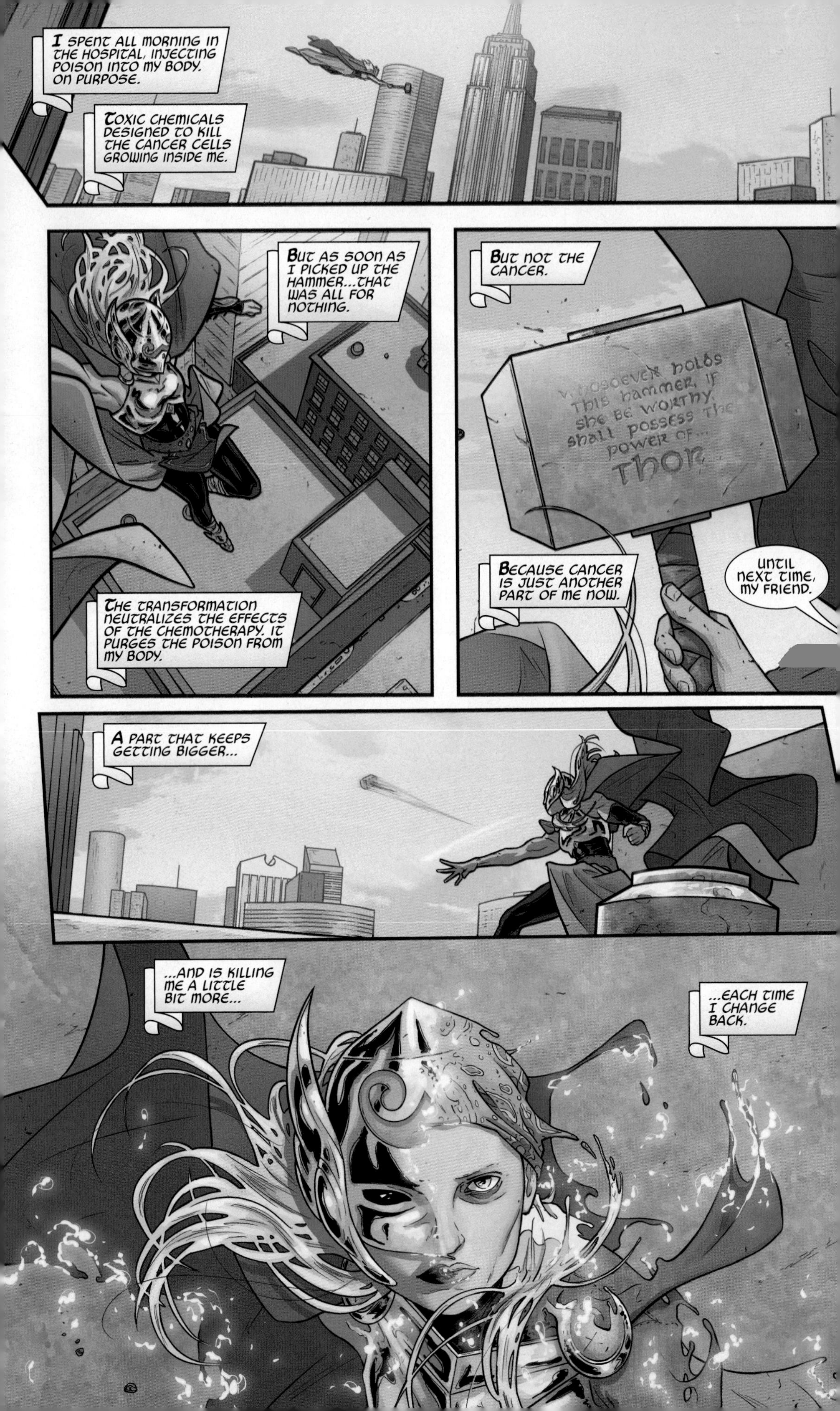
I SPENT ALL MORNING IN THE HOSPITAL, INJECTING POISON INTO MY BODY. ON PURPOSE.
TOXIC CHEMICALS DESIGNED TO KILL THE CANCER CELLS GROWING INSIDE ME.
BUT AS SOON AS I PICKED UP THE HAMMER...THAT WAS ALL FOR NOTHING.
THE TRANSFORMATION NEUTRALIZES THE EFFECTS OF THE CHEMOTHERAPY. IT PURGES THE POISON FROM MY BODY.
BUT NOT THE CANCER.
WHOSOEVER HOLDS THIS HAMMER, IF SHE BE WORTHY, SHALL POSSESS THE POWER OF... THOR
BECAUSE CANCER IS JUST ANOTHER PART OF ME NOW.
UNTIL NEXT TIME, MY FRIEND.
A PART THAT KEEPS GETTING BIGGER...
...AND IS KILLING ME A LITTLE BIT MORE...
...EACH TIME I CHANGE BACK.

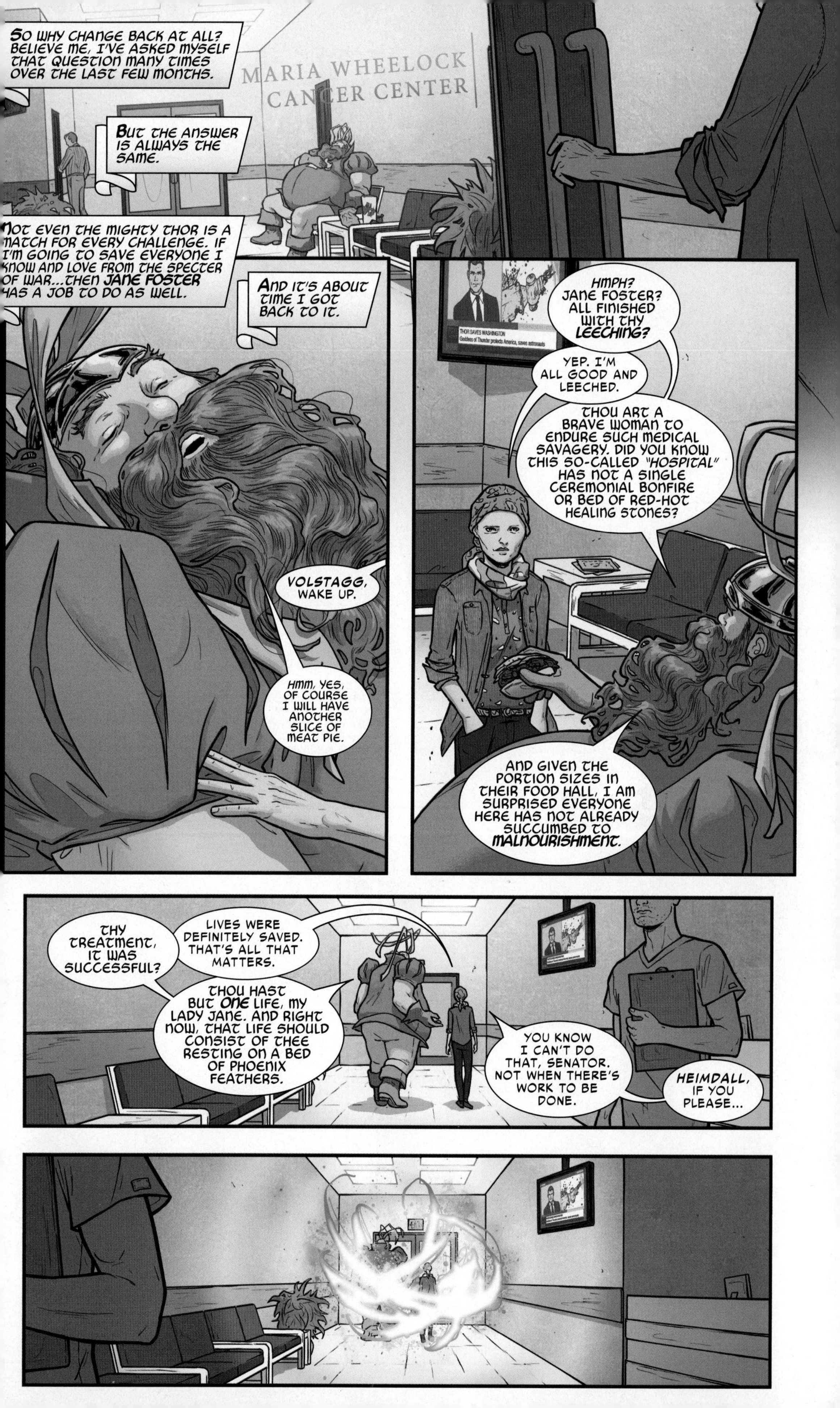

SO WHY CHANGE BACK AT ALL? BELIEVE ME, I'VE ASKED MYSELF THAT QUESTION MANY TIMES OVER THE LAST FEW MONTHS.
MARIA WHEELOCK CANCER CENTER
BUT THE ANSWER IS ALWAYS THE SAME.
NOT EVEN THE MIGHTY THOR IS A MATCH FOR EVERY CHALLENGE. IF I'M GOING TO SAVE EVERYONE I KNOW AND LOVE FROM THE SPECTER OF WAR...THEN JANE FOSTER HAS A JOB TO DO AS WELL.
AND IT'S ABOUT TIME I GOT BACK TO IT.
VOLSTAGG, WAKE UP.
HMM, YES, OF COURSE I WILL HAVE ANOTHER SLICE OF MEAT PIE.
THOR SAVES WASHINGTON
Goddess of Thunder protects America, saves astronauts
HMPH? JANE FOSTER? ALL FINISHED WITH THY LEECHING?
YEP. I'M ALL GOOD AND LEECHED.
THOU ART A BRAVE WOMAN TO ENDURE SUCH MEDICAL SAVAGERY. DID YOU KNOW THIS SO-CALLED "HOSPITAL" HAS NOT A SINGLE CEREMONIAL BONFIRE OR BED OF RED-HOT HEALING STONES?
AND GIVEN THE PORTION SIZES IN THEIR FOOD HALL, I AM SURPRISED EVERYONE HERE HAS NOT ALREADY SUCCUMBED TO MALNOURISHMENT.
THY TREATMENT, IT WAS SUCCESSFUL?
LIVES WERE DEFINITELY SAVED. THAT'S ALL THAT MATTERS.
THOU HAST BUT ONE LIFE, MY LADY JANE. AND RIGHT NOW, THAT LIFE SHOULD CONSIST OF THEE RESTING ON A BED OF PHOENIX FEATHERS.
YOU KNOW I CAN'T DO THAT, SENATOR. NOT WHEN THERE'S WORK TO BE DONE.
HEIMDALL, IF YOU PLEASE...

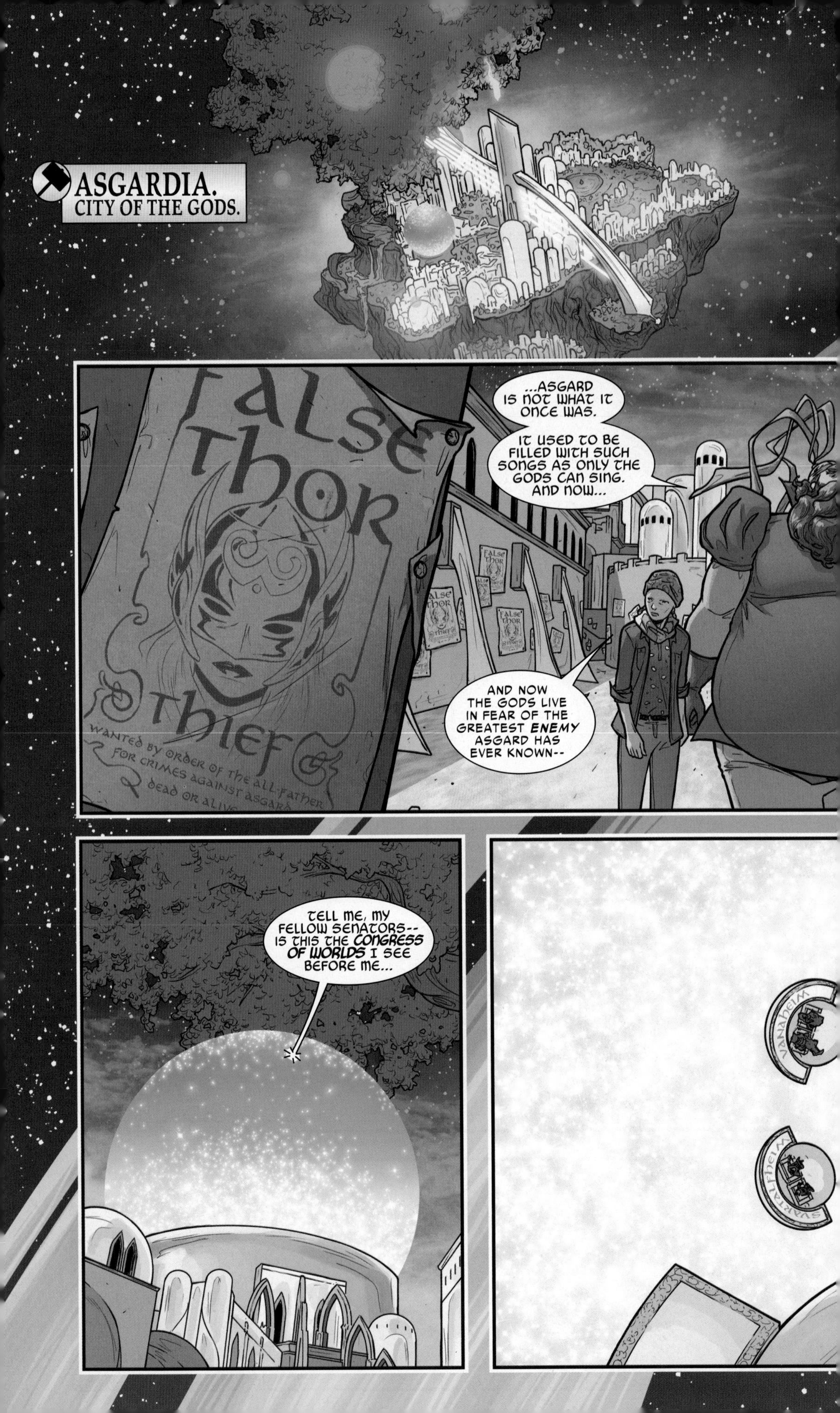
ASGARDIA.
CITY OF THE GODS.
FALSE THOR
THIEF
WANTED BY ORDER OF THE ALL-FATHER FOR CRIMES AGAINST ASGARD
DEAD OR ALIVE
...ASGARD IS NOT WHAT IT ONCE WAS.
IT USED TO BE FILLED WITH SUCH SONGS AS ONLY THE GODS CAN SING. AND NOW...
AND NOW THE GODS LIVE IN FEAR OF THE GREATEST ENEMY ASGARD HAS EVER KNOWN--
TELL ME, MY FELLOW SENATORS-- IS THIS THE CONGRESS OF WORLDS I SEE BEFORE ME...
VANAHEIM
SVARTALFHEIM

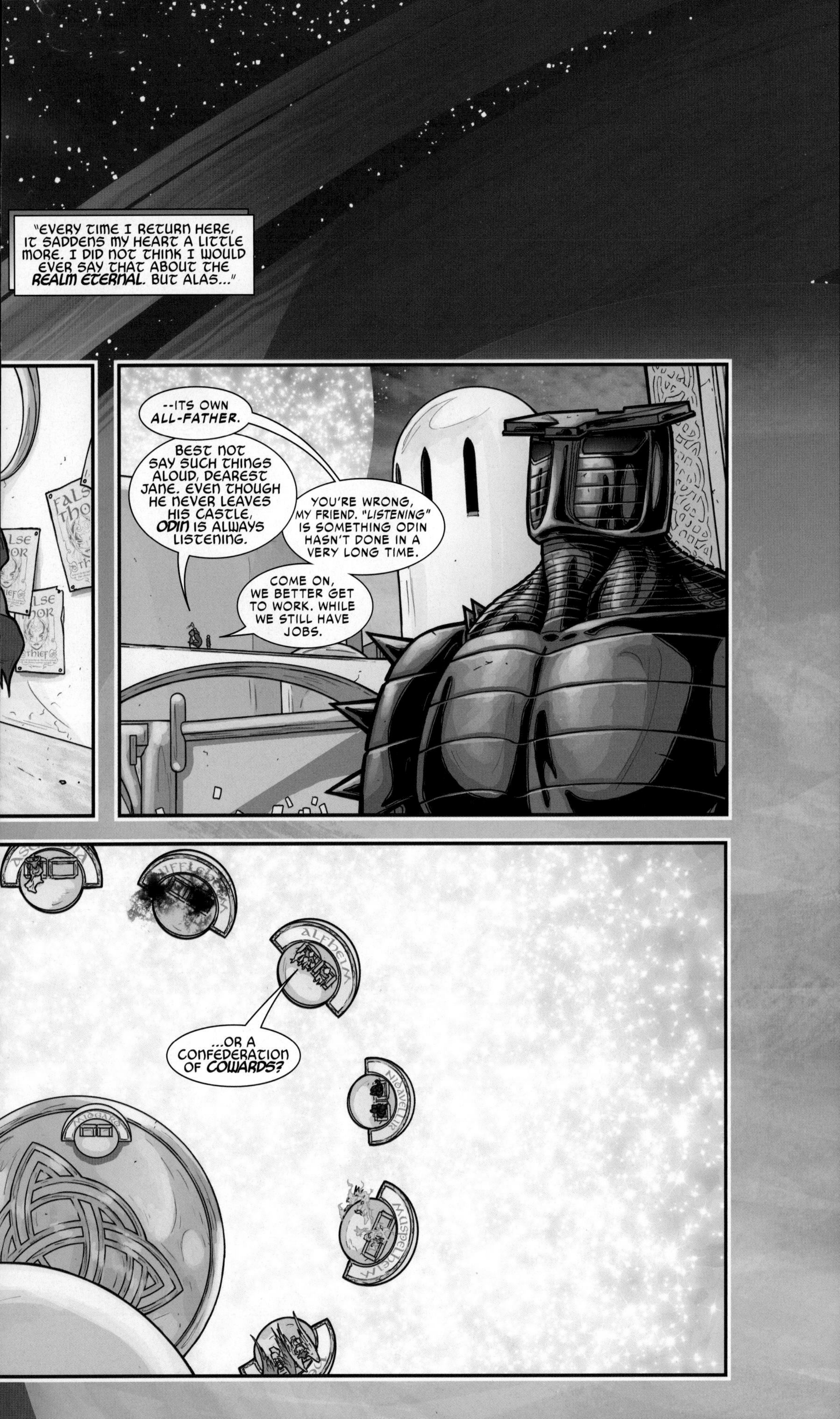
"EVERY TIME I RETURN HERE, IT SADDENS MY HEART A LITTLE MORE. I DID NOT THINK I WOULD EVER SAY THAT ABOUT THE REALM ETERNAL. BUT ALAS..."
FALSE THOR THIEF
--ITS OWN ALL-FATHER.
BEST NOT SAY SUCH THINGS ALOUD, DEAREST JANE. EVEN THOUGH HE NEVER LEAVES HIS CASTLE, ODIN IS ALWAYS LISTENING.
YOU'RE WRONG, MY FRIEND. "LISTENING" IS SOMETHING ODIN HASN'T DONE IN A VERY LONG TIME.
COME ON, WE BETTER GET TO WORK. WHILE WE STILL HAVE JOBS.
ALFHEIM
...OR A CONFEDERATION OF COWARDS?
NIDAVELLIR
MIDGARD
MUSPELHEIM

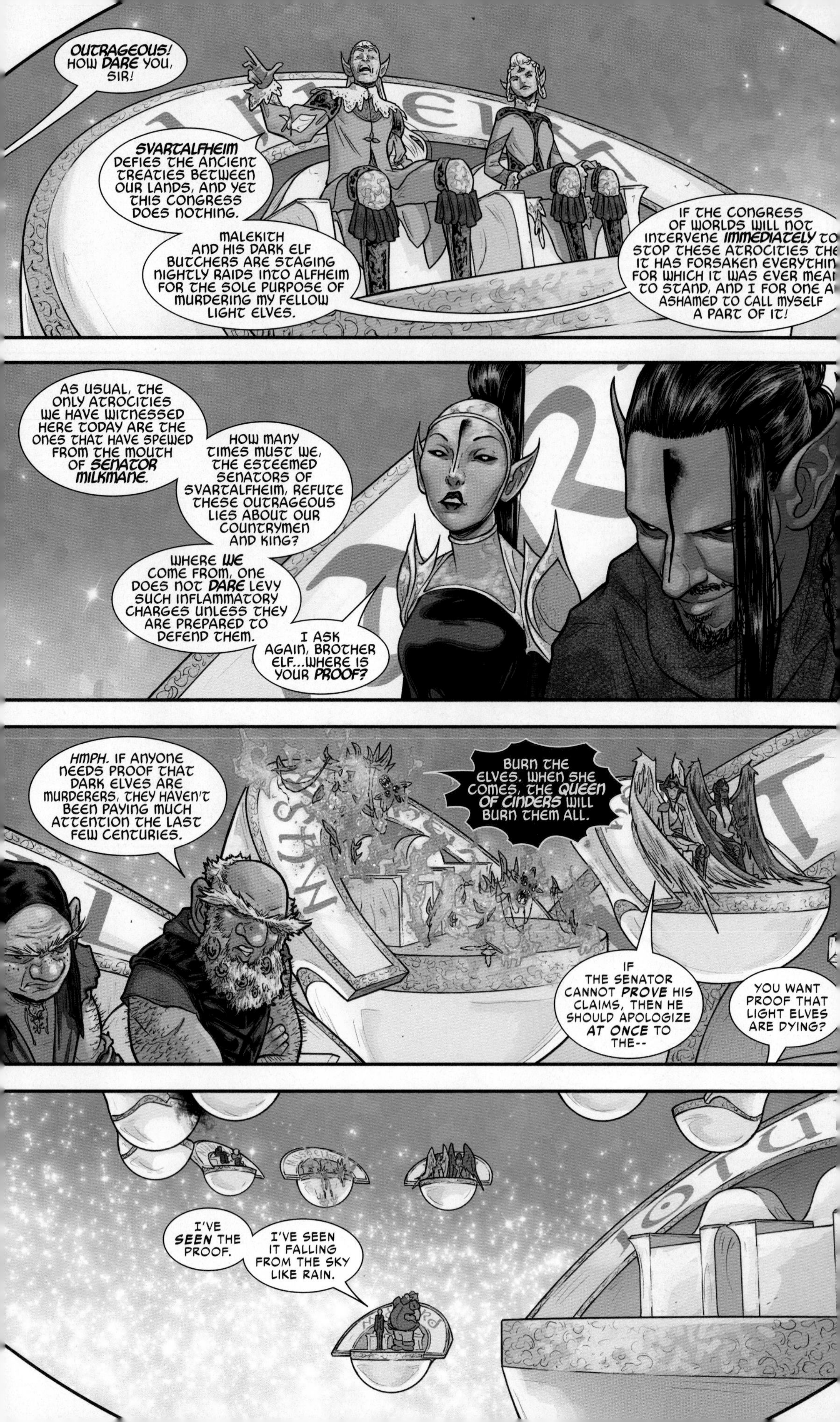
OUTRAGEOUS! HOW DARE YOU, SIR!
SVARTALFHEIM DEFIES THE ANCIENT TREATIES BETWEEN OUR LANDS, AND YET THIS CONGRESS DOES NOTHING.
MALEKITH AND HIS DARK ELF BUTCHERS ARE STAGING NIGHTLY RAIDS INTO ALFHEIM FOR THE SOLE PURPOSE OF MURDERING MY FELLOW LIGHT ELVES.
IF THE CONGRESS OF WORLDS WILL NOT INTERVENE IMMEDIATELY TO STOP THESE ATROCITIES THE IT HAS FORSAKEN EVERYTHIN FOR WHICH IT WAS EVER MEAN TO STAND, AND I FOR ONE A ASHAMED TO CALL MYSELF A PART OF IT!
AS USUAL, THE ONLY ATROCITIES WE HAVE WITNESSED HERE TODAY ARE THE ONES THAT HAVE SPEWED FROM THE MOUTH OF SENATOR MILKMANE.
HOW MANY TIMES MUST WE, THE ESTEEMED SENATORS OF SVARTALFHEIM, REFUTE THESE OUTRAGEOUS LIES ABOUT OUR COUNTRYMEN AND KING?
WHERE WE COME FROM, ONE DOES NOT DARE LEVY SUCH INFLAMMATORY CHARGES UNLESS THEY ARE PREPARED TO DEFEND THEM.
I ASK AGAIN, BROTHER ELF...WHERE IS YOUR PROOF?
HMPH. IF ANYONE NEEDS PROOF THAT DARK ELVES ARE MURDERERS, THEY HAVEN'T BEEN PAYING MUCH ATTENTION THE LAST FEW CENTURIES.
BURN THE ELVES. WHEN SHE COMES, THE QUEEN OF CINDERS WILL BURN THEM ALL.
IF THE SENATOR CANNOT PROVE HIS CLAIMS, THEN HE SHOULD APOLOGIZE AT ONCE TO THE--
YOU WANT PROOF THAT LIGHT ELVES ARE DYING?
I'VE SEEN THE PROOF.
I'VE SEEN IT FALLING FROM THE SKY LIKE RAIN.

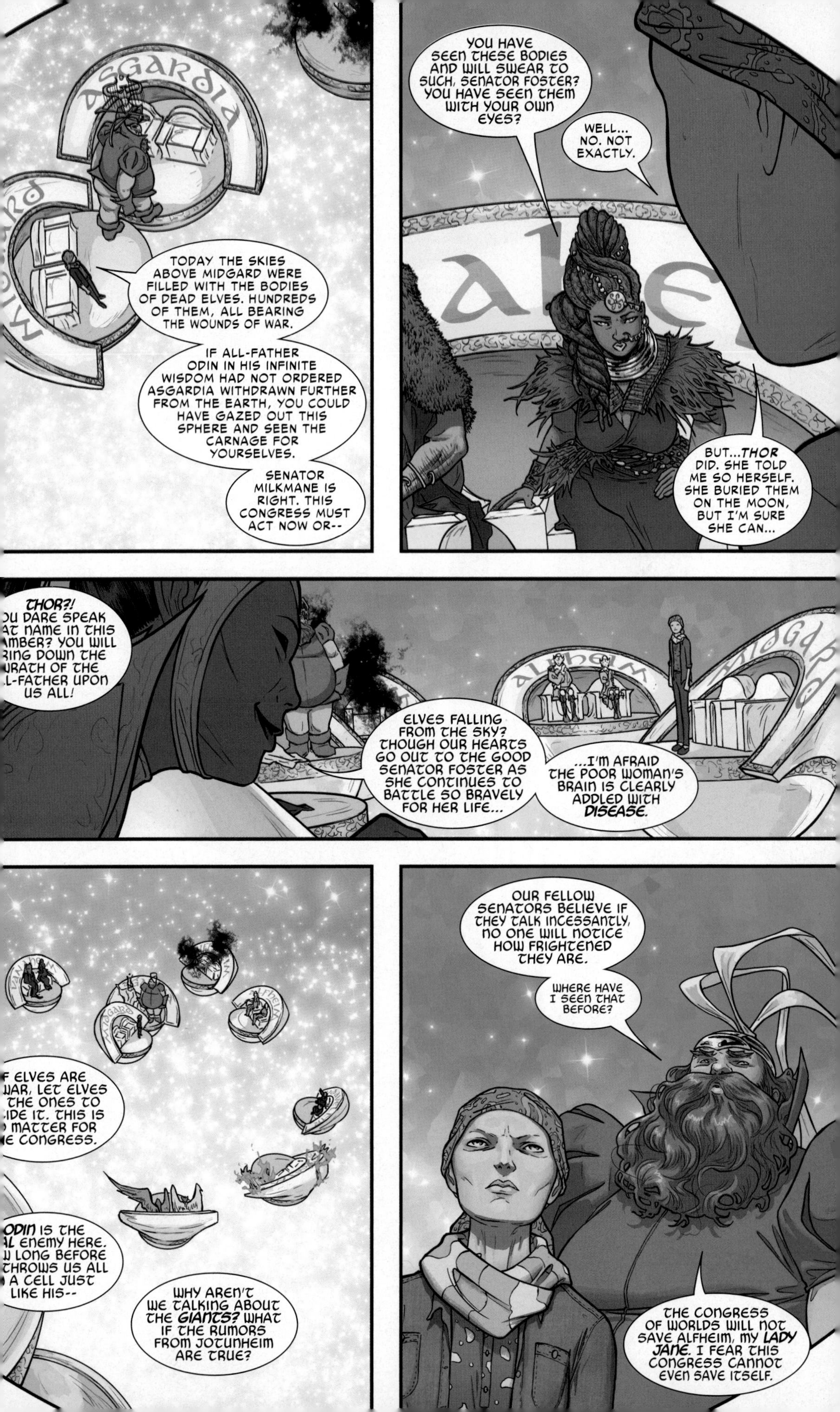
ASGARDIA
MIDGARD
TODAY THE SKIES ABOVE MIDGARD WERE FILLED WITH THE BODIES OF DEAD ELVES. HUNDREDS OF THEM, ALL BEARING THE WOUNDS OF WAR.
IF ALL-FATHER ODIN IN HIS INFINITE WISDOM HAD NOT ORDERED ASGARDIA WITHDRAWN FURTHER FROM THE EARTH, YOU COULD HAVE GAZED OUT THIS SPHERE AND SEEN THE CARNAGE FOR YOURSELVES.
SENATOR MILKMANE IS RIGHT. THIS CONGRESS MUST ACT NOW OR--
YOU HAVE SEEN THESE BODIES AND WILL SWEAR TO SUCH, SENATOR FOSTER? YOU HAVE SEEN THEM WITH YOUR OWN EYES?
WELL... NO. NOT EXACTLY.
BUT...THOR DID. SHE TOLD ME SO HERSELF. SHE BURIED THEM ON THE MOON, BUT I'M SURE SHE CAN...
THOR?! OU DARE SPEAK AT NAME IN THIS AMBER? YOU WILL RING DOWN THE WRATH OF THE L-FATHER UPON US ALL!
ALFHEIM
MIDGARD
ELVES FALLING FROM THE SKY? THOUGH OUR HEARTS GO OUT TO THE GOOD SENATOR FOSTER AS SHE CONTINUES TO BATTLE SO BRAVELY FOR HER LIFE...
...I'M AFRAID THE POOR WOMAN'S BRAIN IS CLEARLY ADDLED WITH DISEASE.
F ELVES ARE WAR, LET ELVES THE ONES TO IDE IT. THIS IS MATTER FOR E CONGRESS.
ODIN IS THE AL ENEMY HERE. N LONG BEFORE THROWS US ALL A CELL JUST LIKE HIS--
WHY AREN'T WE TALKING ABOUT THE GIANTS? WHAT IF THE RUMORS FROM JOTUNHEIM ARE TRUE?
OUR FELLOW SENATORS BELIEVE IF THEY TALK INCESSANTLY, NO ONE WILL NOTICE HOW FRIGHTENED THEY ARE.
WHERE HAVE I SEEN THAT BEFORE?
THE CONGRESS OF WORLDS WILL NOT SAVE ALFHEIM, MY LADY JANE. I FEAR THIS CONGRESS CANNOT EVEN SAVE ITSELF.

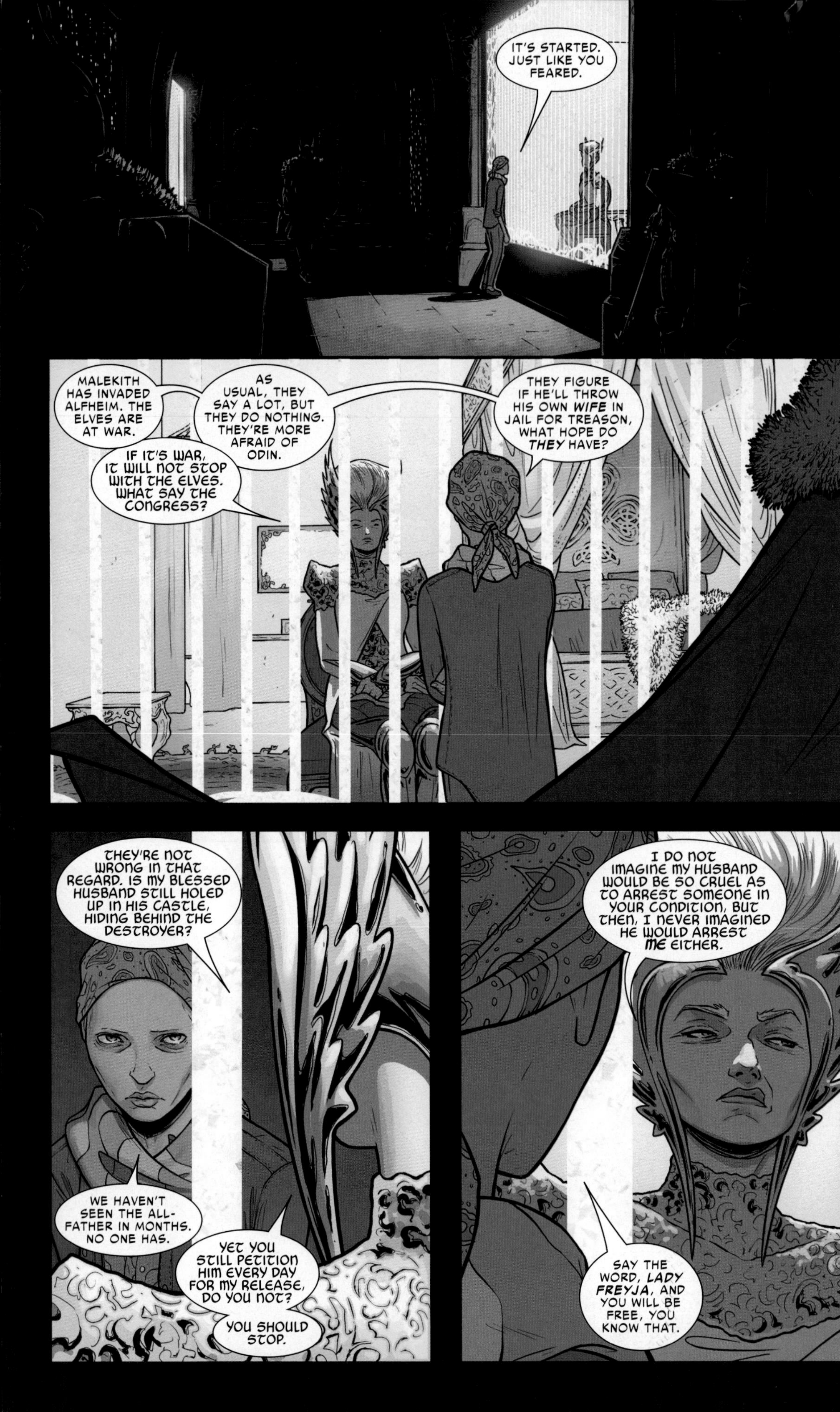
IT'S STARTED. JUST LIKE YOU FEARED.
MALEKITH HAS INVADED ALFHEIM. THE ELVES ARE AT WAR.
IF IT'S WAR, IT WILL NOT STOP WITH THE ELVES. WHAT SAY THE CONGRESS?
AS USUAL, THEY SAY A LOT, BUT THEY DO NOTHING. THEY'RE MORE AFRAID OF ODIN.
THEY FIGURE IF HE'LL THROW HIS OWN WIFE IN JAIL FOR TREASON, WHAT HOPE DO THEY HAVE?
THEY'RE NOT WRONG IN THAT REGARD. IS MY BLESSED HUSBAND STILL HOLED UP IN HIS CASTLE, HIDING BEHIND THE DESTROYER?
WE HAVEN'T SEEN THE ALL-FATHER IN MONTHS. NO ONE HAS.
YET YOU STILL PETITION HIM EVERY DAY FOR MY RELEASE, DO YOU NOT?
YOU SHOULD STOP.
I DO NOT IMAGINE MY HUSBAND WOULD BE SO CRUEL AS TO ARREST SOMEONE IN YOUR CONDITION, BUT THEN, I NEVER IMAGINED HE WOULD ARREST ME EITHER.
SAY THE WORD, LADY FREYJA, AND YOU WILL BE FREE, YOU KNOW THAT.

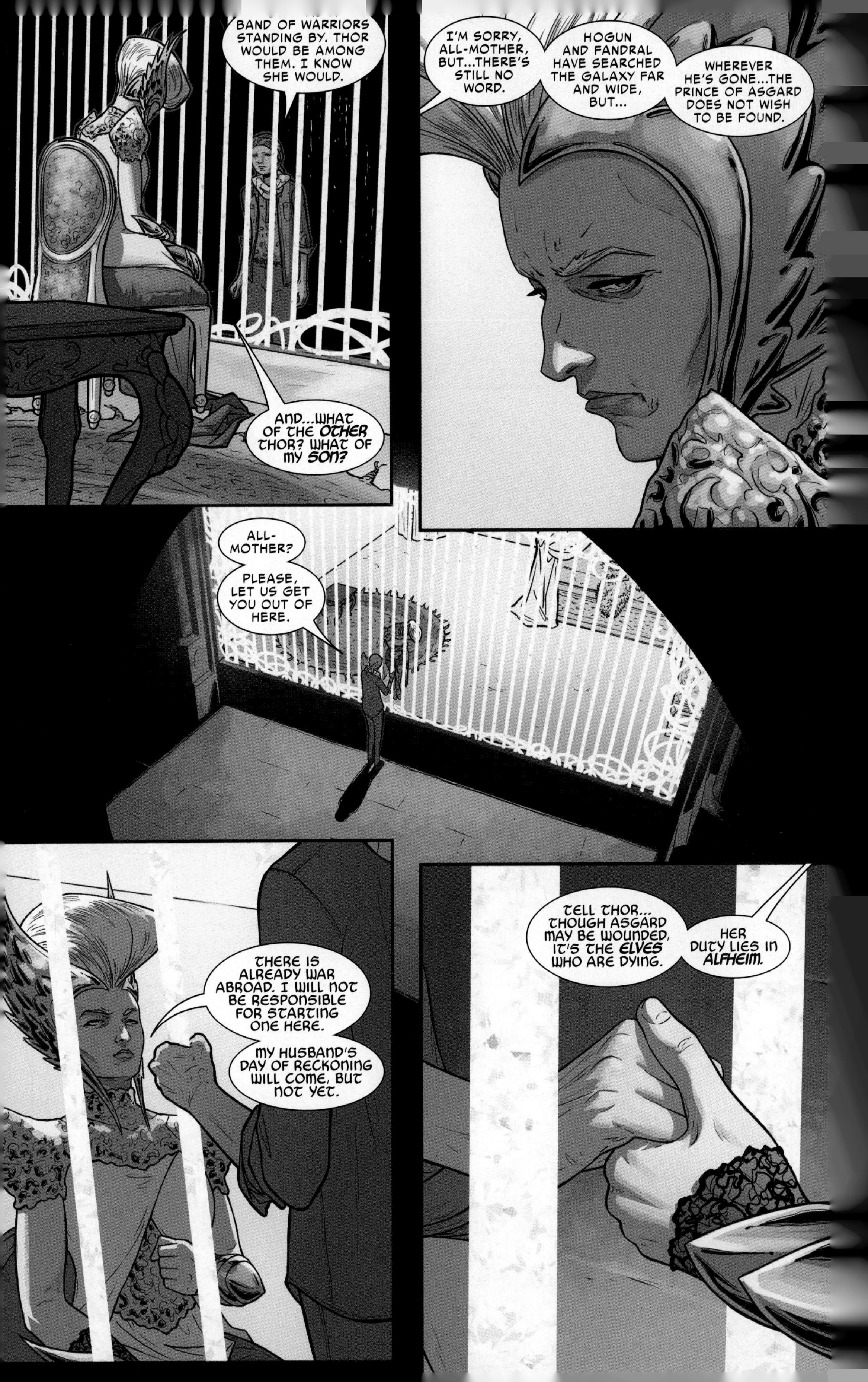
BAND OF WARRIORS STANDING BY. THOR WOULD BE AMONG THEM. I KNOW SHE WOULD.
AND...WHAT OF THE OTHER THOR? WHAT OF MY SON?
I'M SORRY, ALL-MOTHER, BUT...THERE'S STILL NO WORD.
HOGUN AND FANDRAL HAVE SEARCHED THE GALAXY FAR AND WIDE, BUT...
WHEREVER HE'S GONE...THE PRINCE OF ASGARD DOES NOT WISH TO BE FOUND.
ALL-MOTHER?
PLEASE, LET US GET YOU OUT OF HERE.
THERE IS ALREADY WAR ABROAD. I WILL NOT BE RESPONSIBLE FOR STARTING ONE HERE.
MY HUSBAND'S DAY OF RECKONING WILL COME, BUT NOT YET.
TELL THOR... THOUGH ASGARD MAY BE WOUNDED, IT'S THE ELVES WHO ARE DYING.
HER DUTY LIES IN ALFHEIM.

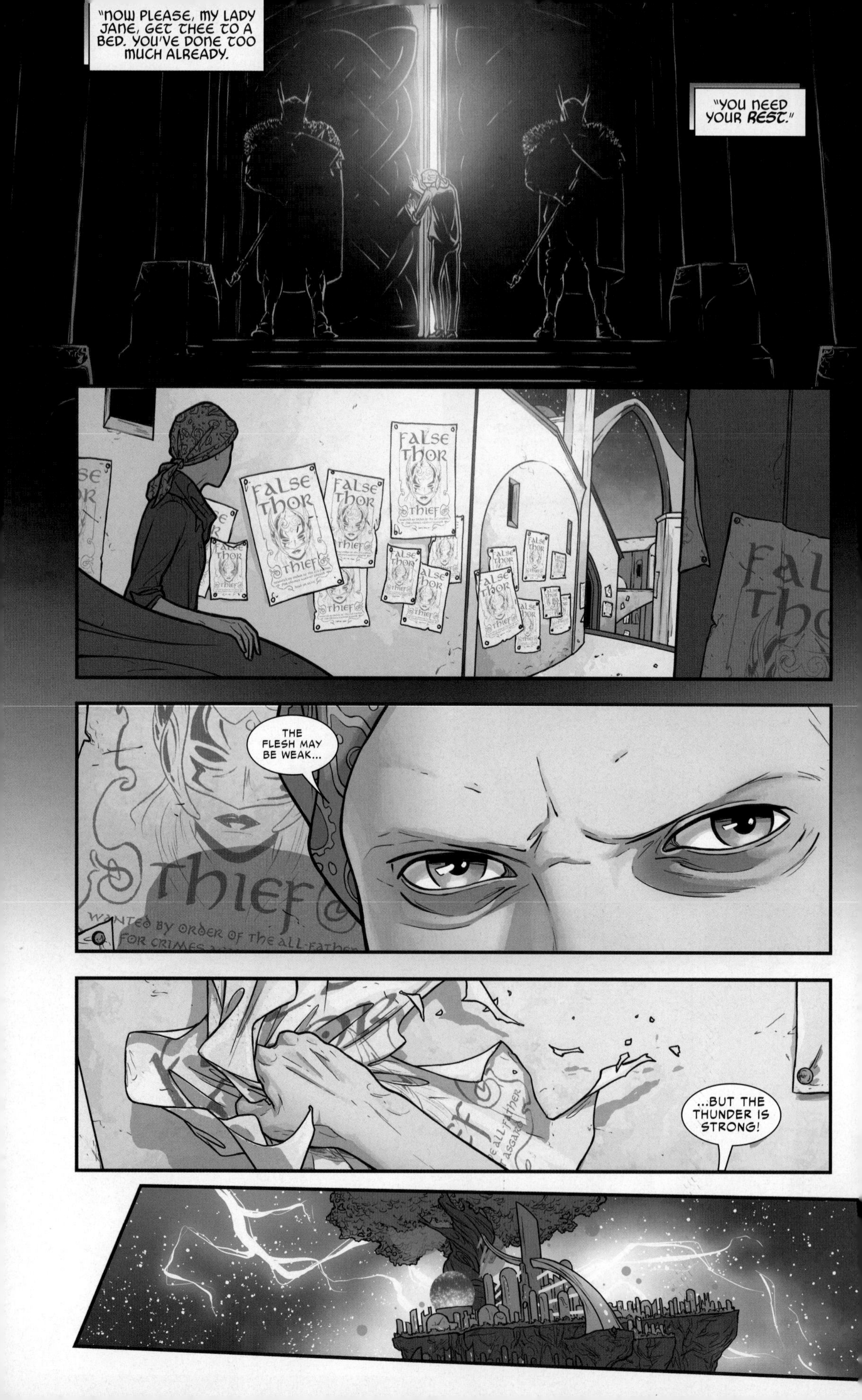
"NOW PLEASE, MY LADY JANE, GET THEE TO A BED. YOU'VE DONE TOO MUCH ALREADY.
"YOU NEED YOUR REST."
FALSE THOR
THIEF
THE FLESH MAY BE WEAK...
WANTED BY ORDER OF THE ALL-FATHER
FOR CRIMES
...BUT THE THUNDER IS STRONG!

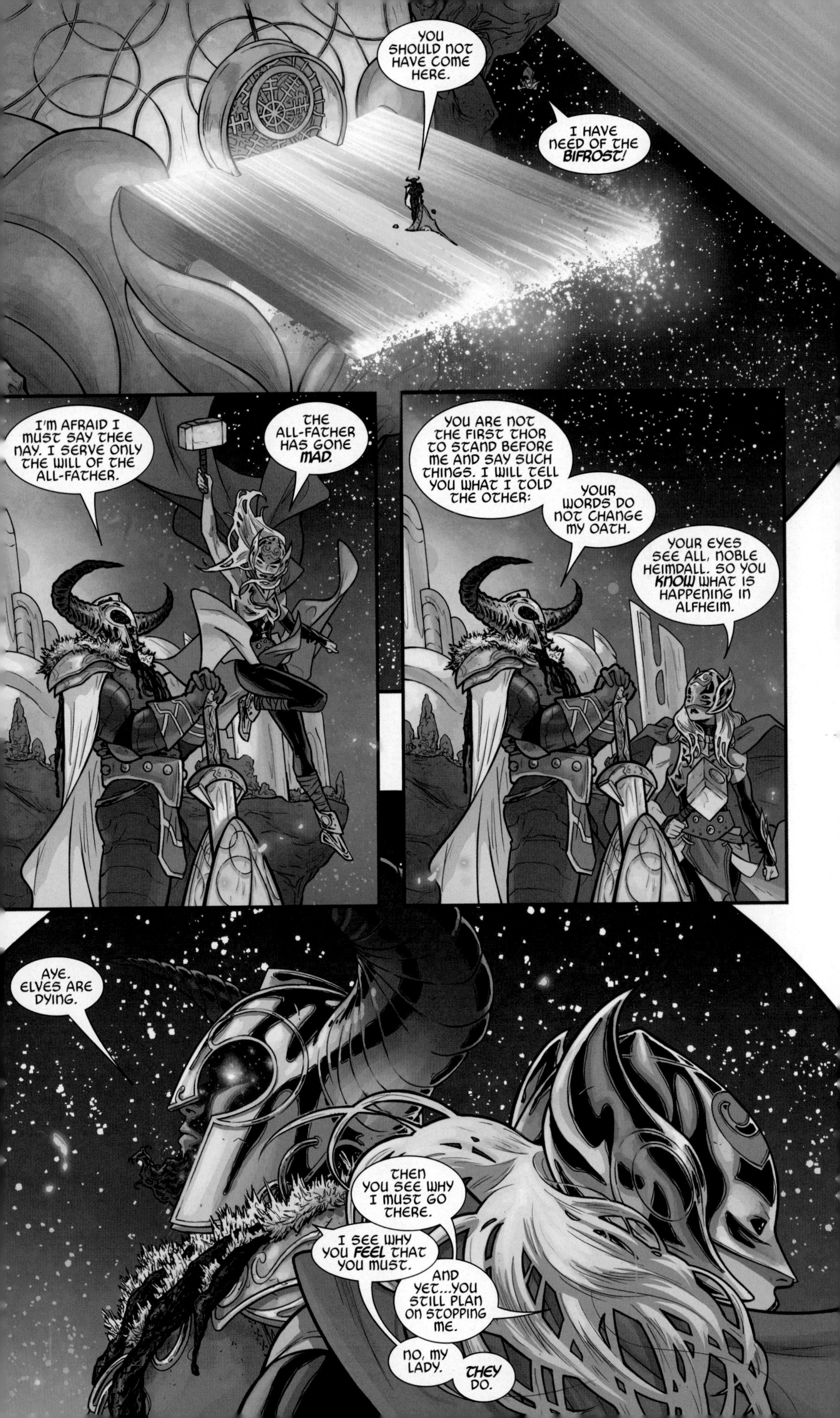

YOU SHOULD NOT HAVE COME HERE.
I HAVE NEED OF THE BIFROST!
I'M AFRAID I MUST SAY THEE NAY. I SERVE ONLY THE WILL OF THE ALL-FATHER.
THE ALL-FATHER HAS GONE MAD.
YOU ARE NOT THE FIRST THOR TO STAND BEFORE ME AND SAY SUCH THINGS. I WILL TELL YOU WHAT I TOLD THE OTHER:
YOUR WORDS DO NOT CHANGE MY OATH.
YOUR EYES SEE ALL, NOBLE HEIMDALL. SO YOU KNOW WHAT IS HAPPENING IN ALFHEIM.
AYE. ELVES ARE DYING.
THEN YOU SEE WHY I MUST GO THERE.
I SEE WHY YOU FEEL THAT YOU MUST.
AND YET...YOU STILL PLAN ON STOPPING ME.
NO, MY LADY.
THEY DO.

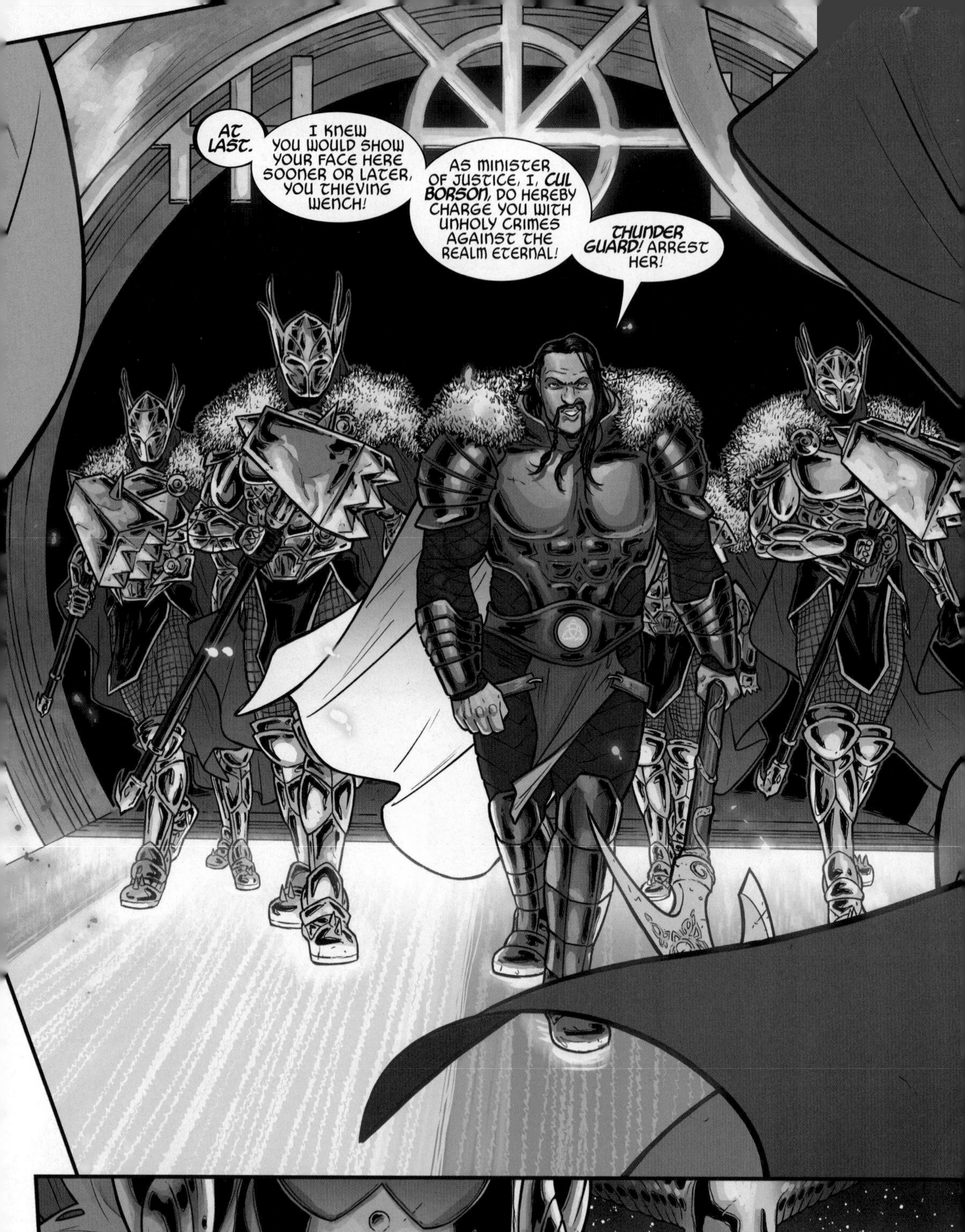
AT LAST.
I KNEW YOU WOULD SHOW YOUR FACE HERE SOONER OR LATER, YOU THIEVING WENCH!
AS MINISTER OF JUSTICE, I, CUL BORSON, DO HEREBY CHARGE YOU WITH UNHOLY CRIMES AGAINST THE REALM ETERNAL!
THUNDER GUARD! ARREST HER!

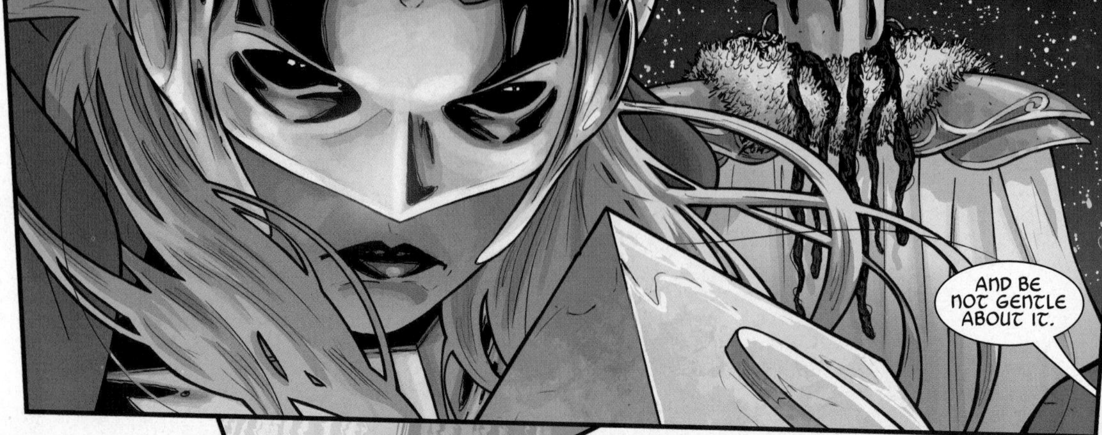
AND BE NOT GENTLE ABOUT IT.

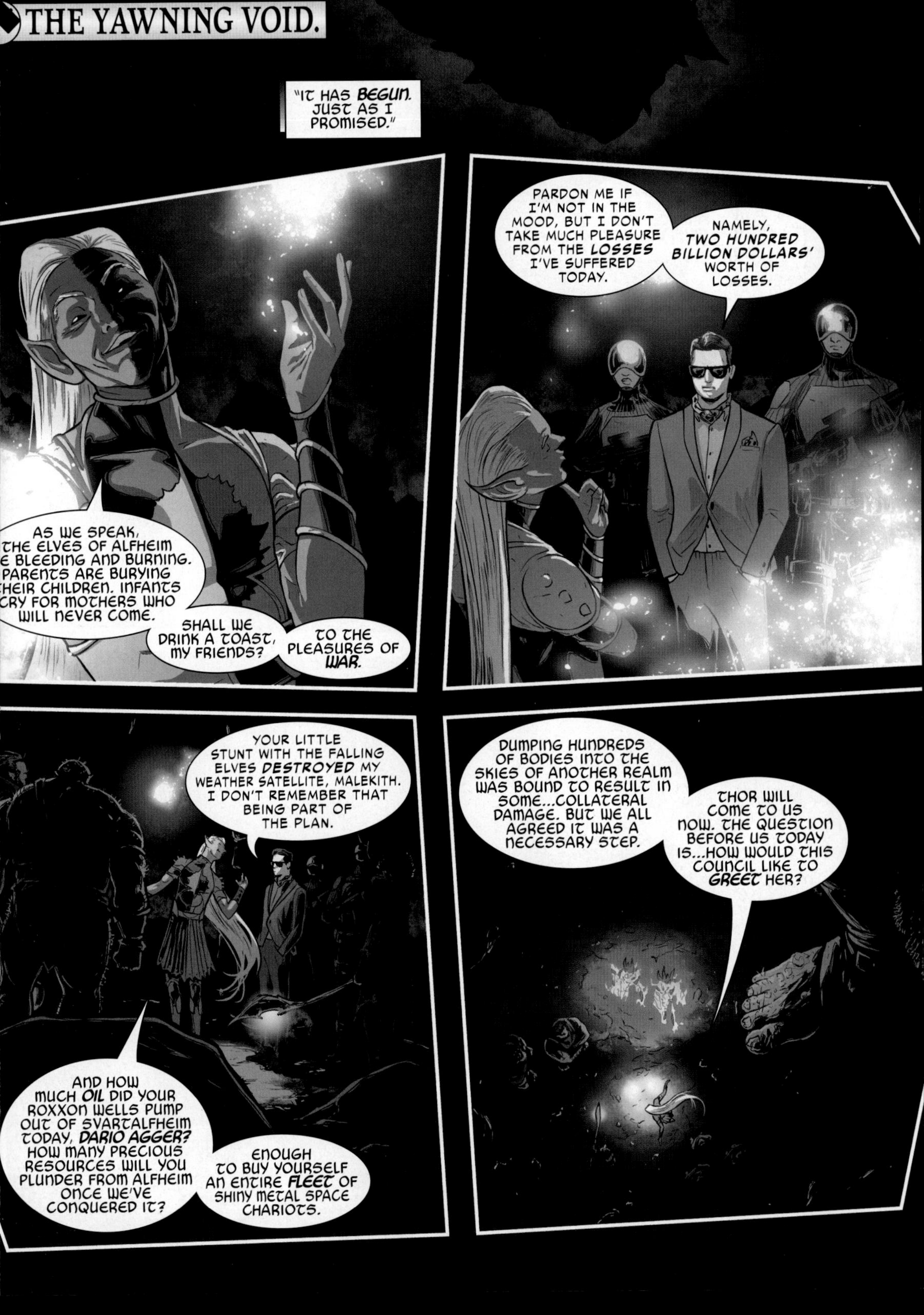
THE YAWNING VOID.
"IT HAS BEGUN. JUST AS I PROMISED."
AS WE SPEAK, THE ELVES OF ALFHEIM E BLEEDING AND BURNING. PARENTS ARE BURYING HEIR CHILDREN. INFANTS CRY FOR MOTHERS WHO WILL NEVER COME.
SHALL WE DRINK A TOAST, MY FRIENDS?
TO THE PLEASURES OF WAR.
PARDON ME IF I'M NOT IN THE MOOD, BUT I DON'T TAKE MUCH PLEASURE FROM THE LOSSES I'VE SUFFERED TODAY.
NAMELY, TWO HUNDRED BILLION DOLLARS' WORTH OF LOSSES.
YOUR LITTLE STUNT WITH THE FALLING ELVES DESTROYED MY WEATHER SATELLITE, MALEKITH. I DON'T REMEMBER THAT BEING PART OF THE PLAN.
AND HOW MUCH OIL DID YOUR ROXXON WELLS PUMP OUT OF SVARTALFHEIM TODAY, DARIO AGGER? HOW MANY PRECIOUS RESOURCES WILL YOU PLUNDER FROM ALFHEIM ONCE WE'VE CONQUERED IT?
ENOUGH TO BUY YOURSELF AN ENTIRE FLEET OF SHINY METAL SPACE CHARIOTS.
DUMPING HUNDREDS OF BODIES INTO THE SKIES OF ANOTHER REALM WAS BOUND TO RESULT IN SOME...COLLATERAL DAMAGE. BUT WE ALL AGREED IT WAS A NECESSARY STEP.
THOR WILL COME TO US NOW. THE QUESTION BEFORE US TODAY IS...HOW WOULD THIS COUNCIL LIKE TO GREET HER?

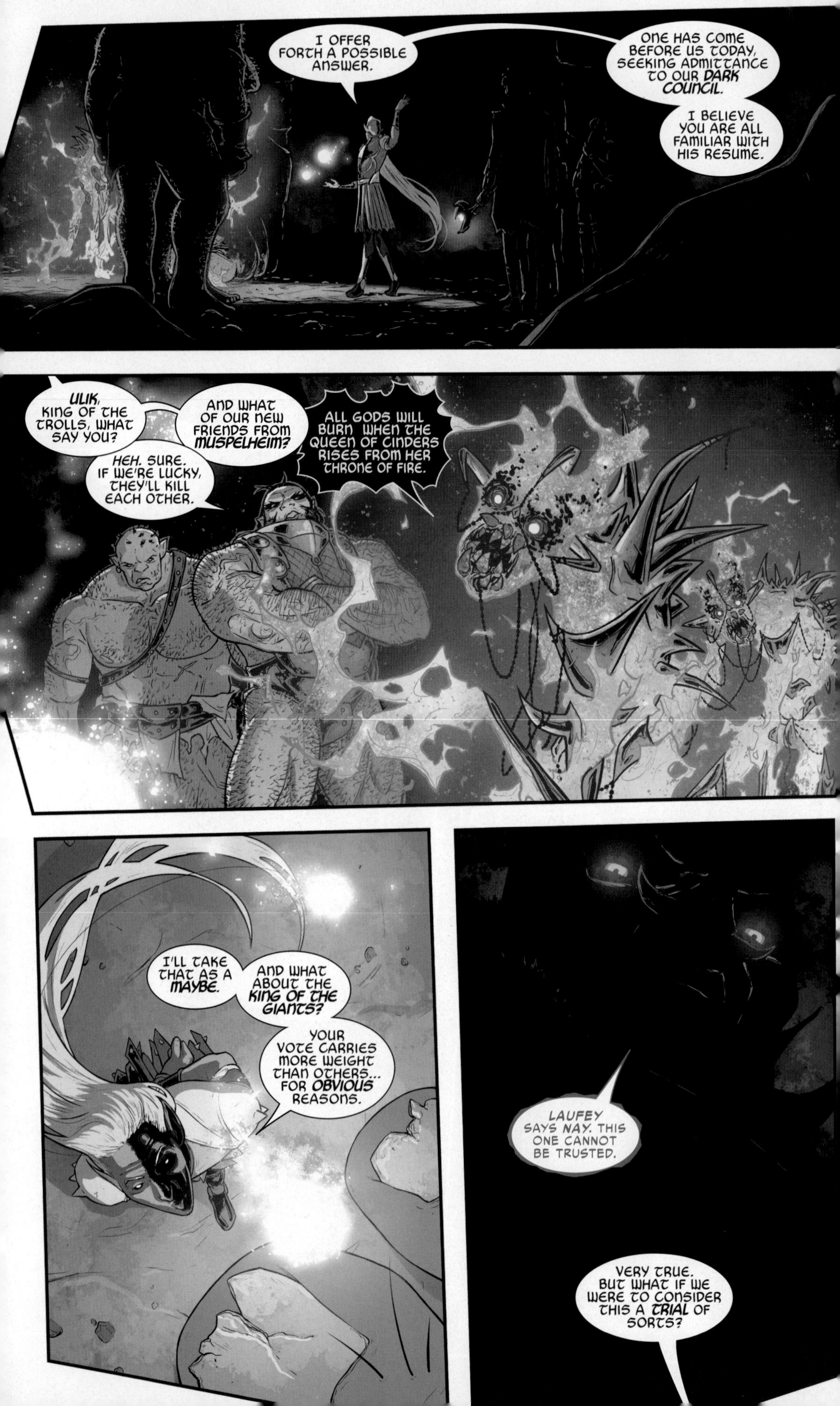
I OFFER FORTH A POSSIBLE ANSWER.
ONE HAS COME BEFORE US TODAY, SEEKING ADMITTANCE TO OUR DARK COUNCIL.
I BELIEVE YOU ARE ALL FAMILIAR WITH HIS RESUME.
ULIK, KING OF THE TROLLS, WHAT SAY YOU?
HEH. SURE. IF WE'RE LUCKY, THEY'LL KILL EACH OTHER.
AND WHAT OF OUR NEW FRIENDS FROM MUSPELHEIM?
ALL GODS WILL BURN WHEN THE QUEEN OF CINDERS RISES FROM HER THRONE OF FIRE.
I'LL TAKE THAT AS A MAYBE.
AND WHAT ABOUT THE KING OF THE GIANTS?
YOUR VOTE CARRIES MORE WEIGHT THAN OTHERS... FOR OBVIOUS REASONS.
LAUFEY SAYS NAY. THIS ONE CANNOT BE TRUSTED.
VERY TRUE. BUT WHAT IF WE WERE TO CONSIDER THIS A TRIAL OF SORTS?

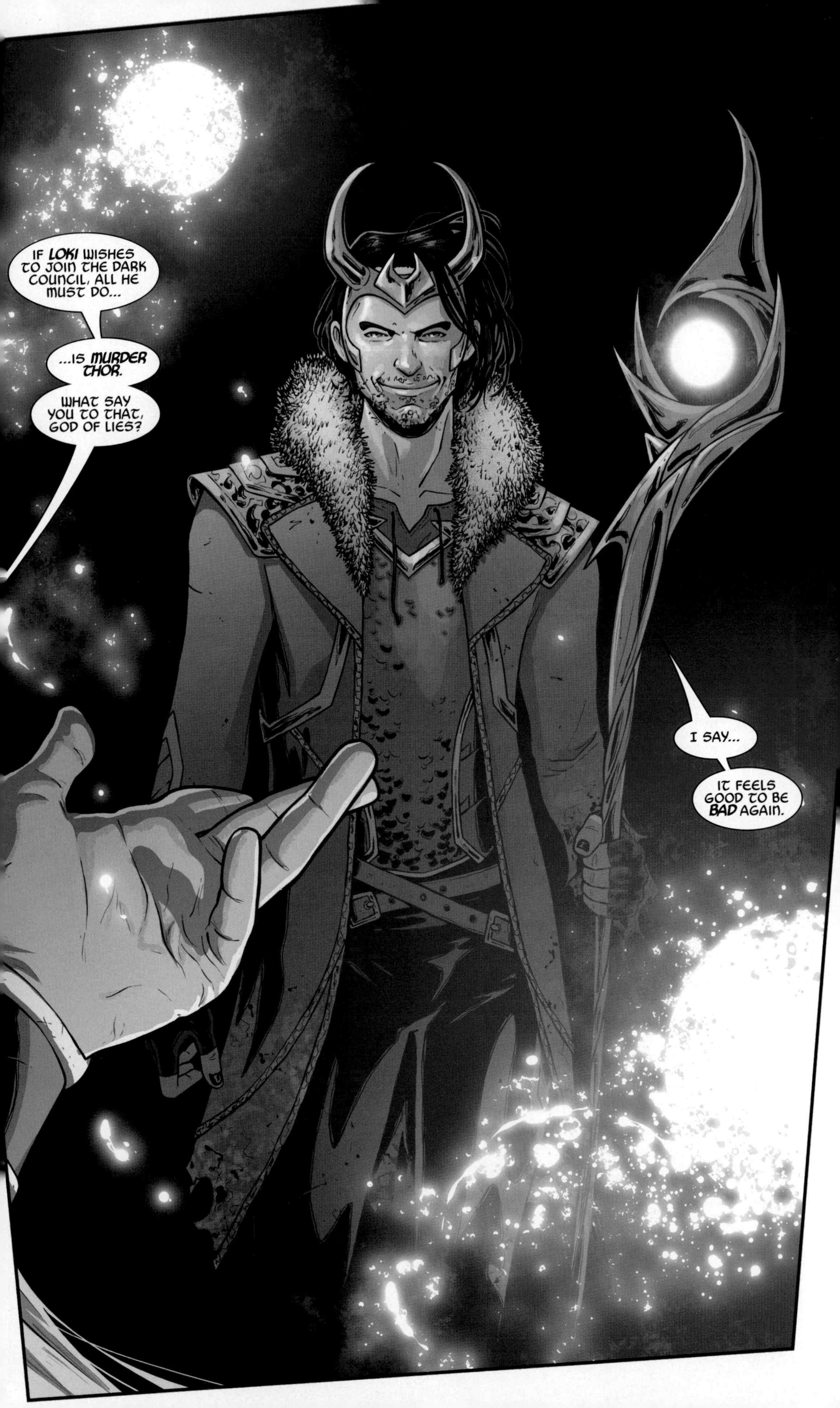
IF **LOKI** WISHES TO JOIN THE DARK COUNCIL, ALL HE MUST DO...
...IS **MURDER THOR.**
WHAT SAY YOU TO THAT, GOD OF LIES?
I SAY...
IT FEELS GOOD TO BE **BAD** AGAIN.

2

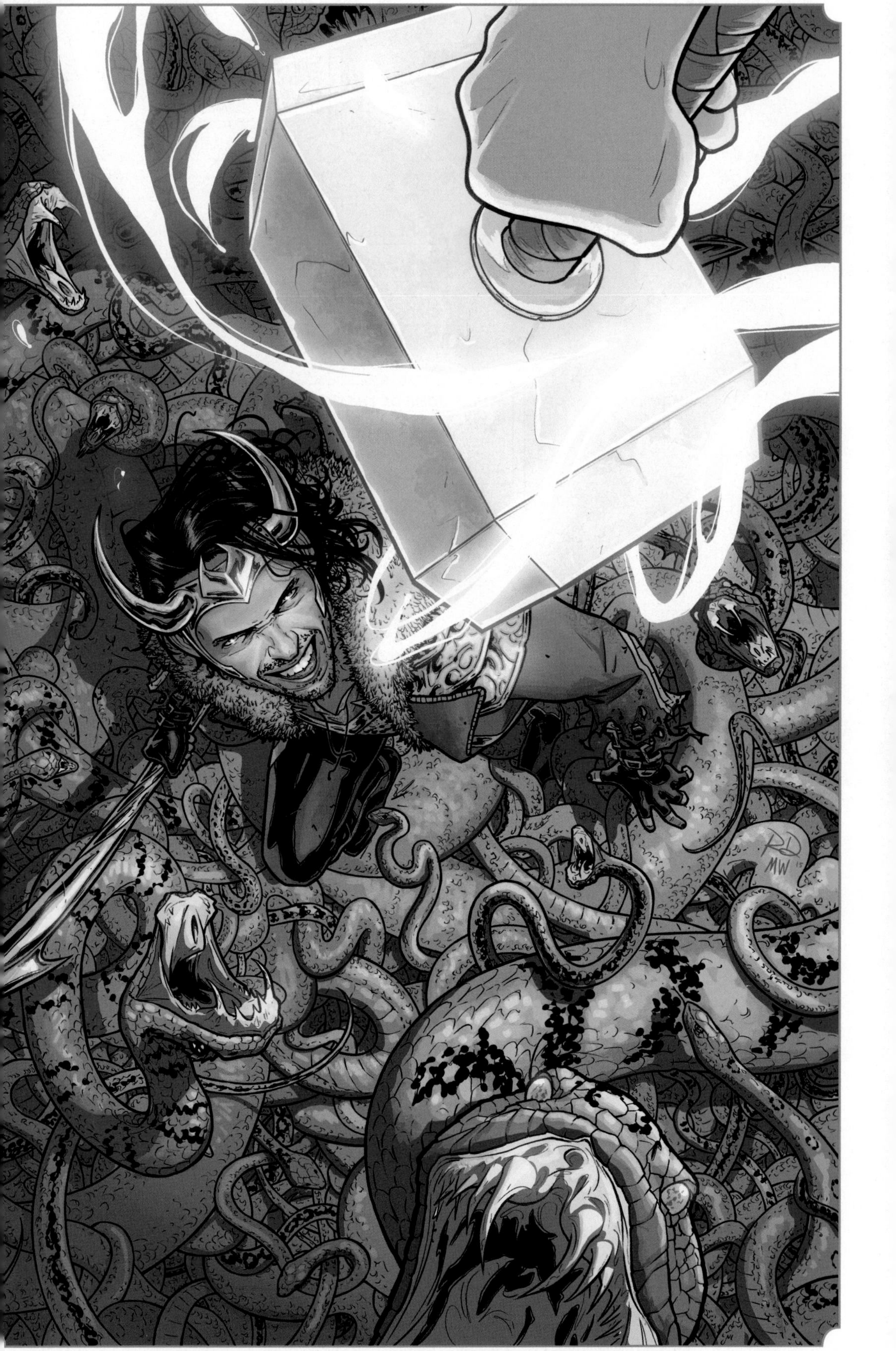

THE WAR OF THE ELVES

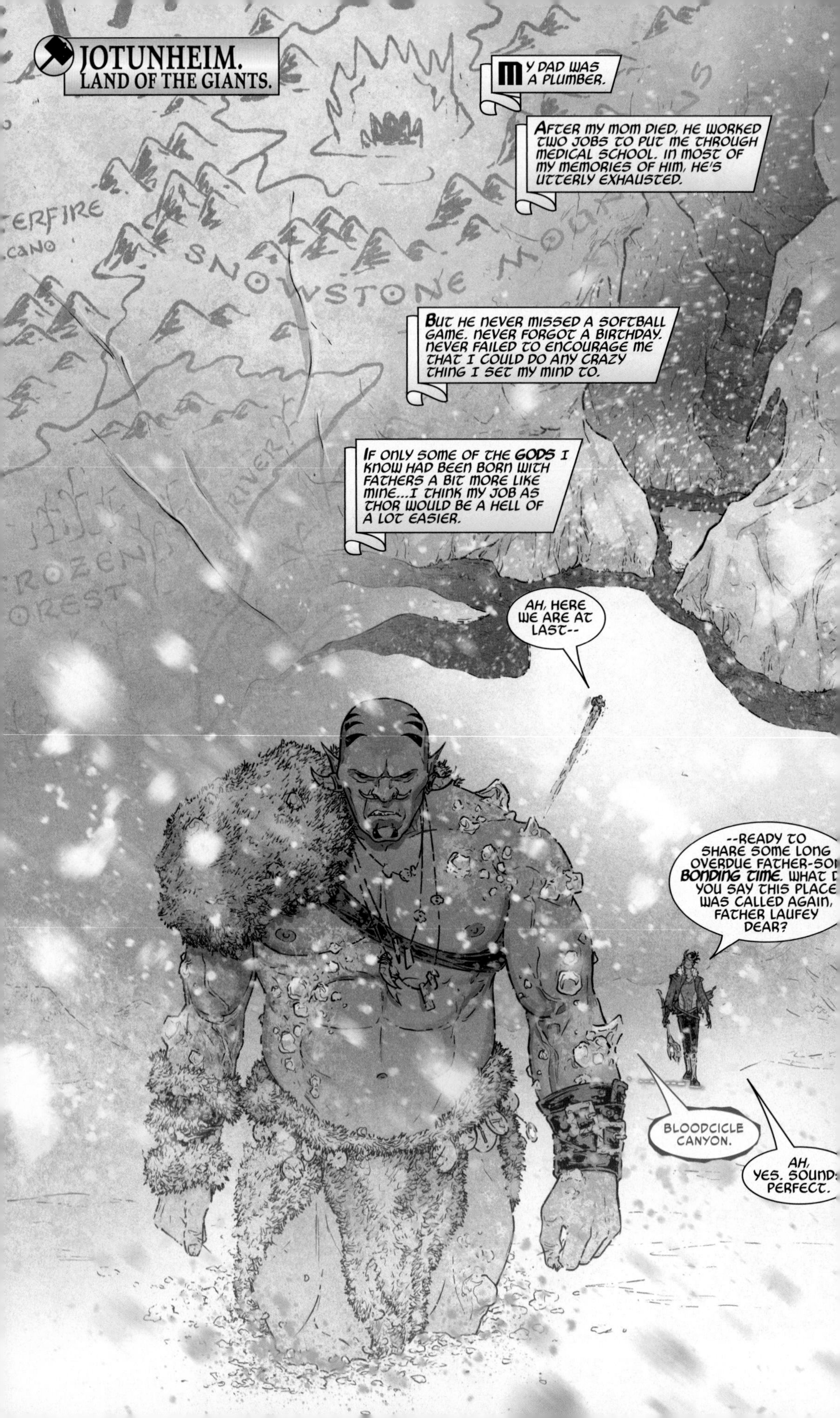
JOTUNHEIM. LAND OF THE GIANTS.
MY DAD WAS A PLUMBER.
AFTER MY MOM DIED, HE WORKED TWO JOBS TO PUT ME THROUGH MEDICAL SCHOOL. IN MOST OF MY MEMORIES OF HIM, HE'S UTTERLY EXHAUSTED.
BUT HE NEVER MISSED A SOFTBALL GAME. NEVER FORGOT A BIRTHDAY. NEVER FAILED TO ENCOURAGE ME THAT I COULD DO ANY CRAZY THING I SET MY MIND TO.
IF ONLY SOME OF THE GODS I KNOW HAD BEEN BORN WITH FATHERS A BIT MORE LIKE MINE...I THINK MY JOB AS THOR WOULD BE A HELL OF A LOT EASIER.
SNOWSTONE
RIVER
AH, HERE WE ARE AT LAST--
--READY TO SHARE SOME LONG OVERDUE FATHER-SO BONDING TIME. WHAT D YOU SAY THIS PLACE WAS CALLED AGAIN, FATHER LAUFEY DEAR?
BLOODCICLE CANYON.
AH, YES. SOUND PERFECT.

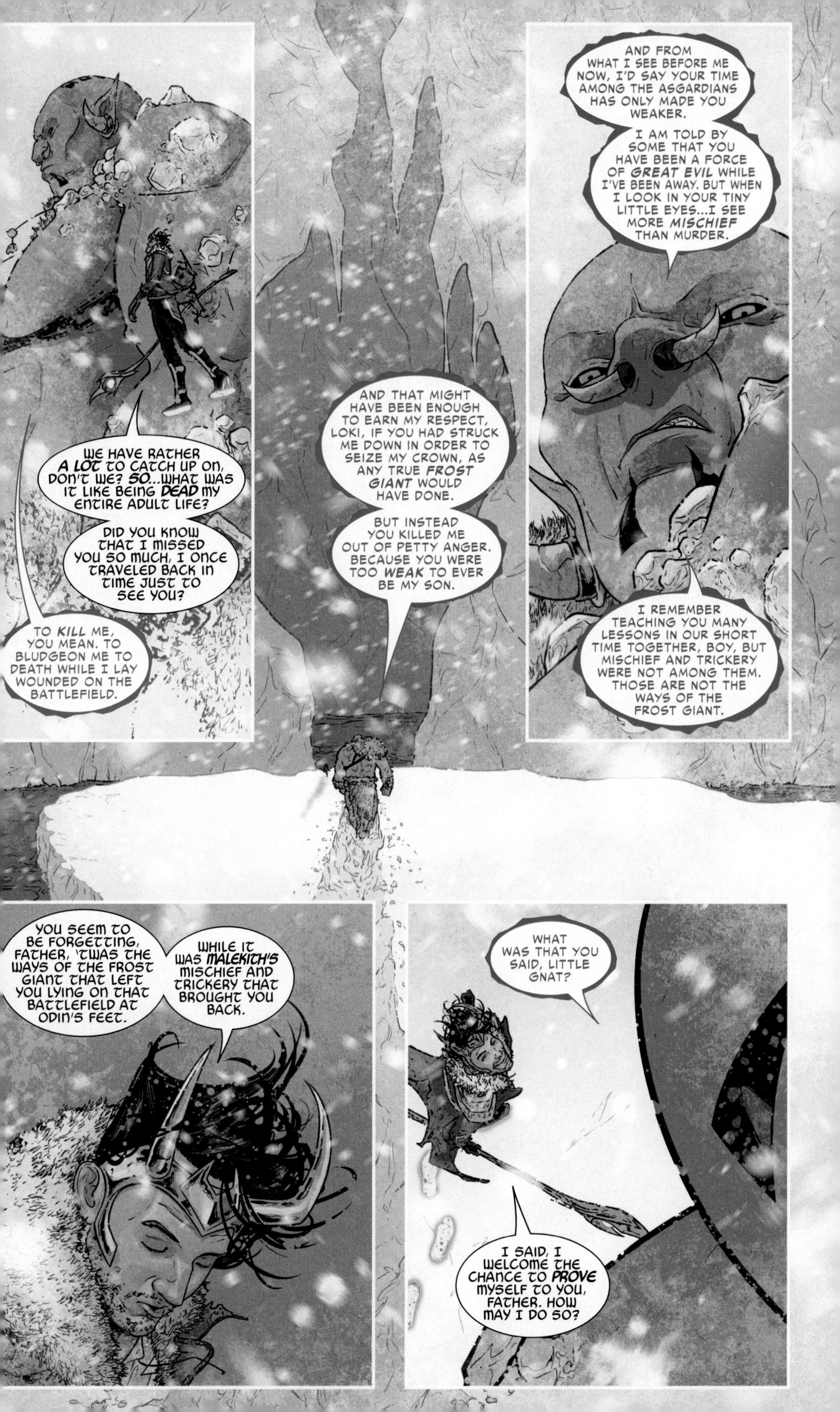
WE HAVE RATHER A LOT TO CATCH UP ON, DON'T WE? SO...WHAT WAS IT LIKE BEING DEAD MY ENTIRE ADULT LIFE?
DID YOU KNOW THAT I MISSED YOU SO MUCH, I ONCE TRAVELED BACK IN TIME JUST TO SEE YOU?
TO KILL ME, YOU MEAN. TO BLUDGEON ME TO DEATH WHILE I LAY WOUNDED ON THE BATTLEFIELD.
AND THAT MIGHT HAVE BEEN ENOUGH TO EARN MY RESPECT, LOKI, IF YOU HAD STRUCK ME DOWN IN ORDER TO SEIZE MY CROWN, AS ANY TRUE FROST GIANT WOULD HAVE DONE.
BUT INSTEAD YOU KILLED ME OUT OF PETTY ANGER. BECAUSE YOU WERE TOO WEAK TO EVER BE MY SON.
AND FROM WHAT I SEE BEFORE ME NOW, I'D SAY YOUR TIME AMONG THE ASGARDIANS HAS ONLY MADE YOU WEAKER.
I AM TOLD BY SOME THAT YOU HAVE BEEN A FORCE OF GREAT EVIL WHILE I'VE BEEN AWAY. BUT WHEN I LOOK IN YOUR TINY LITTLE EYES...I SEE MORE MISCHIEF THAN MURDER.
I REMEMBER TEACHING YOU MANY LESSONS IN OUR SHORT TIME TOGETHER, BOY, BUT MISCHIEF AND TRICKERY WERE NOT AMONG THEM. THOSE ARE NOT THE WAYS OF THE FROST GIANT.
YOU SEEM TO BE FORGETTING, FATHER, 'TWAS THE WAYS OF THE FROST GIANT THAT LEFT YOU LYING ON THAT BATTLEFIELD AT ODIN'S FEET.
WHILE IT WAS MALEKITH'S MISCHIEF AND TRICKERY THAT BROUGHT YOU BACK.
WHAT WAS THAT YOU SAID, LITTLE GNAT?
I SAID, I WELCOME THE CHANCE TO PROVE MYSELF TO YOU, FATHER. HOW MAY I DO SO?

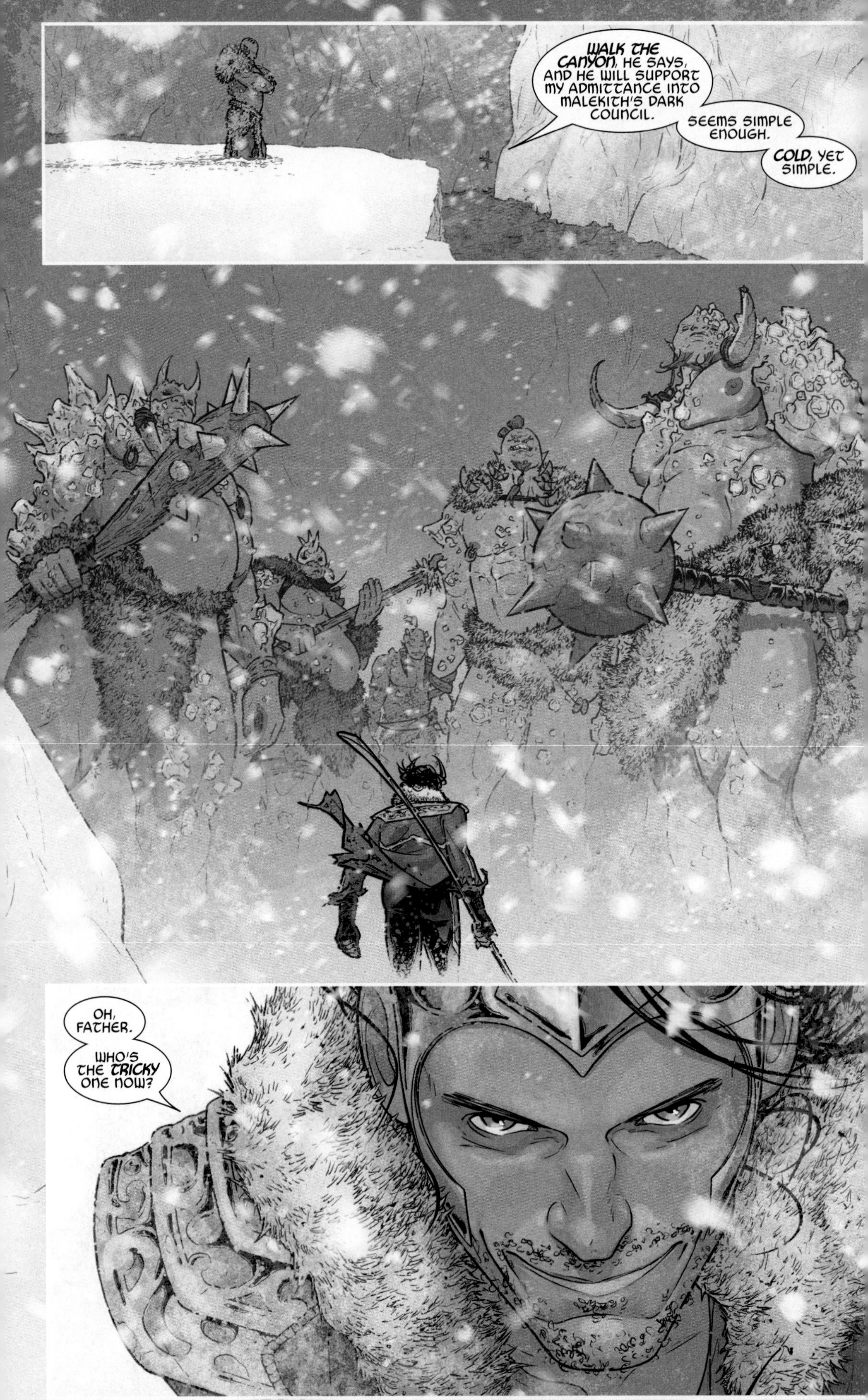
WALK THE CANYON, HE SAYS, AND HE WILL SUPPORT MY ADMITTANCE INTO MALEKITH'S DARK COUNCIL.
SEEMS SIMPLE ENOUGH.
COLD, YET SIMPLE.
OH, FATHER.
WHO'S THE TRICKY ONE NOW?

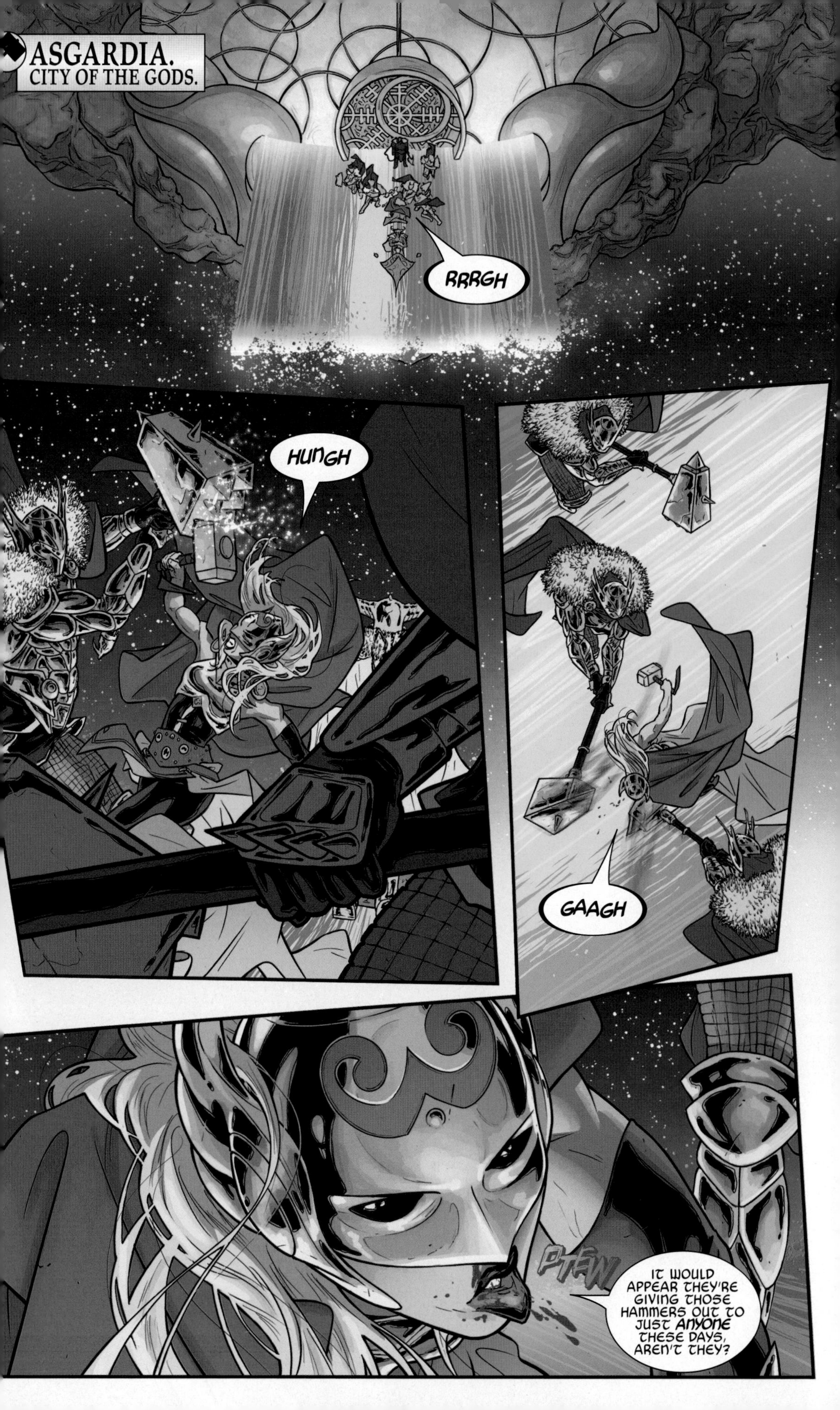
ASGARDIA.
CITY OF THE GODS.
RRRGH
HUNGH
GAAGH
PTEW
IT WOULD APPEAR THEY'RE GIVING THOSE HAMMERS OUT TO JUST ANYONE THESE DAYS, AREN'T THEY?

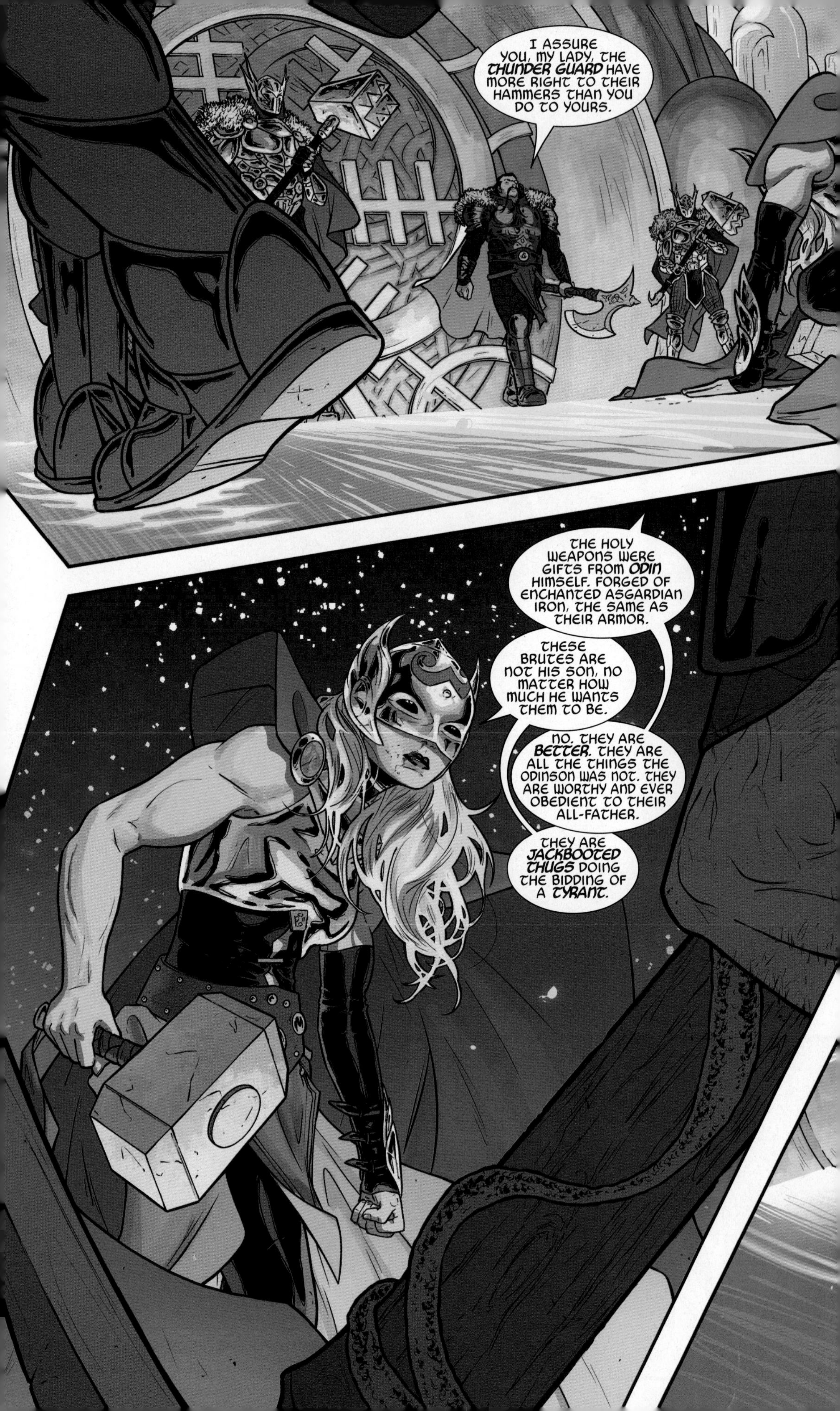
I ASSURE YOU, MY LADY, THE THUNDER GUARD HAVE MORE RIGHT TO THEIR HAMMERS THAN YOU DO TO YOURS.
THE HOLY WEAPONS WERE GIFTS FROM ODIN HIMSELF. FORGED OF ENCHANTED ASGARDIAN IRON, THE SAME AS THEIR ARMOR.
THESE BRUTES ARE NOT HIS SON, NO MATTER HOW MUCH HE WANTS THEM TO BE.
NO. THEY ARE BETTER. THEY ARE ALL THE THINGS THE ODINSON WAS NOT. THEY ARE WORTHY AND EVER OBEDIENT TO THEIR ALL-FATHER.
THEY ARE JACKBOOTED THUGS DOING THE BIDDING OF A TYRANT.

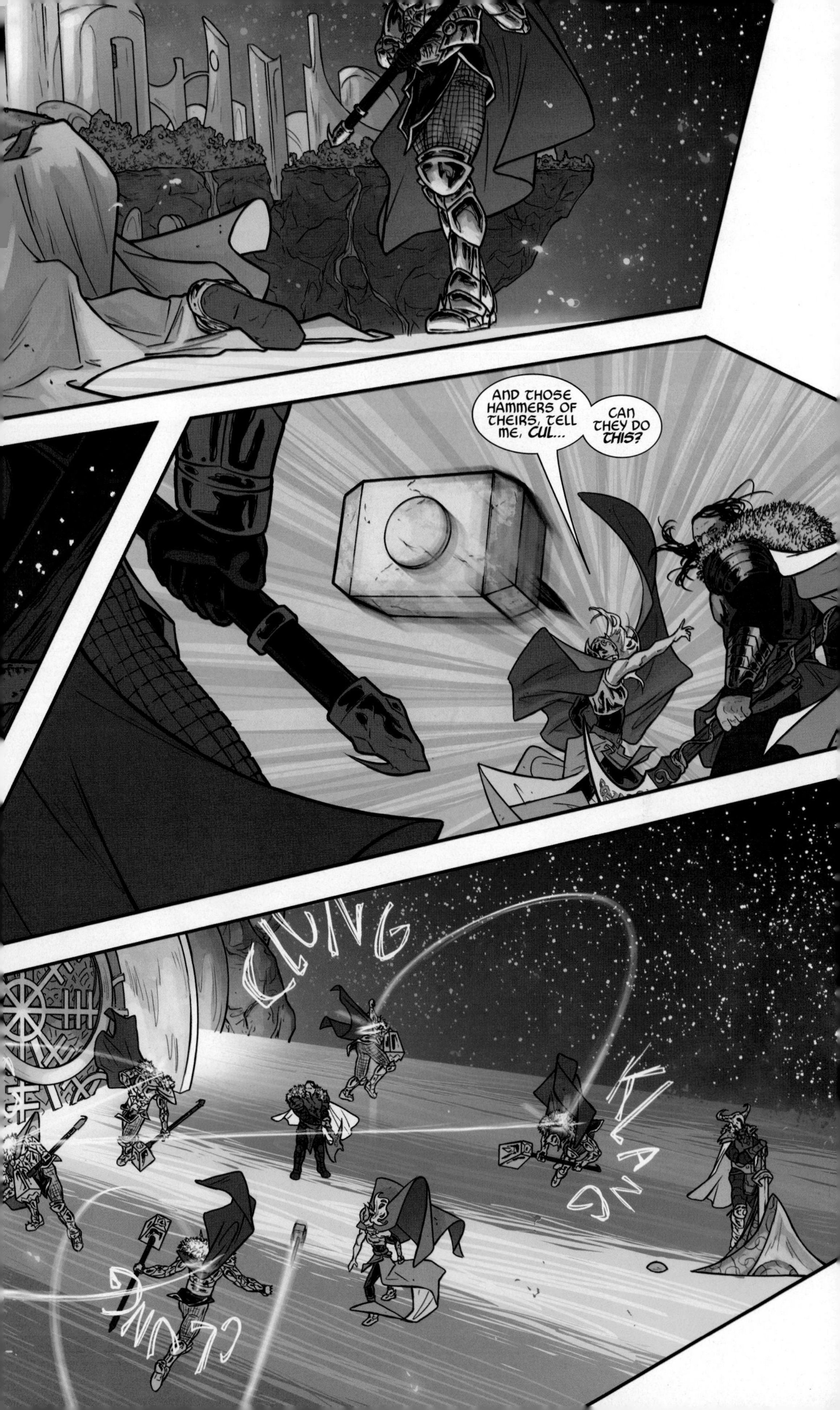

AND THOSE HAMMERS OF THEIRS, TELL ME, CUL...
CAN THEY DO THIS?
CLUNG
KLANG
CLUNG

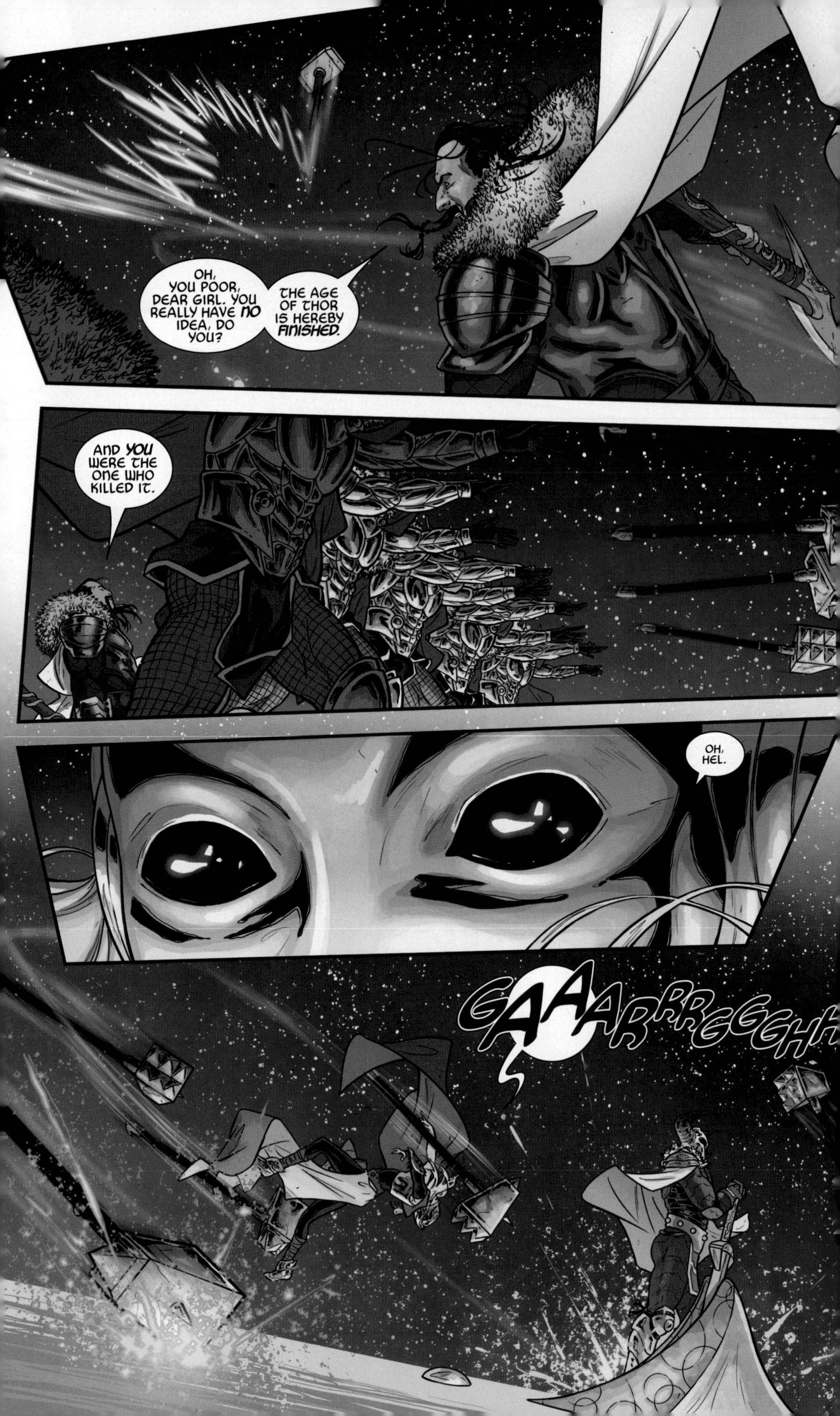
OH, YOU POOR, DEAR GIRL. YOU REALLY HAVE NO IDEA, DO YOU?
THE AGE OF THOR IS HEREBY FINISHED.
AND YOU WERE THE ONE WHO KILLED IT.
OH, HEL.
GAAARRRGGGHH

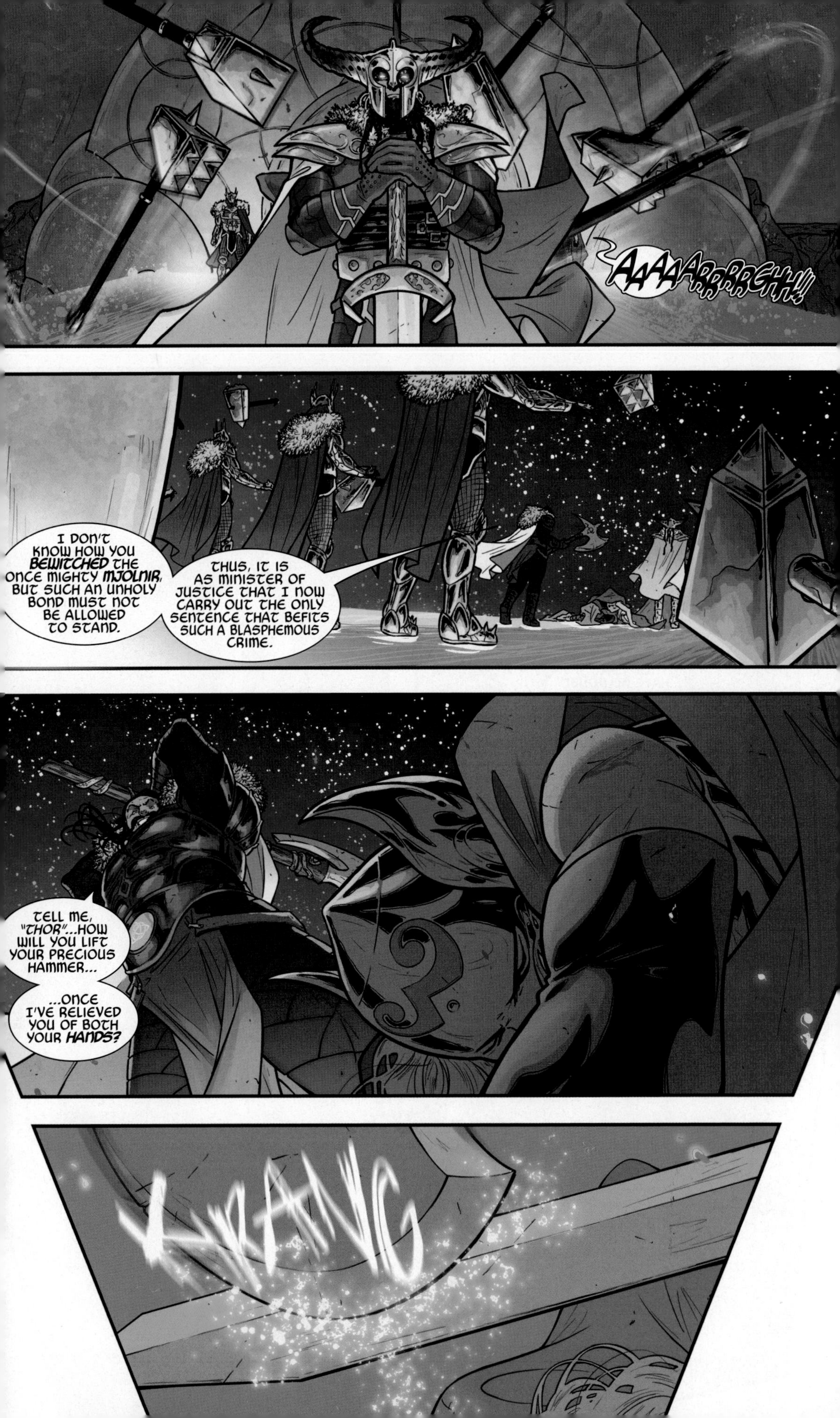
AAAAARRRRGHH!!
I DON'T KNOW HOW YOU BEWITCHED THE ONCE MIGHTY MJOLNIR, BUT SUCH AN UNHOLY BOND MUST NOT BE ALLOWED TO STAND.
THUS, IT IS AS MINISTER OF JUSTICE THAT I NOW CARRY OUT THE ONLY SENTENCE THAT BEFITS SUCH A BLASPHEMOUS CRIME.
TELL ME, "THOR"...HOW WILL YOU LIFT YOUR PRECIOUS HAMMER...
...ONCE I'VE RELIEVED YOU OF BOTH YOUR HANDS?
KRANG

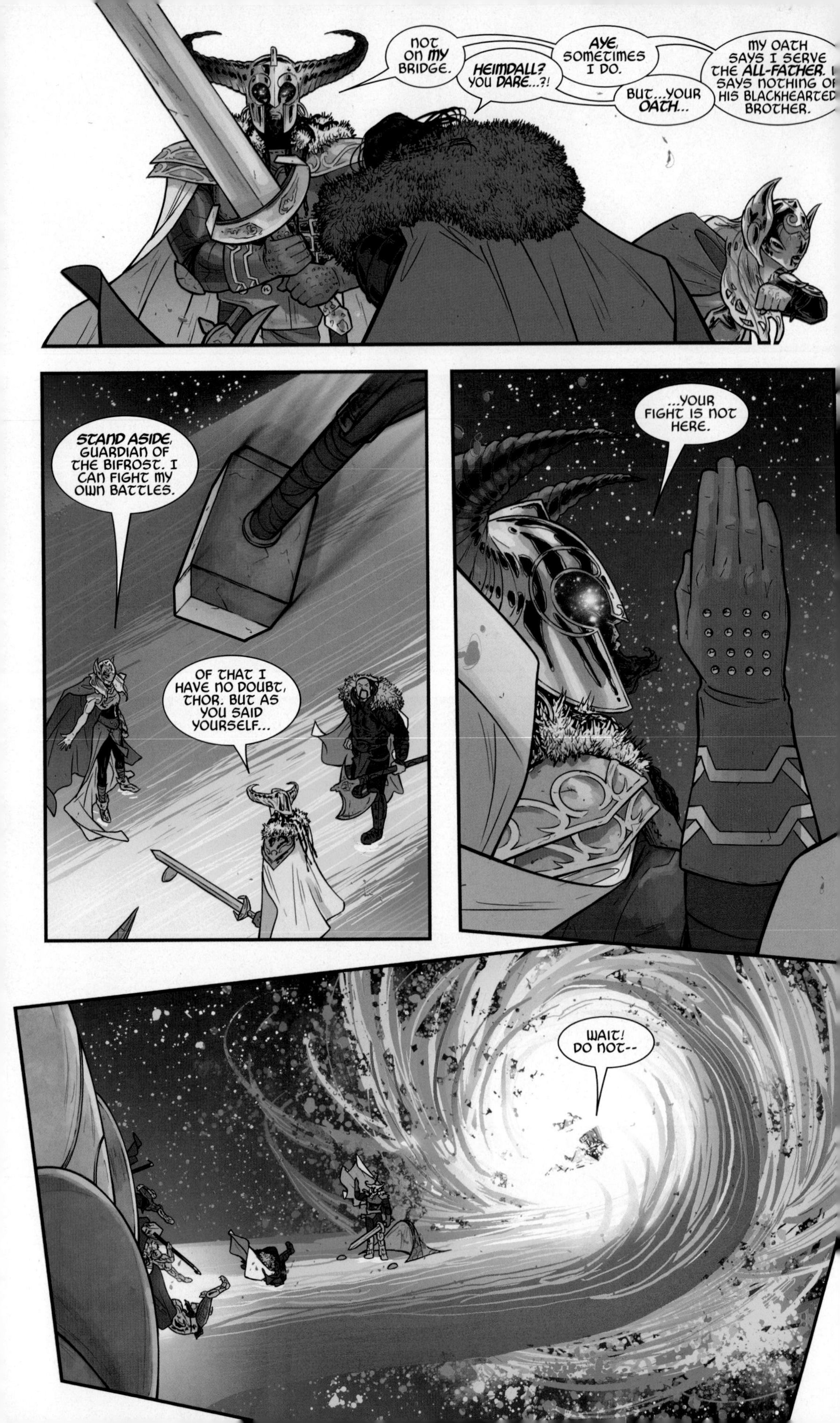
NOT ON MY BRIDGE.
HEIMDALL? YOU DARE...?!
AYE, SOMETIMES I DO.
BUT...YOUR OATH...
MY OATH SAYS I SERVE THE ALL-FATHER. I SAYS NOTHING OF HIS BLACKHEARTED BROTHER.
STAND ASIDE, GUARDIAN OF THE BIFROST. I CAN FIGHT MY OWN BATTLES.
OF THAT I HAVE NO DOUBT, THOR. BUT AS YOU SAID YOURSELF...
...YOUR FIGHT IS NOT HERE.
WAIT! DO NOT--

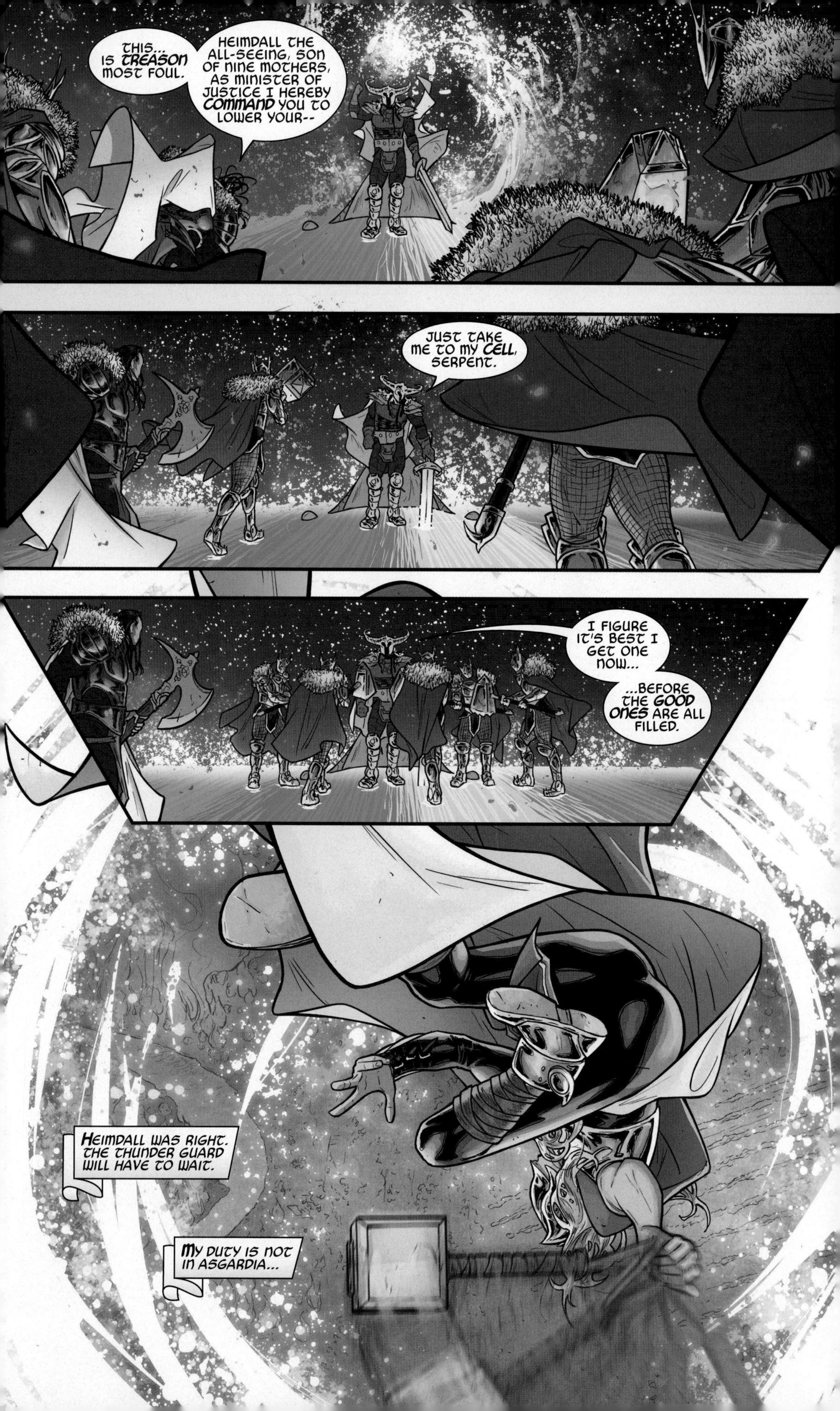
THIS... IS TREASON MOST FOUL.
HEIMDALL THE ALL-SEEING, SON OF NINE MOTHERS, AS MINISTER OF JUSTICE I HEREBY COMMAND YOU TO LOWER YOUR--
JUST TAKE ME TO MY CELL, SERPENT.
I FIGURE IT'S BEST I GET ONE NOW...
...BEFORE THE GOOD ONES ARE ALL FILLED.
HEIMDALL WAS RIGHT. THE THUNDER GUARD WILL HAVE TO WAIT.
MY DUTY IS NOT IN ASGARDIA...

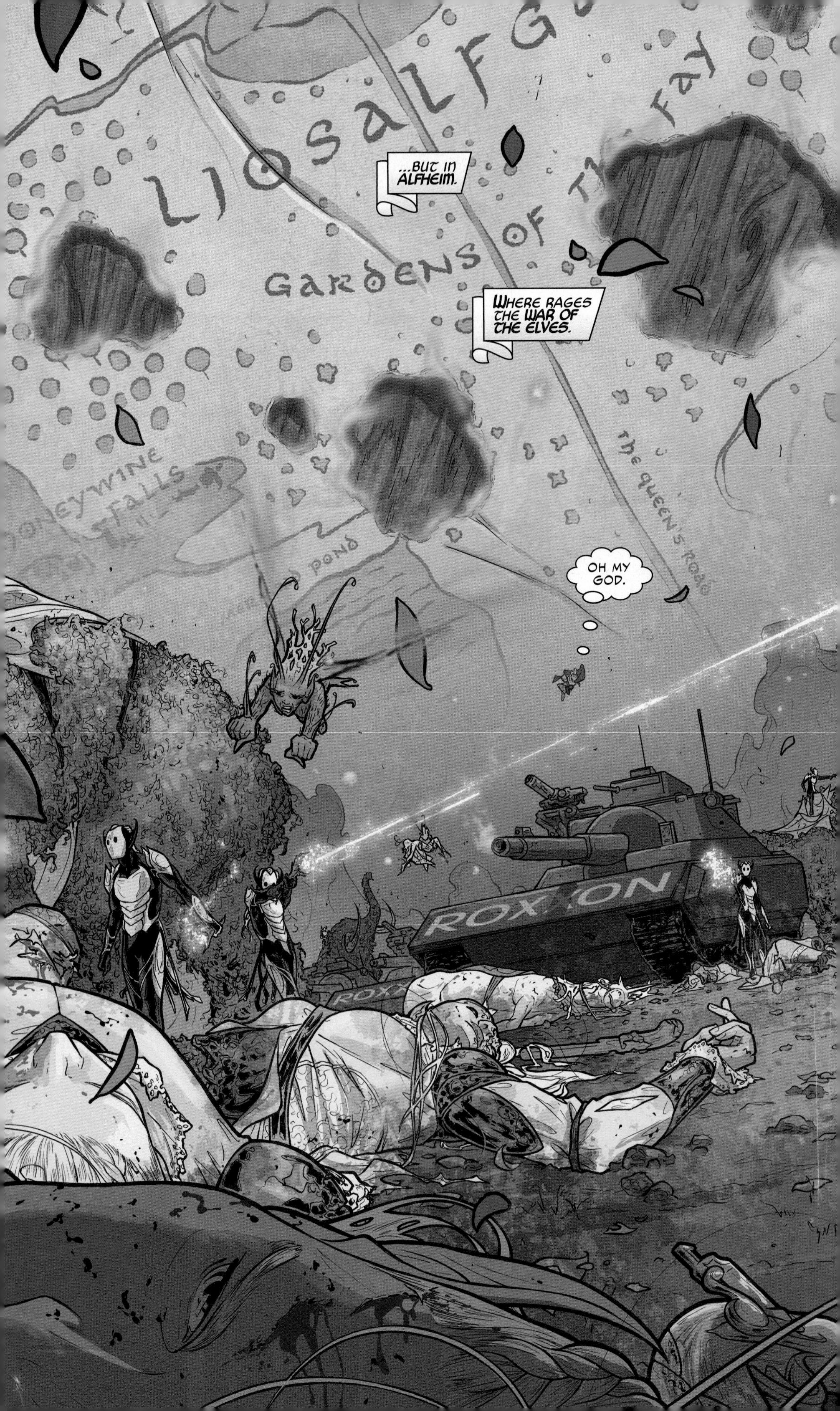
...BUT IN ALFHEIM.
WHERE RAGES THE WAR OF THE ELVES.
OH MY GOD.
the queen's road
ROXXON

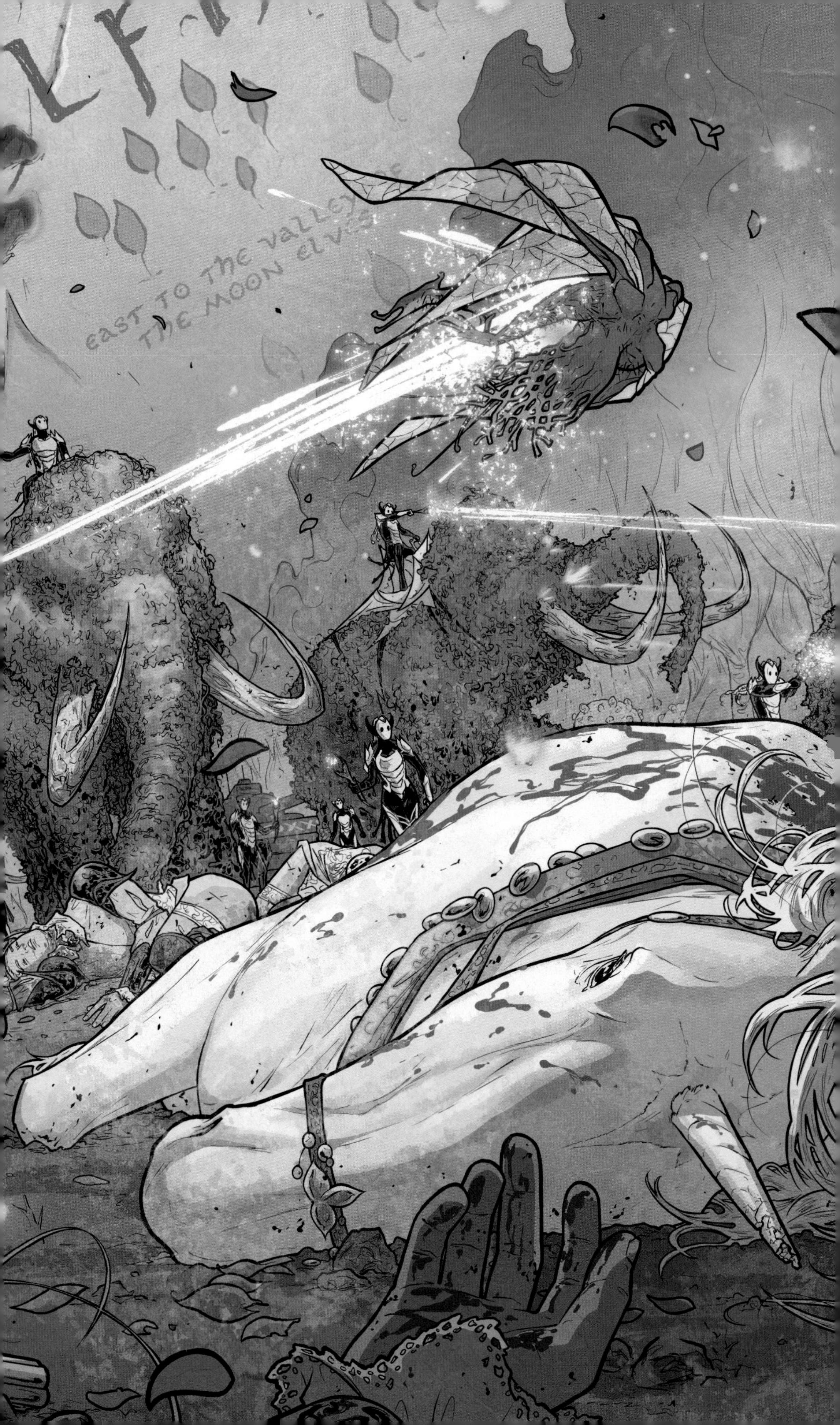

East to the valley of
The Moon Elves

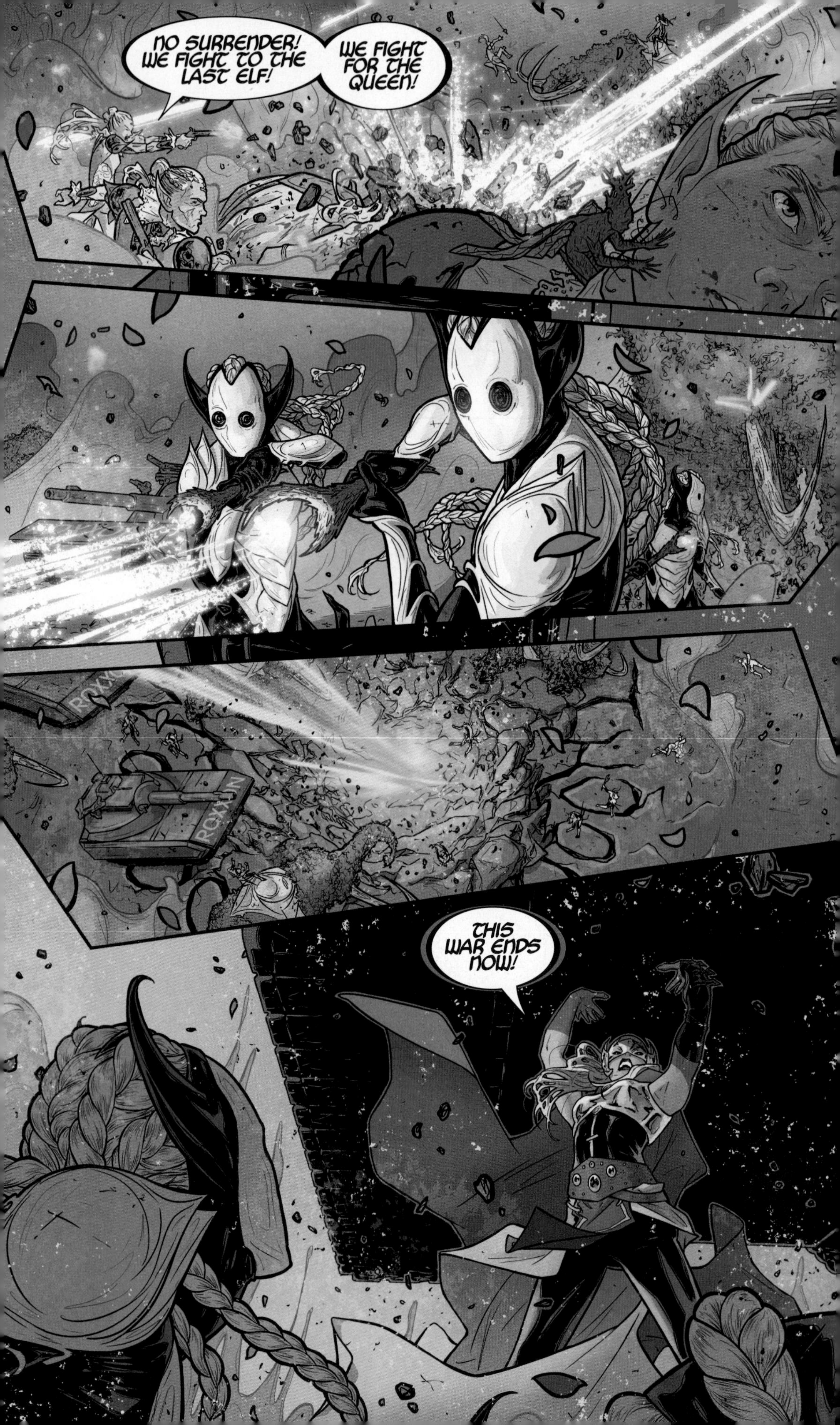
NO SURRENDER! WE FIGHT TO THE LAST ELF!
WE FIGHT FOR THE QUEEN!
ROXXON
THIS WAR ENDS NOW!

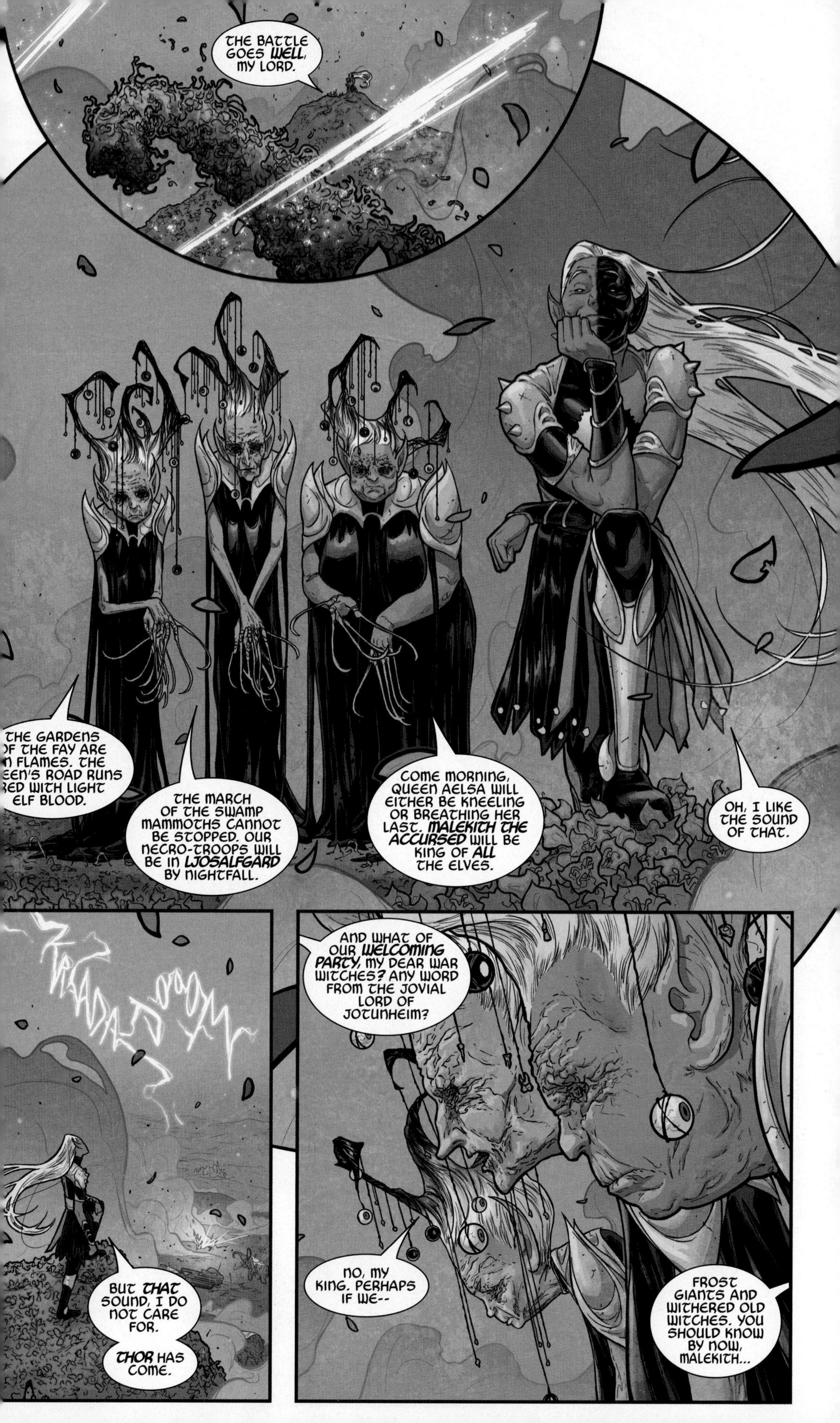
THE BATTLE GOES WELL, MY LORD.
THE GARDENS OF THE FAY ARE IN FLAMES. THE QUEEN'S ROAD RUNS RED WITH LIGHT ELF BLOOD.
THE MARCH OF THE SWAMP MAMMOTHS CANNOT BE STOPPED. OUR NECRO-TROOPS WILL BE IN LJOSALFGARD BY NIGHTFALL.
COME MORNING, QUEEN AELSA WILL EITHER BE KNEELING OR BREATHING HER LAST. MALEKITH THE ACCURSED WILL BE KING OF ALL THE ELVES.
OH, I LIKE THE SOUND OF THAT.
KRAAKA-DOOOM
BUT THAT SOUND, I DO NOT CARE FOR.
THOR HAS COME.
AND WHAT OF OUR WELCOMING PARTY, MY DEAR WAR WITCHES? ANY WORD FROM THE JOVIAL LORD OF JOTUNHEIM?
NO, MY KING. PERHAPS IF WE--
FROST GIANTS AND WITHERED OLD WITCHES. YOU SHOULD KNOW BY NOW, MALEKITH...

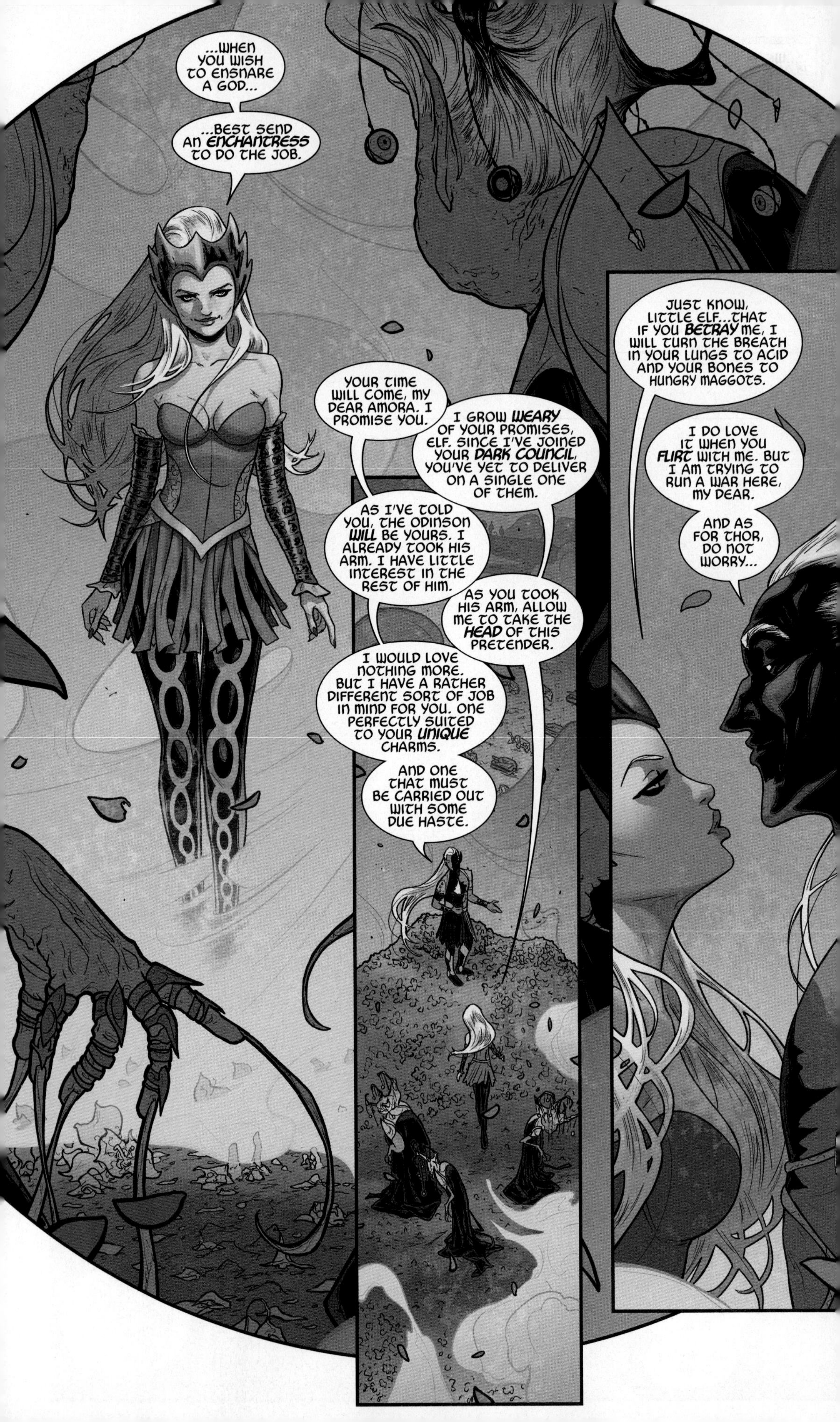

...WHEN YOU WISH TO ENSNARE A GOD...
...BEST SEND AN ENCHANTRESS TO DO THE JOB.
YOUR TIME WILL COME, MY DEAR AMORA. I PROMISE YOU.
I GROW WEARY OF YOUR PROMISES, ELF. SINCE I'VE JOINED YOUR DARK COUNCIL, YOU'VE YET TO DELIVER ON A SINGLE ONE OF THEM.
AS I'VE TOLD YOU, THE ODINSON WILL BE YOURS. I ALREADY TOOK HIS ARM. I HAVE LITTLE INTEREST IN THE REST OF HIM.
AS YOU TOOK HIS ARM, ALLOW ME TO TAKE THE HEAD OF THIS PRETENDER.
I WOULD LOVE NOTHING MORE. BUT I HAVE A RATHER DIFFERENT SORT OF JOB IN MIND FOR YOU. ONE PERFECTLY SUITED TO YOUR UNIQUE CHARMS.
AND ONE THAT MUST BE CARRIED OUT WITH SOME DUE HASTE.
JUST KNOW, LITTLE ELF...THAT IF YOU BETRAY ME, I WILL TURN THE BREATH IN YOUR LUNGS TO ACID AND YOUR BONES TO HUNGRY MAGGOTS.
I DO LOVE IT WHEN YOU FLIRT WITH ME. BUT I AM TRYING TO RUN A WAR HERE, MY DEAR.
AND AS FOR THOR, DO NOT WORRY...

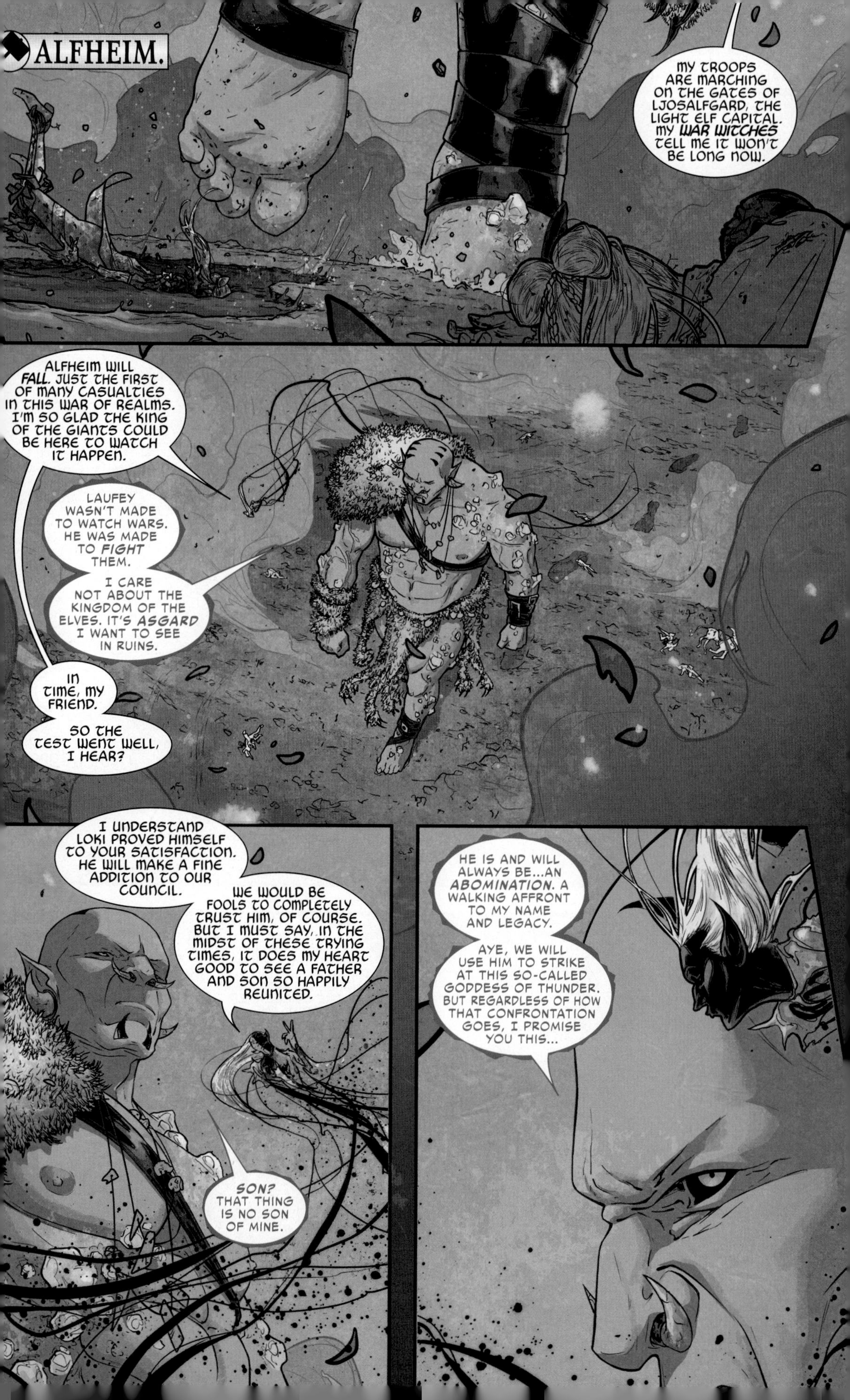
ALFHEIM.
MY TROOPS ARE MARCHING ON THE GATES OF LJOSALFGARD, THE LIGHT ELF CAPITAL. MY WAR WITCHES TELL ME IT WON'T BE LONG NOW.
ALFHEIM WILL FALL. JUST THE FIRST OF MANY CASUALTIES IN THIS WAR OF REALMS. I'M SO GLAD THE KING OF THE GIANTS COULD BE HERE TO WATCH IT HAPPEN.
LAUFEY WASN'T MADE TO WATCH WARS. HE WAS MADE TO FIGHT THEM.
I CARE NOT ABOUT THE KINGDOM OF THE ELVES. IT'S ASGARD I WANT TO SEE IN RUINS.
IN TIME, MY FRIEND.
SO THE TEST WENT WELL, I HEAR?
I UNDERSTAND LOKI PROVED HIMSELF TO YOUR SATISFACTION. HE WILL MAKE A FINE ADDITION TO OUR COUNCIL.
WE WOULD BE FOOLS TO COMPLETELY TRUST HIM, OF COURSE. BUT I MUST SAY, IN THE MIDST OF THESE TRYING TIMES, IT DOES MY HEART GOOD TO SEE A FATHER AND SON SO HAPPILY REUNITED.
SON? THAT THING IS NO SON OF MINE.
HE IS AND WILL ALWAYS BE...AN ABOMINATION. A WALKING AFFRONT TO MY NAME AND LEGACY.
AYE, WE WILL USE HIM TO STRIKE AT THIS SO-CALLED GODDESS OF THUNDER. BUT REGARDLESS OF HOW THAT CONFRONTATION GOES, I PROMISE YOU THIS...

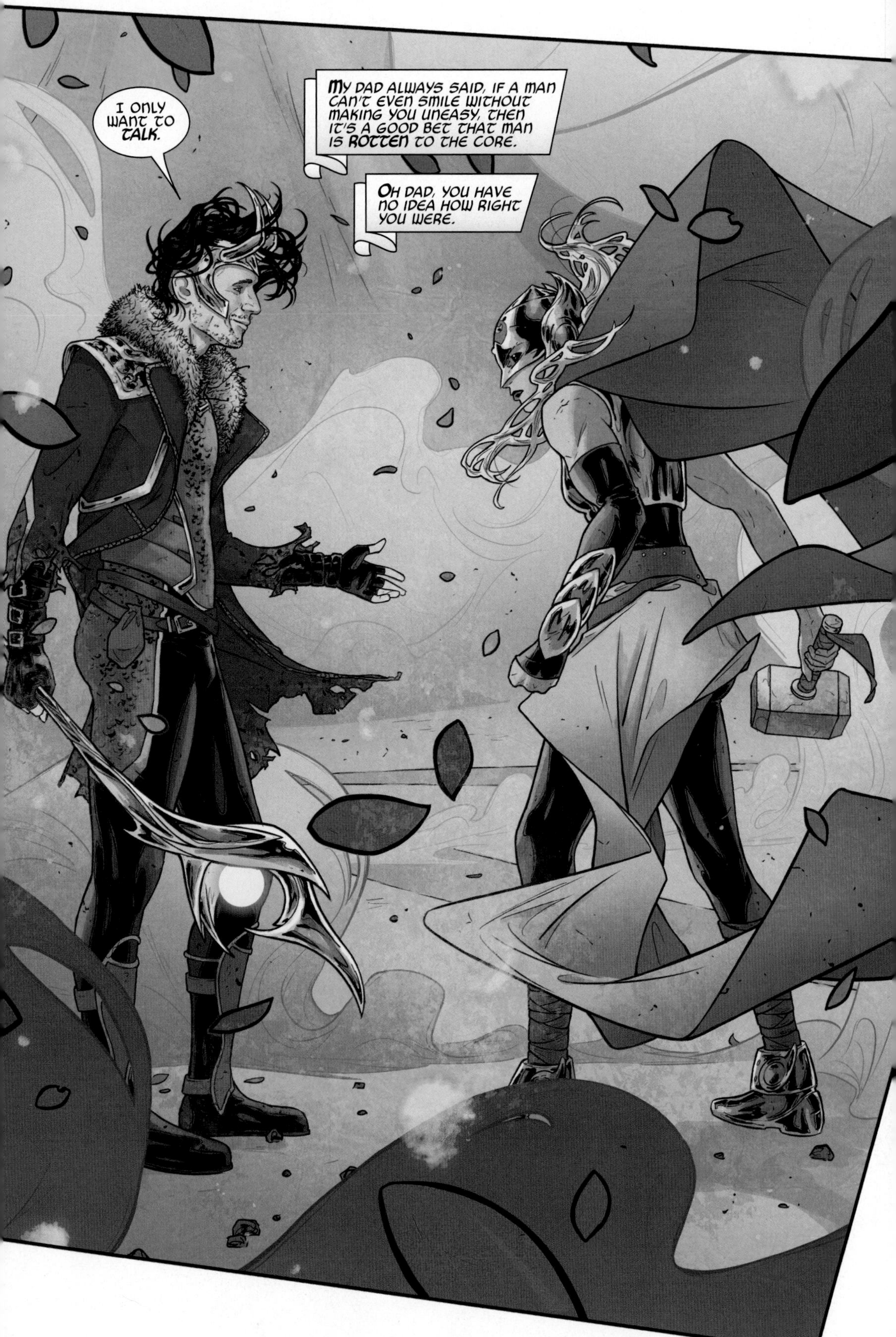
I ONLY WANT TO TALK.
MY DAD ALWAYS SAID, IF A MAN CAN'T EVEN SMILE WITHOUT MAKING YOU UNEASY, THEN IT'S A GOOD BET THAT MAN IS ROTTEN TO THE CORE.
OH DAD, YOU HAVE NO IDEA HOW RIGHT YOU WERE.

3

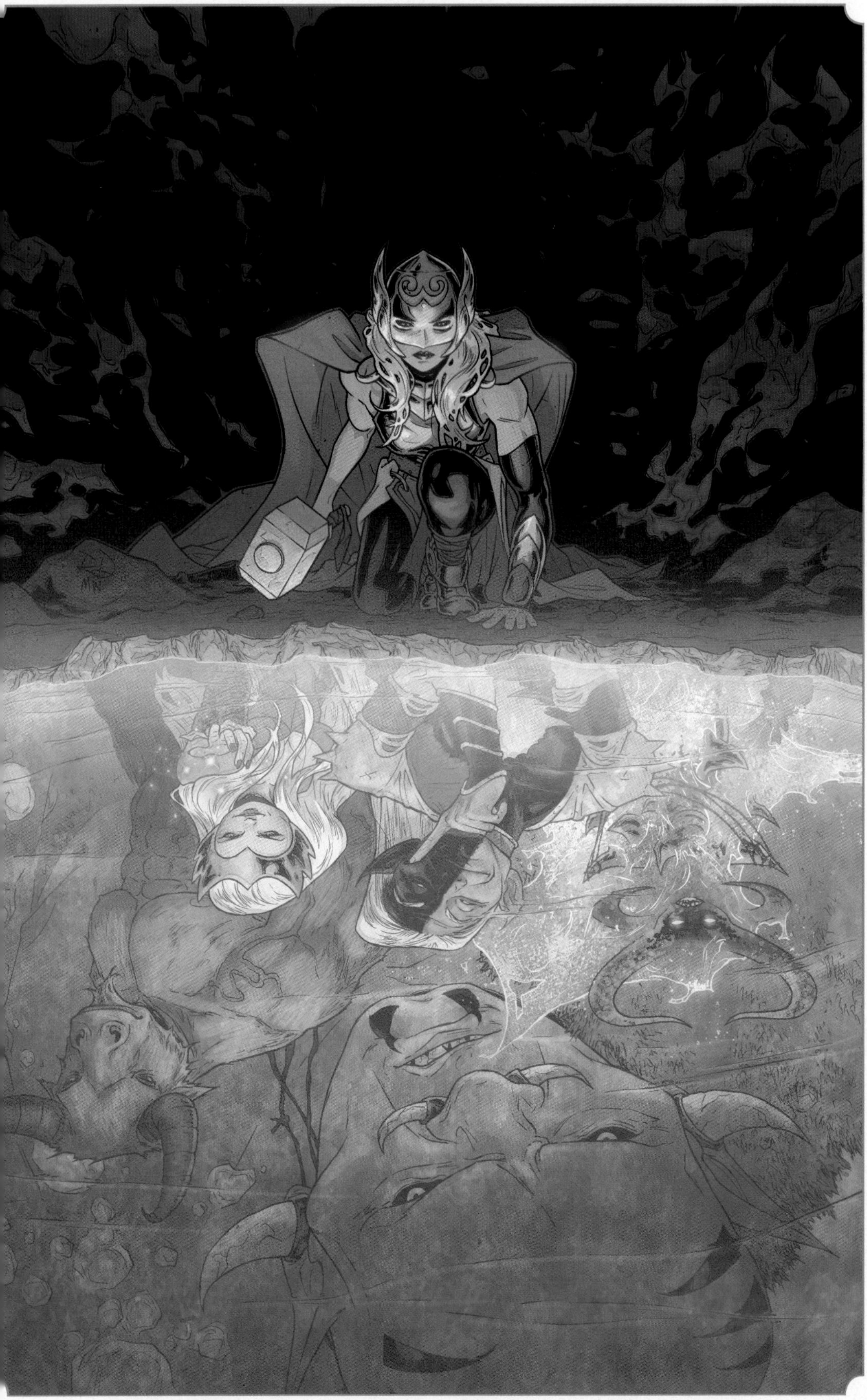

THE SAGA OF THOR AND LOKI

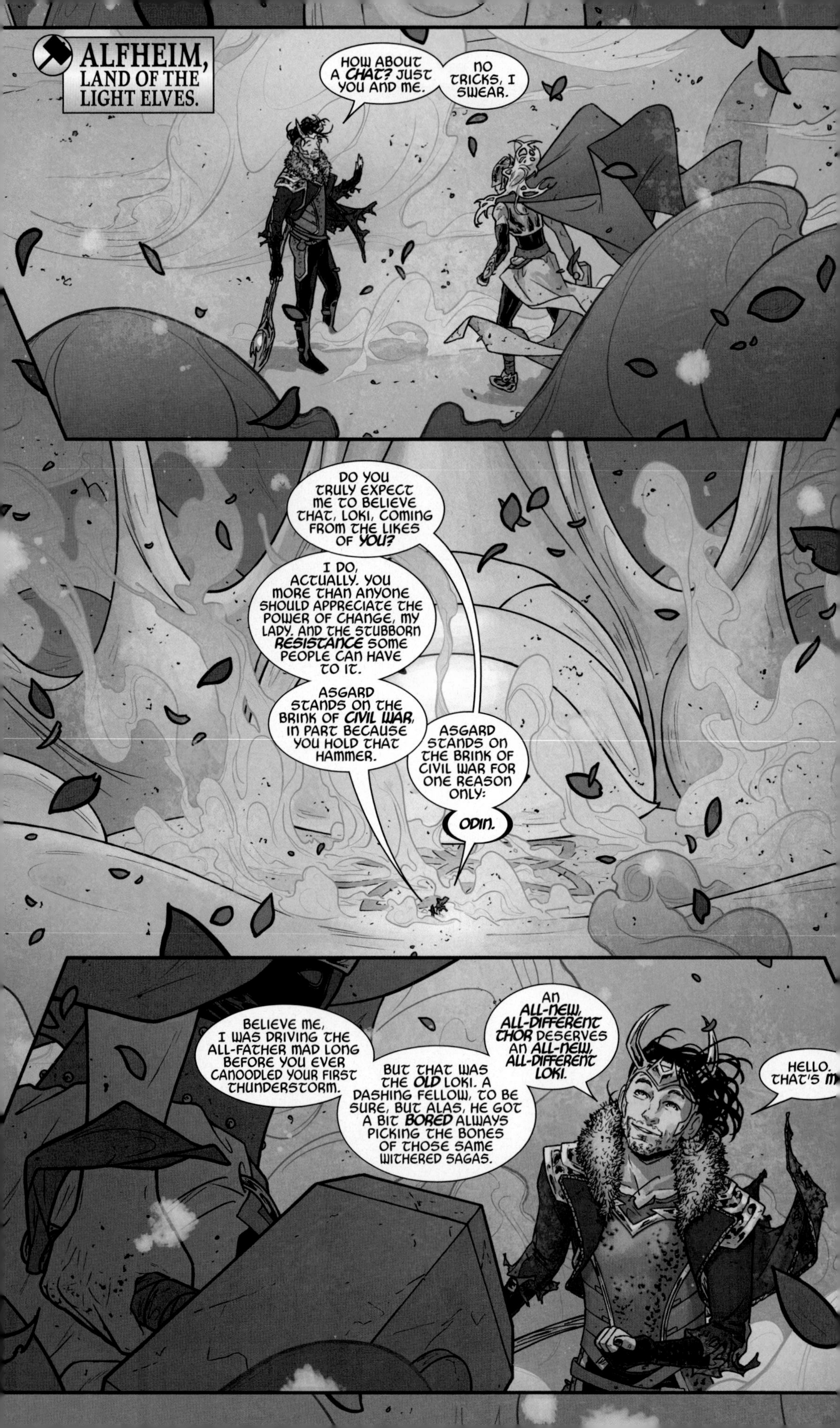
ALFHEIM, LAND OF THE LIGHT ELVES.
HOW ABOUT A CHAT? JUST YOU AND ME.
NO TRICKS, I SWEAR.
DO YOU TRULY EXPECT ME TO BELIEVE THAT, LOKI, COMING FROM THE LIKES OF YOU?
I DO, ACTUALLY. YOU MORE THAN ANYONE SHOULD APPRECIATE THE POWER OF CHANGE, MY LADY. AND THE STUBBORN RESISTANCE SOME PEOPLE CAN HAVE TO IT.
ASGARD STANDS ON THE BRINK OF CIVIL WAR, IN PART BECAUSE YOU HOLD THAT HAMMER.
ASGARD STANDS ON THE BRINK OF CIVIL WAR FOR ONE REASON ONLY:
ODIN.
BELIEVE ME, I WAS DRIVING THE ALL-FATHER MAD LONG BEFORE YOU EVER CANOODLED YOUR FIRST THUNDERSTORM.
BUT THAT WAS THE OLD LOKI. A DASHING FELLOW, TO BE SURE, BUT ALAS, HE GOT A BIT BORED ALWAYS PICKING THE BONES OF THOSE SAME WITHERED SAGAS.
AN ALL-NEW, ALL-DIFFERENT THOR DESERVES AN ALL-NEW, ALL-DIFFERENT LOKI.
HELLO. THAT'S

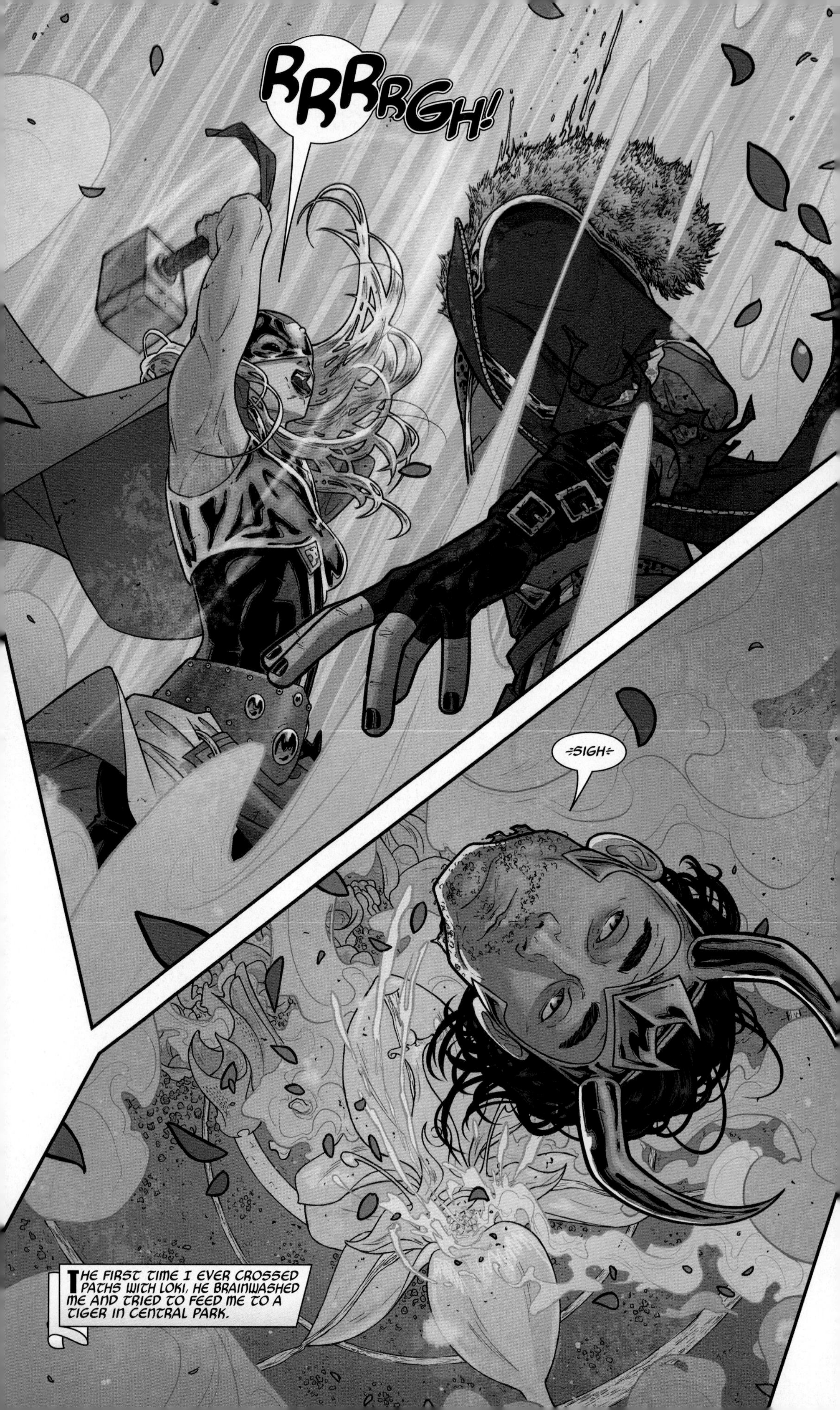
RRRRRGH!
=SIGH=
THE FIRST TIME I EVER CROSSED PATHS WITH LOKI, HE BRAINWASHED ME AND TRIED TO FEED ME TO A TIGER IN CENTRAL PARK.

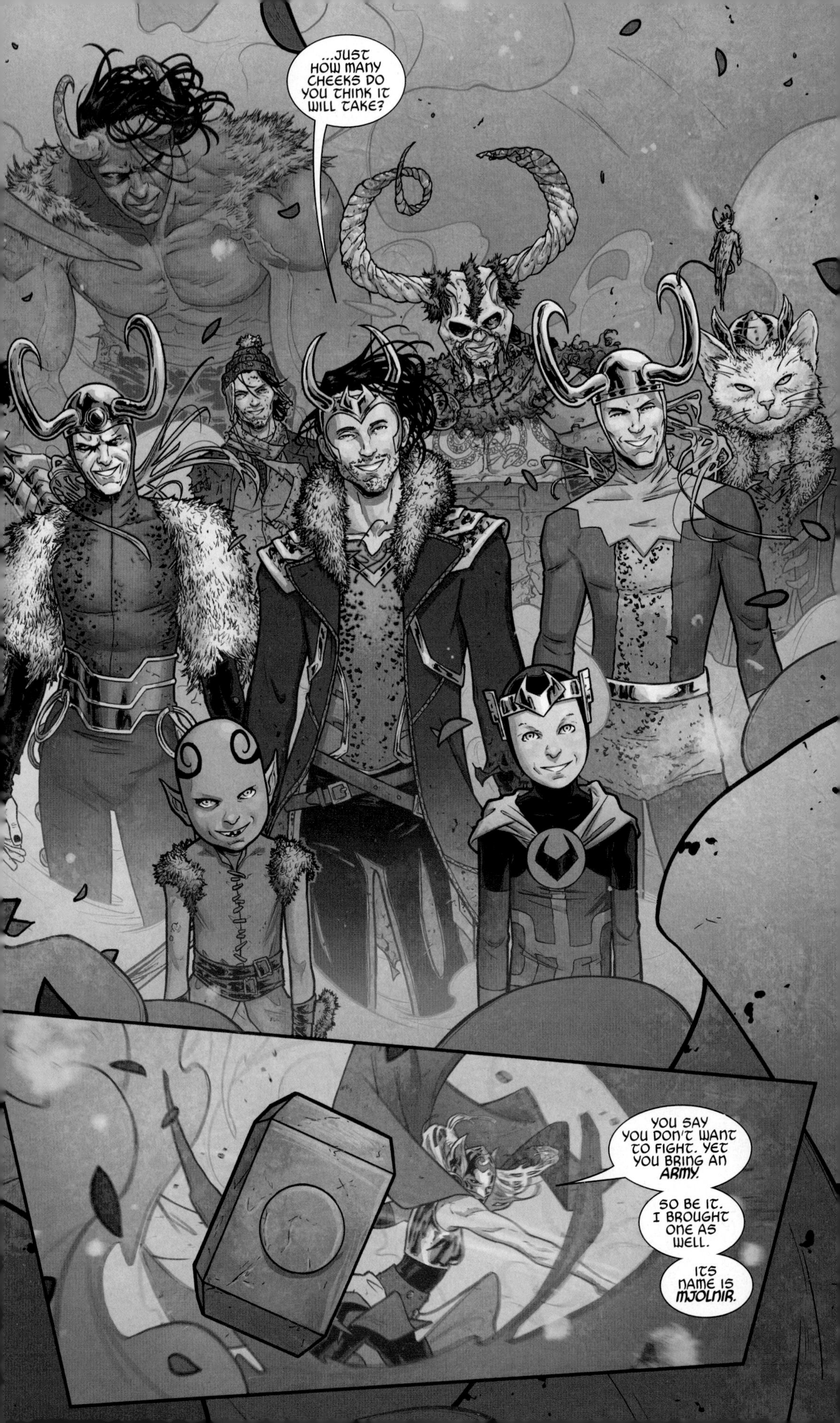

...JUST HOW MANY CHEEKS DO YOU THINK IT WILL TAKE?
YOU SAY YOU DON'T WANT TO FIGHT. YET YOU BRING AN ARMY.
SO BE IT. I BROUGHT ONE AS WELL.
ITS NAME IS MJOLNIR.

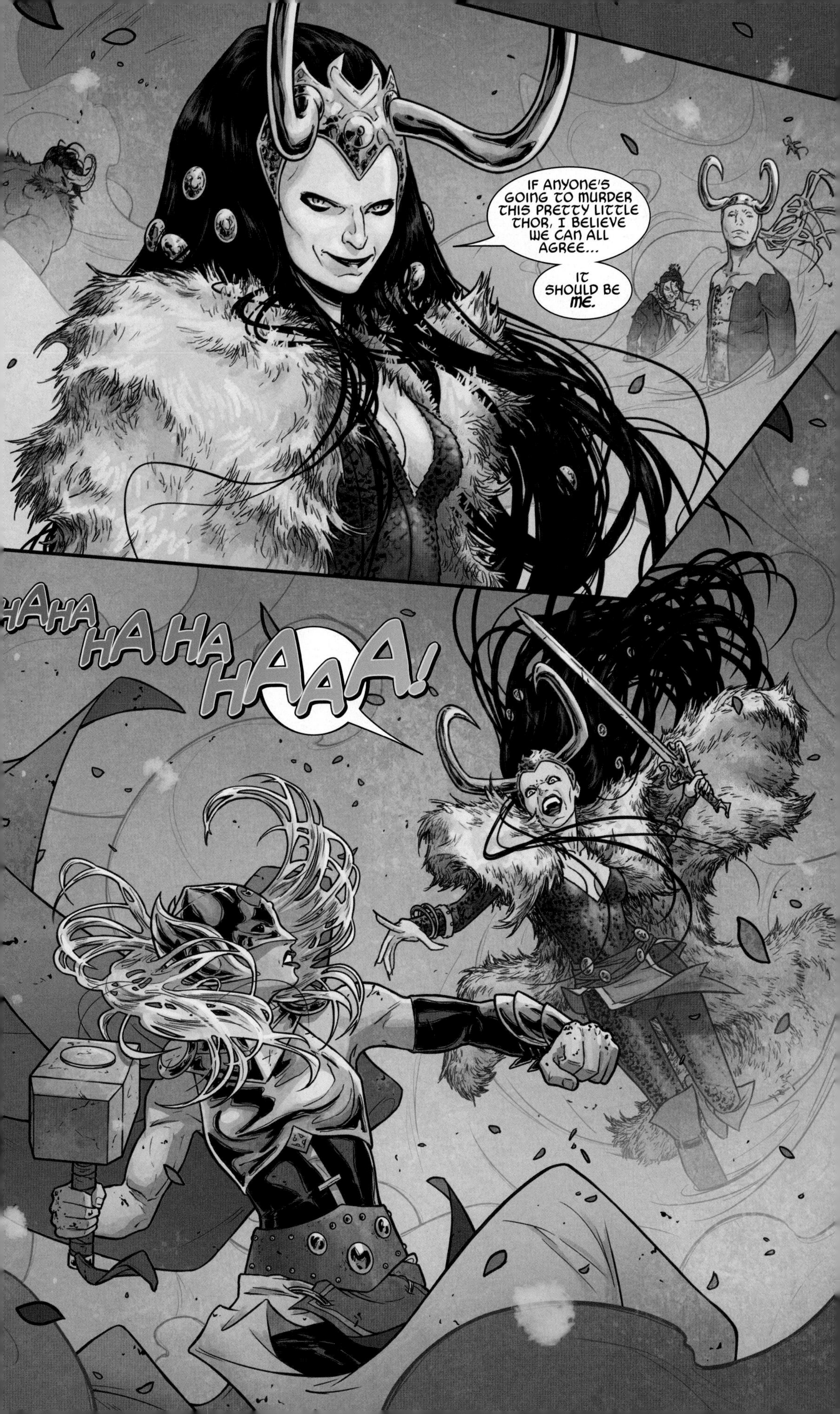
IF ANYONE'S GOING TO MURDER THIS PRETTY LITTLE THOR, I BELIEVE WE CAN ALL AGREE...
IT SHOULD BE ME.
HAHA HA HA HAAAA!

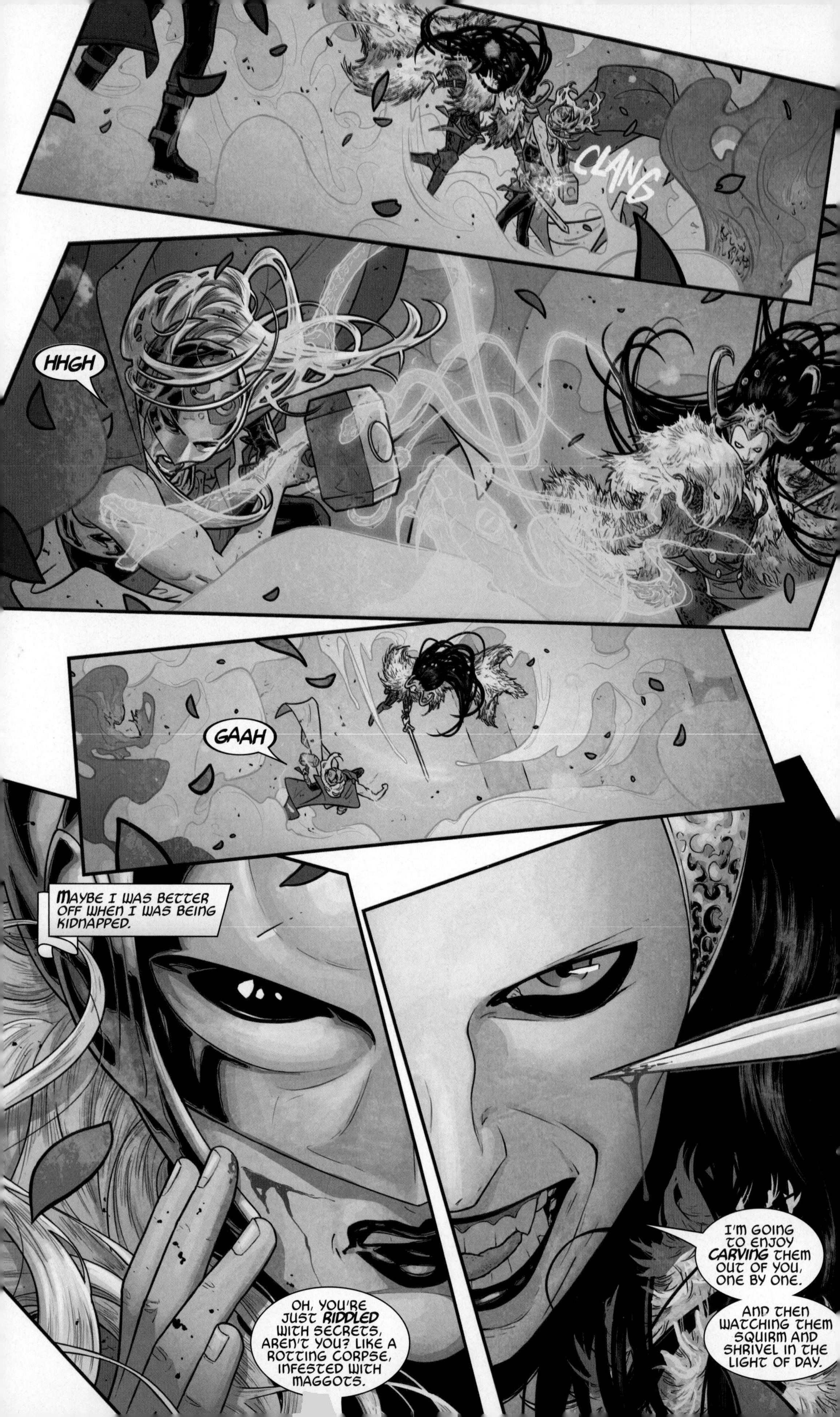
CLANG
HHGH
GAAH
MAYBE I WAS BETTER OFF WHEN I WAS BEING KIDNAPPED.
OH, YOU'RE JUST **RIDDLED** WITH SECRETS, AREN'T YOU? LIKE A ROTTING CORPSE, INFESTED WITH MAGGOTS.
I'M GOING TO ENJOY **CARVING** THEM OUT OF YOU, ONE BY ONE.
AND THEN WATCHING THEM SQUIRM AND SHRIVEL IN THE LIGHT OF DAY.

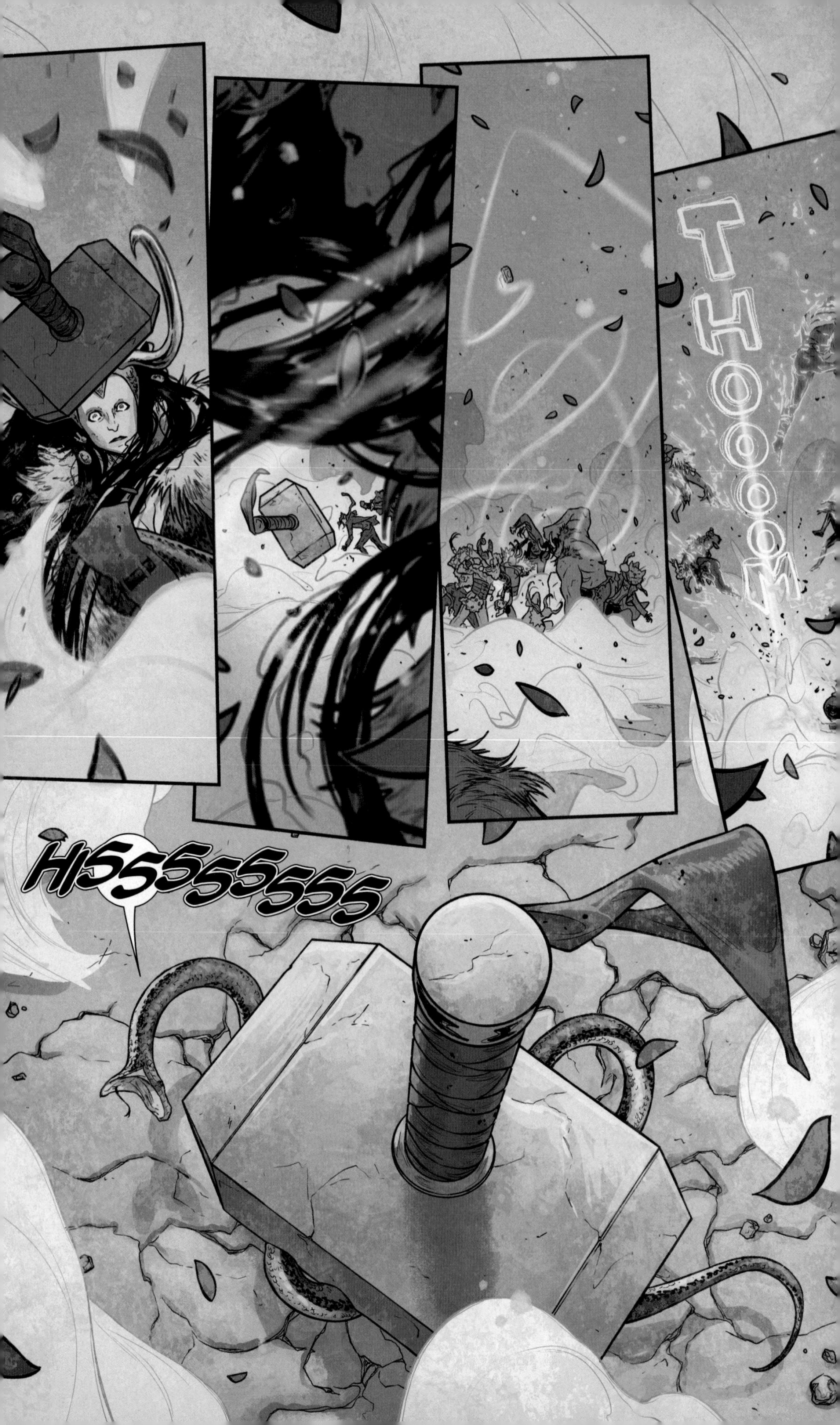
THOOOOM
HISSSSSSSS

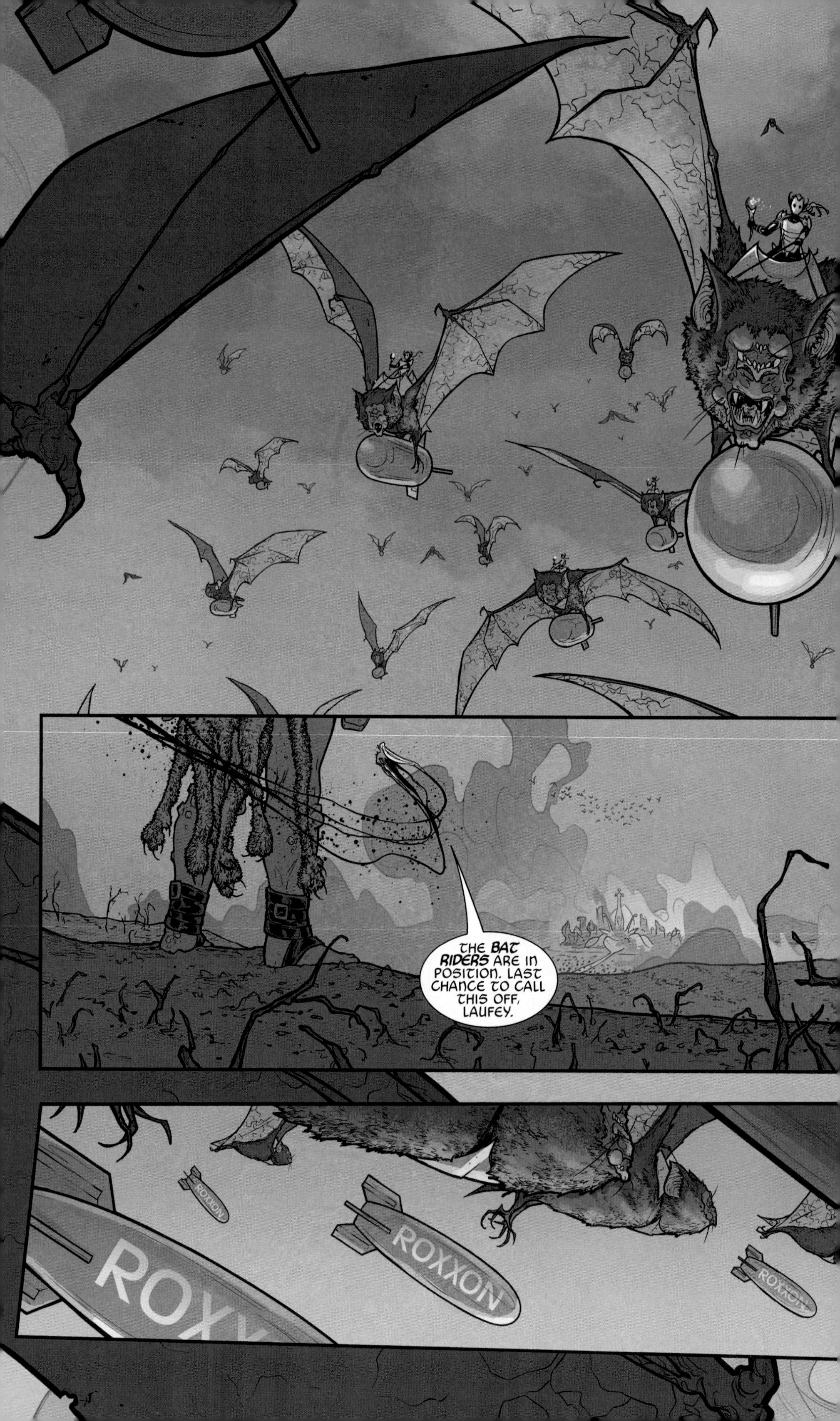
THE BAT RIDERS ARE IN POSITION. LAST CHANCE TO CALL THIS OFF, LAUFEY.
ROXXON
ROXXON
ROXXON
ROXX

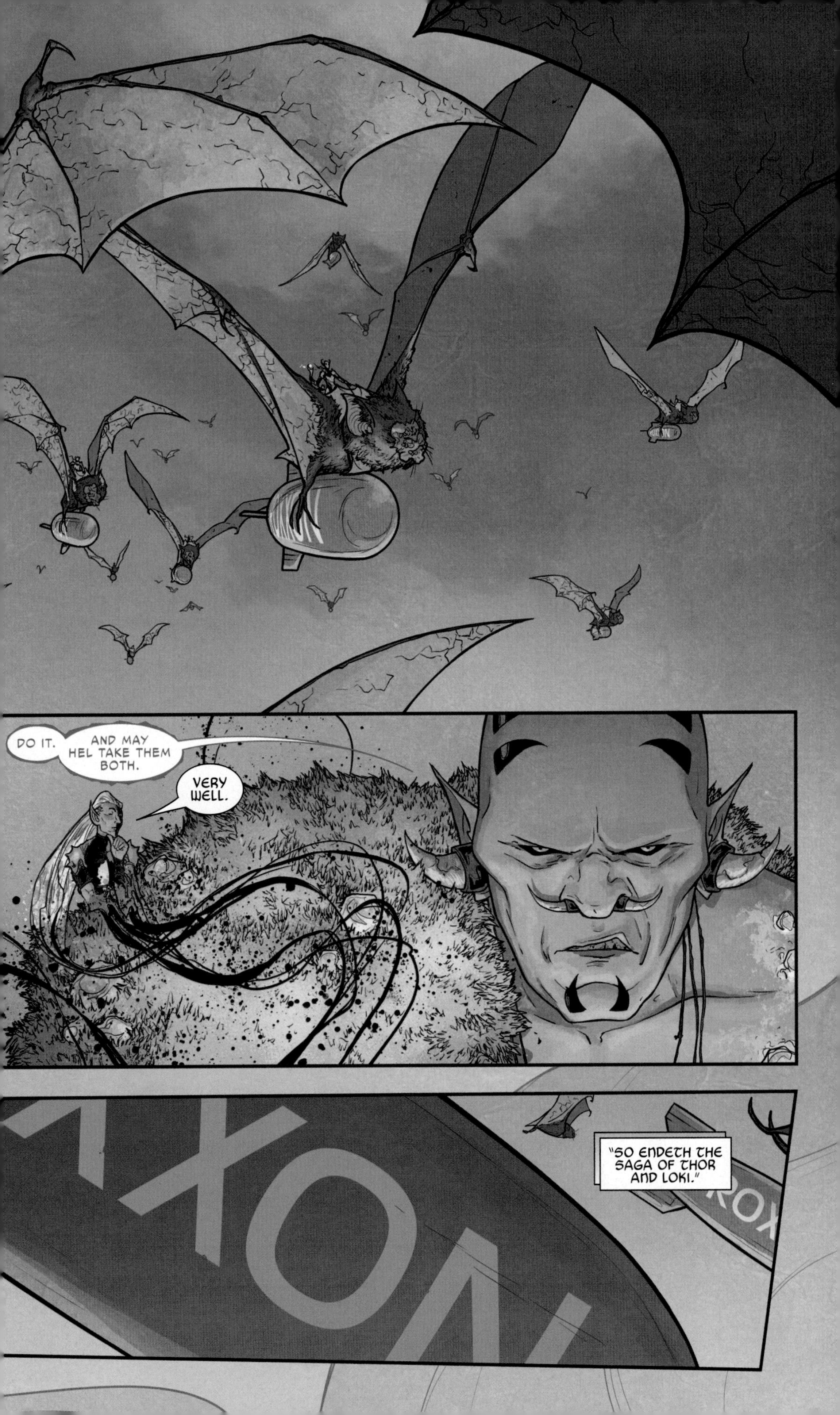
DO IT.
AND MAY HEL TAKE THEM BOTH.
VERY WELL.
"SO ENDETH THE SAGA OF THOR AND LOKI."

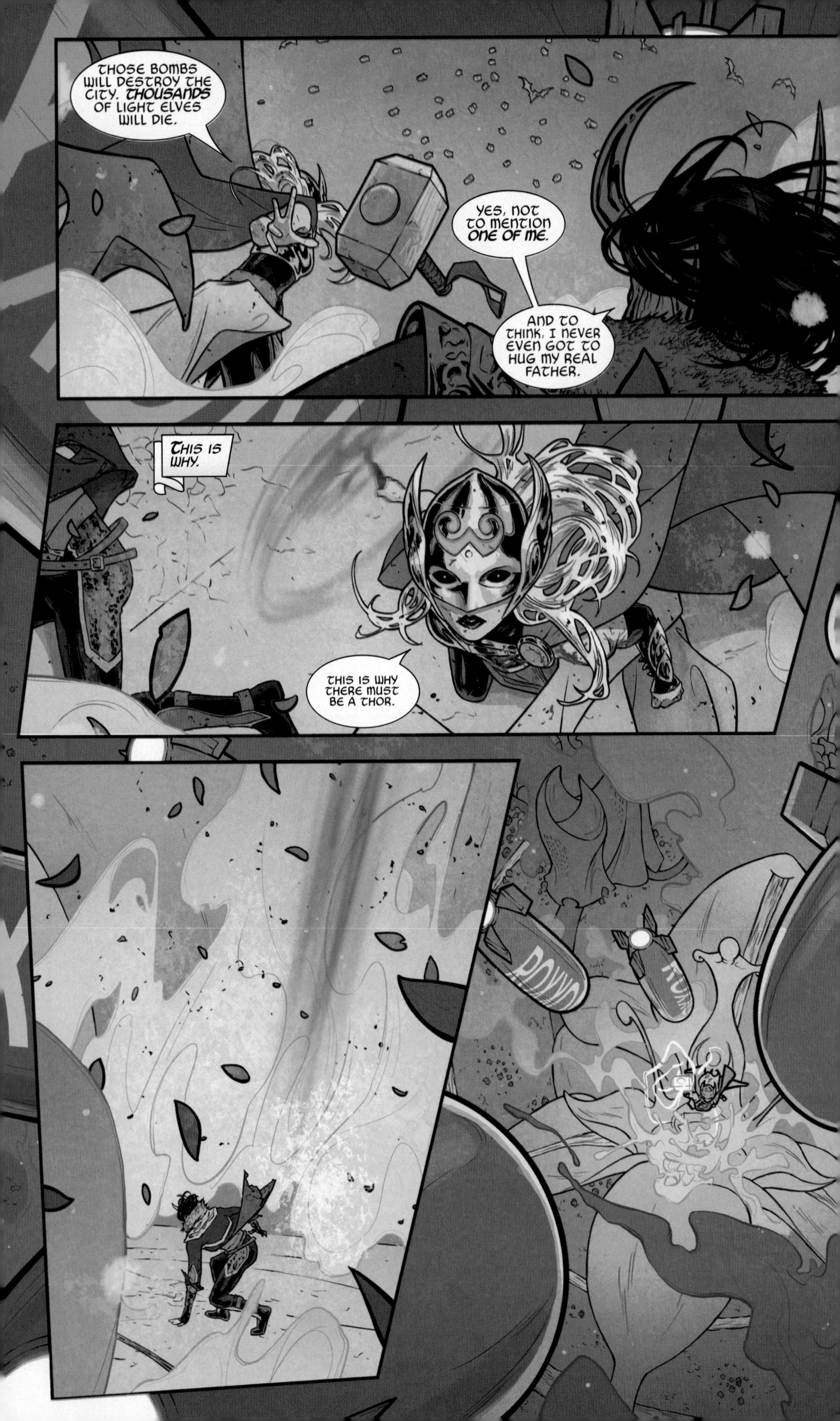
THOSE BOMBS WILL DESTROY THE CITY. THOUSANDS OF LIGHT ELVES WILL DIE.
YES, NOT TO MENTION ONE OF ME.
AND TO THINK, I NEVER EVEN GOT TO HUG MY REAL FATHER.
THIS IS WHY.
THIS IS WHY THERE MUST BE A THOR.

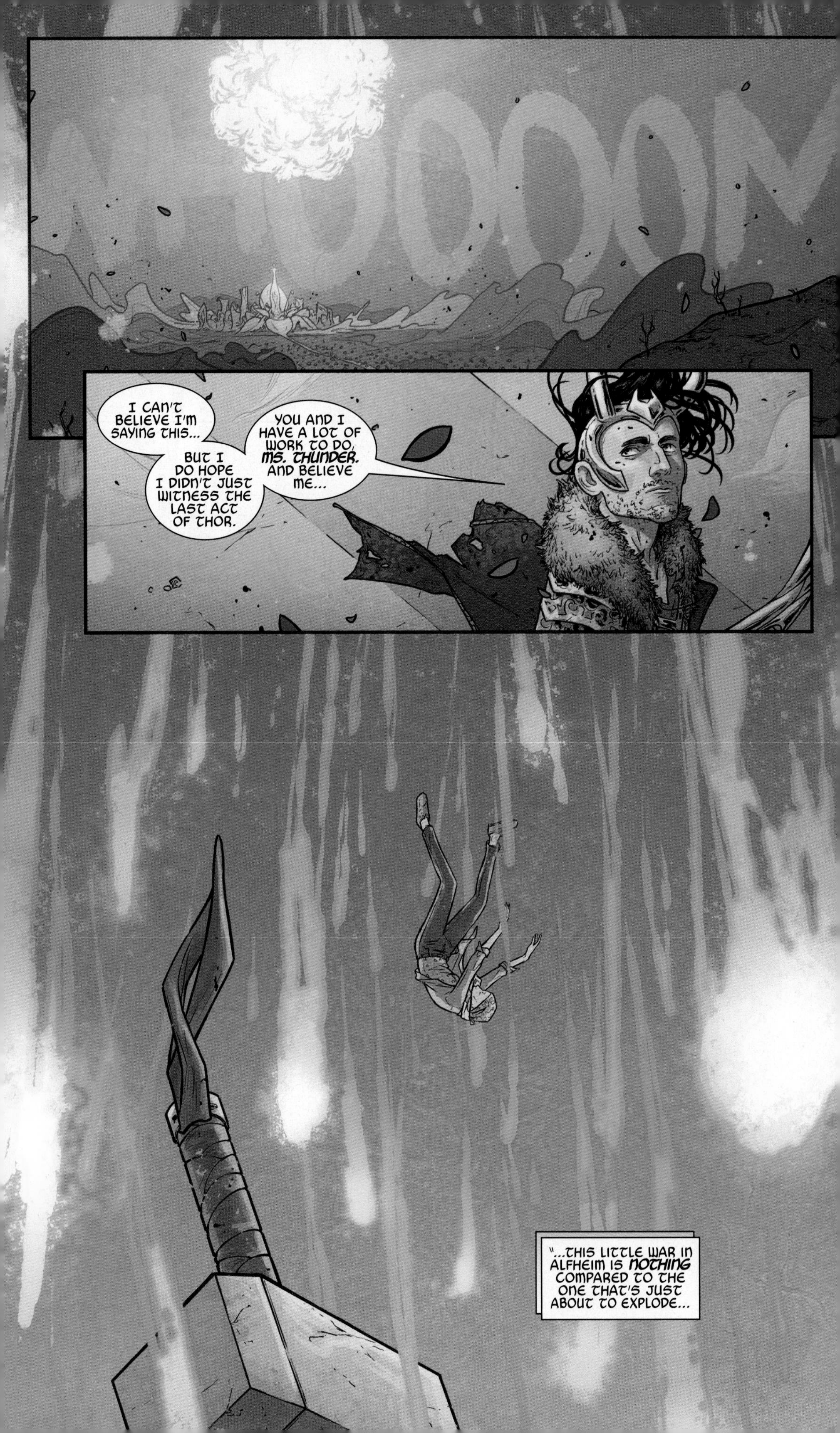
I CAN'T BELIEVE I'M SAYING THIS...
BUT I DO HOPE I DIDN'T JUST WITNESS THE LAST ACT OF THOR.
YOU AND I HAVE A LOT OF WORK TO DO, MS. THUNDER. AND BELIEVE ME...
"...THIS LITTLE WAR IN ALFHEIM IS NOTHING COMPARED TO THE ONE THAT'S JUST ABOUT TO EXPLODE...

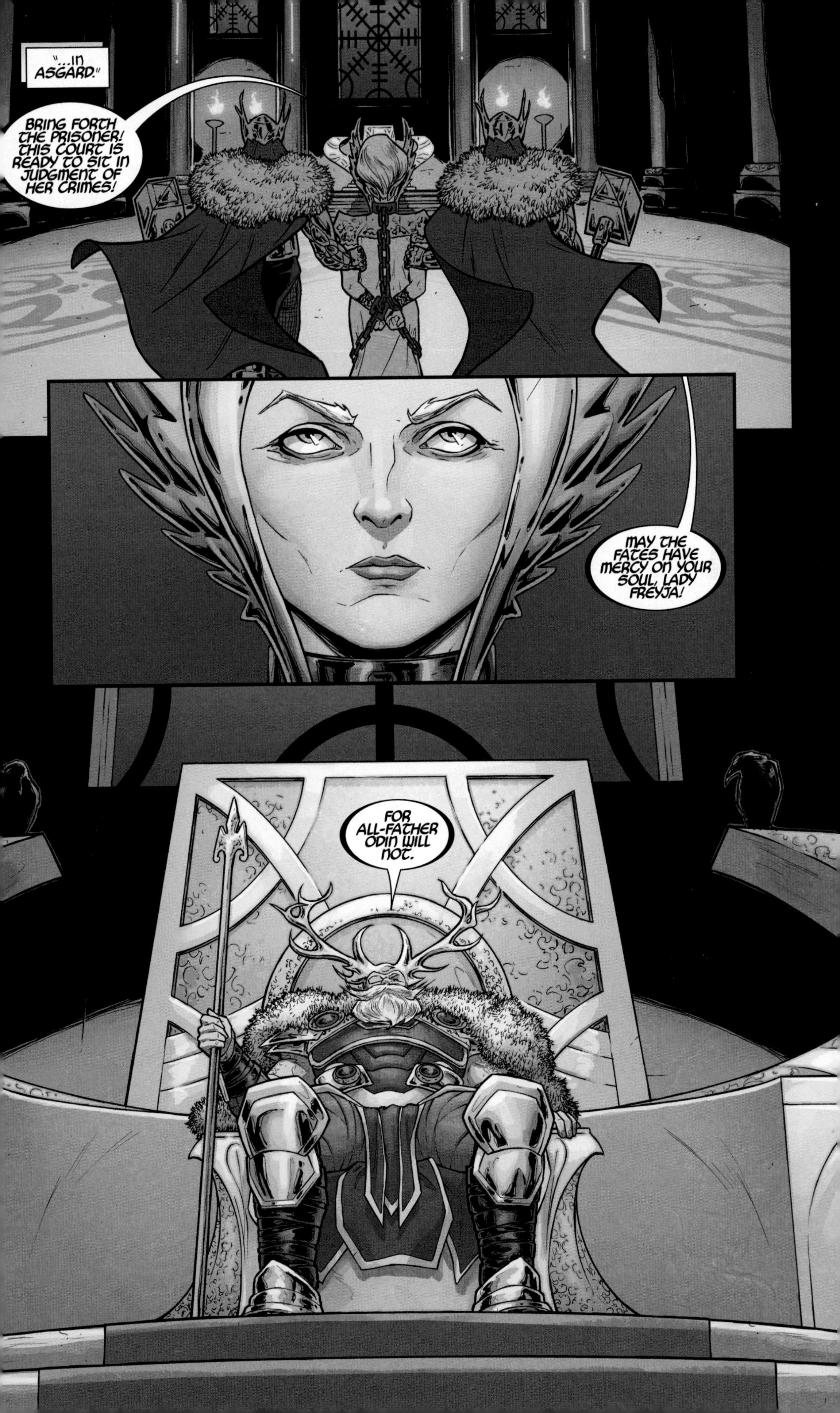
"...IN ASGARD."
BRING FORTH THE PRISONER! THIS COURT IS READY TO SIT IN JUDGMENT OF HER CRIMES!
MAY THE FATES HAVE MERCY ON YOUR SOUL, LADY FREYJA!
FOR ALL-FATHER ODIN WILL NOT.

4

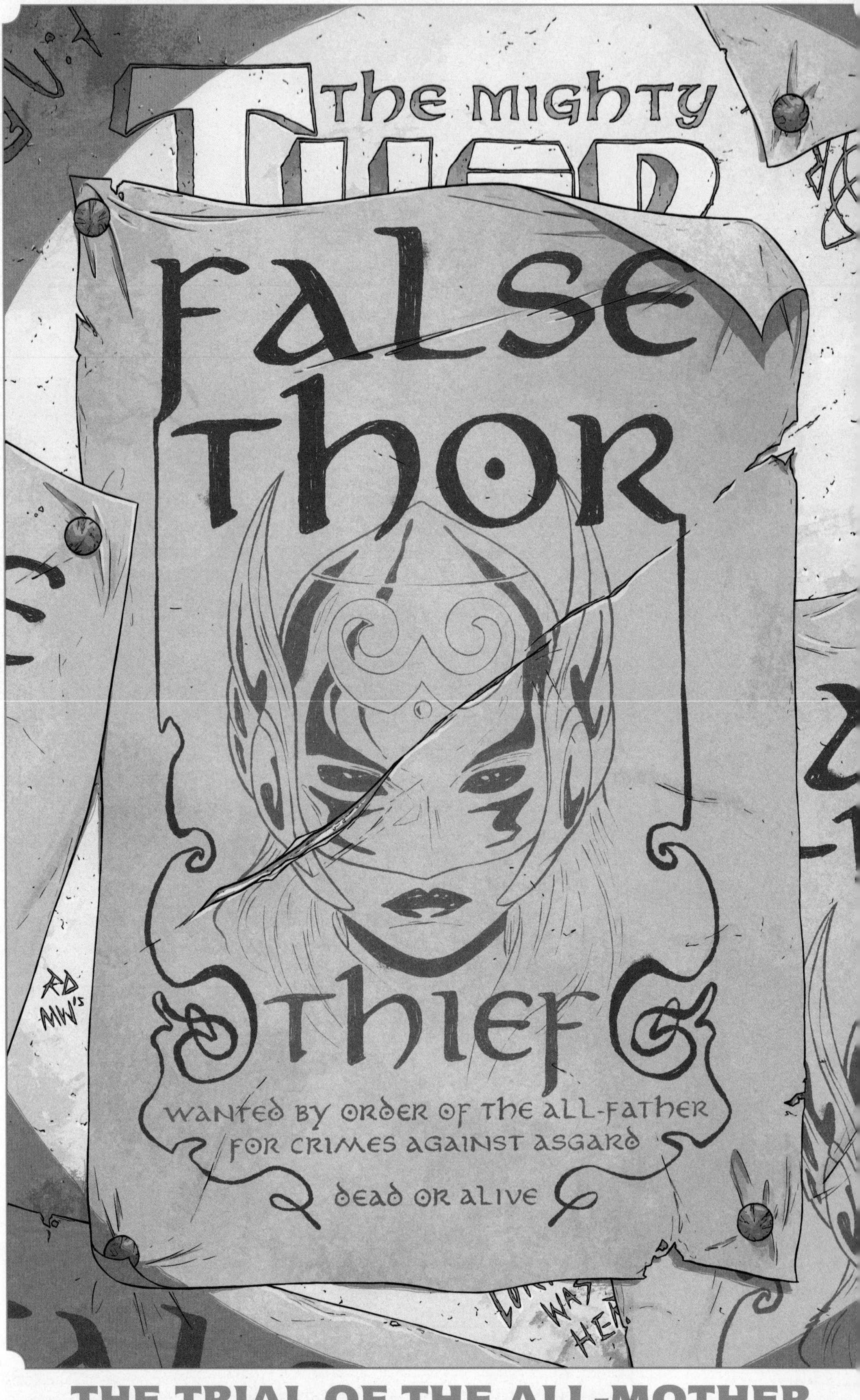
THE MIGHTY
FALSE THOR
THIEF
WANTED BY ORDER OF THE ALL-FATHER
FOR CRIMES AGAINST ASGARD
DEAD OR ALIVE

THE TRIAL OF THE ALL-MOTHER

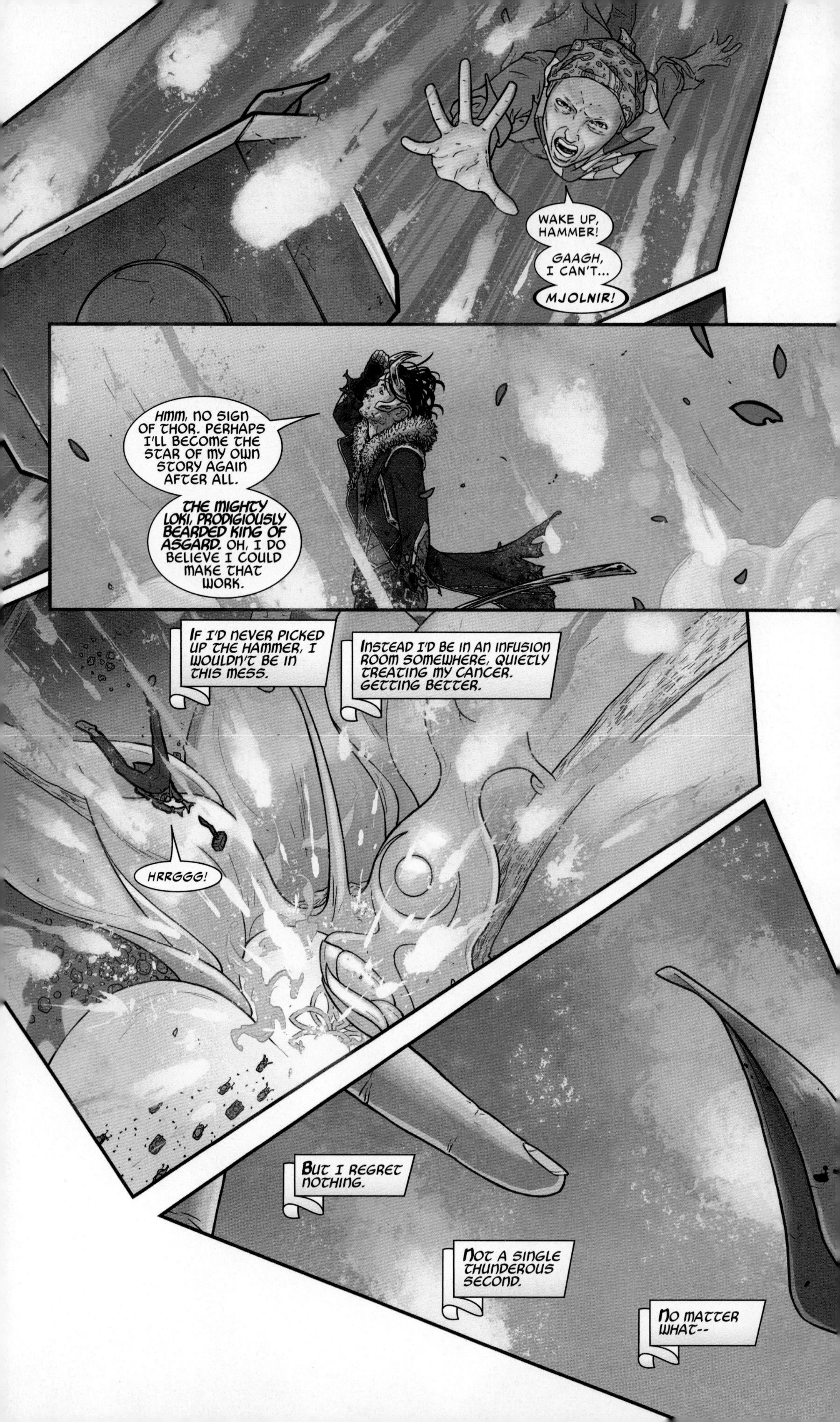
WAKE UP, HAMMER!
GAAGH, I CAN'T...
MJOLNIR!
HMM, NO SIGN OF THOR. PERHAPS I'LL BECOME THE STAR OF MY OWN STORY AGAIN AFTER ALL.
THE MIGHTY LOKI, PRODIGIOUSLY BEARDED KING OF ASGARD. OH, I DO BELIEVE I COULD MAKE THAT WORK.
IF I'D NEVER PICKED UP THE HAMMER, I WOULDN'T BE IN THIS MESS.
INSTEAD I'D BE IN AN INFUSION ROOM SOMEWHERE, QUIETLY TREATING MY CANCER. GETTING BETTER.
HRRGGG!
BUT I REGRET NOTHING.
NOT A SINGLE THUNDEROUS SECOND.
NO MATTER WHAT--

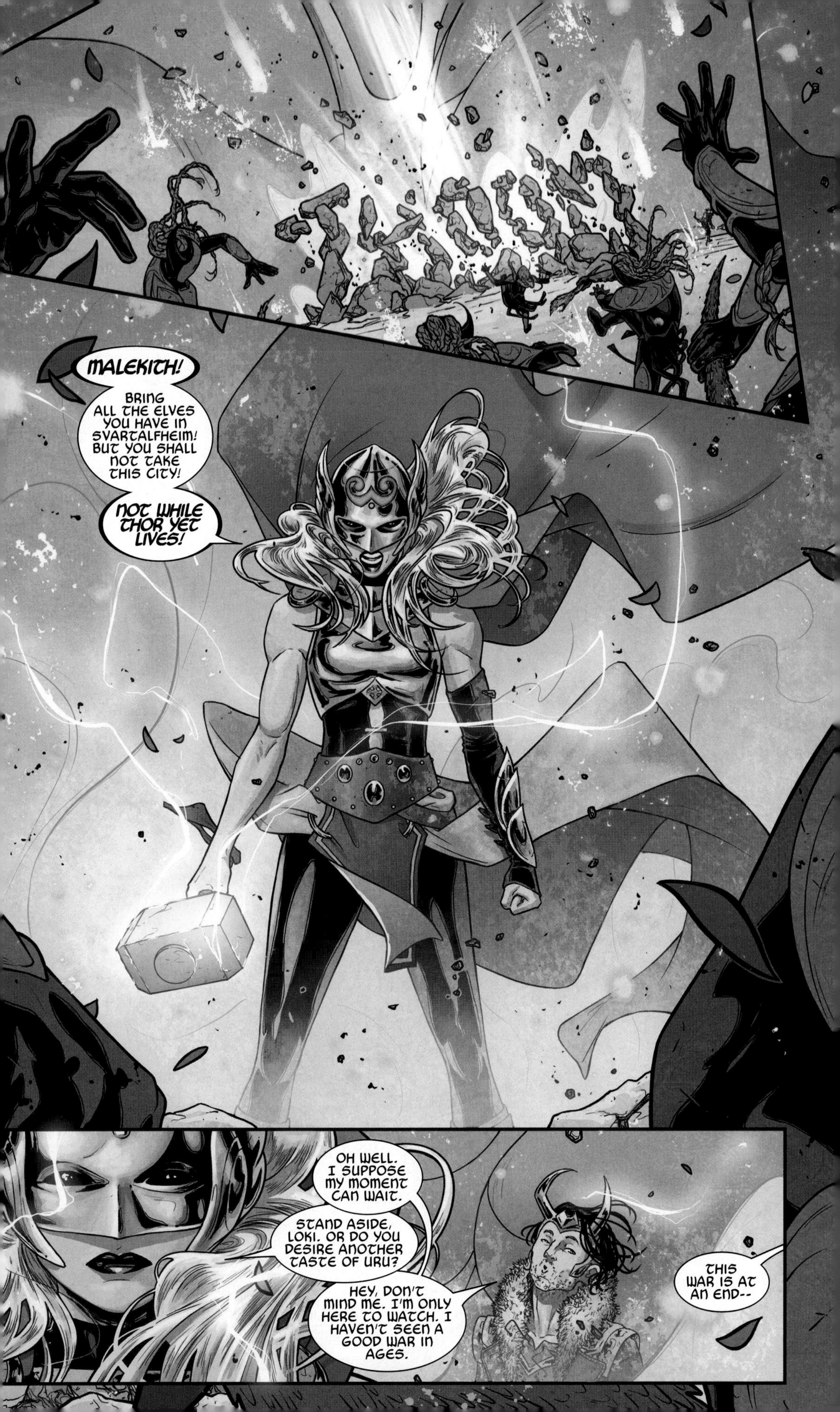
MALEKITH!
BRING ALL THE ELVES YOU HAVE IN SVARTALFHEIM! BUT YOU SHALL NOT TAKE THIS CITY!
NOT WHILE THOR YET LIVES!
OH WELL. I SUPPOSE MY MOMENT CAN WAIT.
STAND ASIDE, LOKI. OR DO YOU DESIRE ANOTHER TASTE OF URU?
HEY, DON'T MIND ME. I'M ONLY HERE TO WATCH. I HAVEN'T SEEN A GOOD WAR IN AGES.
THIS WAR IS AT AN END--

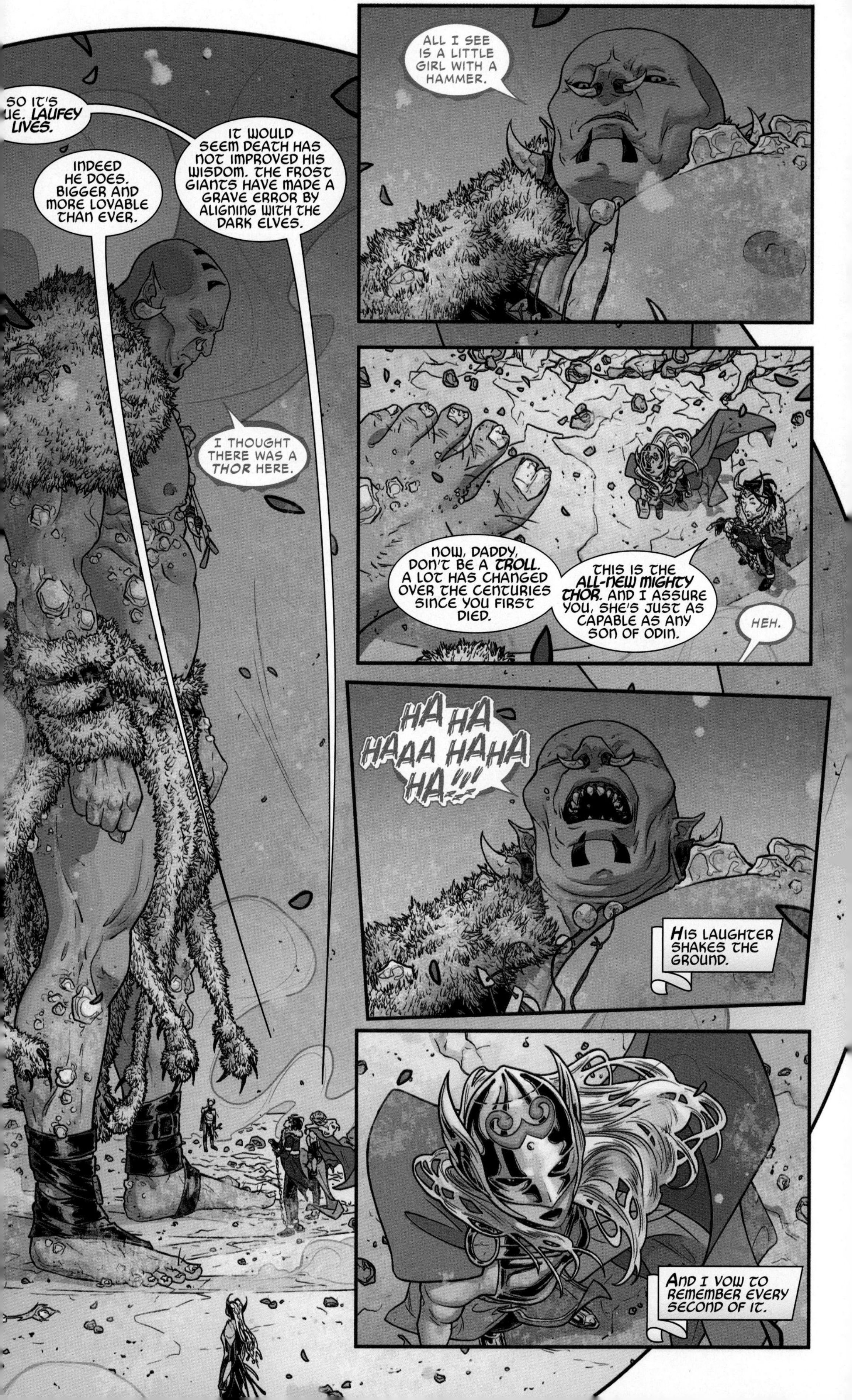

SO IT'S
UE. LAUFEY
LIVES.
INDEED
HE DOES.
BIGGER AND
MORE LOVABLE
THAN EVER.
IT WOULD
SEEM DEATH HAS
NOT IMPROVED HIS
WISDOM. THE FROST
GIANTS HAVE MADE A
GRAVE ERROR BY
ALIGNING WITH THE
DARK ELVES.
I THOUGHT
THERE WAS A
THOR HERE.
ALL I SEE
IS A LITTLE
GIRL WITH A
HAMMER.
NOW, DADDY,
DON'T BE A TROLL.
A LOT HAS CHANGED
OVER THE CENTURIES
SINCE YOU FIRST
DIED.
THIS IS THE
ALL-NEW MIGHTY
THOR. AND I ASSURE
YOU, SHE'S JUST AS
CAPABLE AS ANY
SON OF ODIN.
HEH.
HA HA
HAAA HAHA
HA!!!
HIS LAUGHTER
SHAKES THE
GROUND.
AND I VOW TO
REMEMBER EVERY
SECOND OF IT.

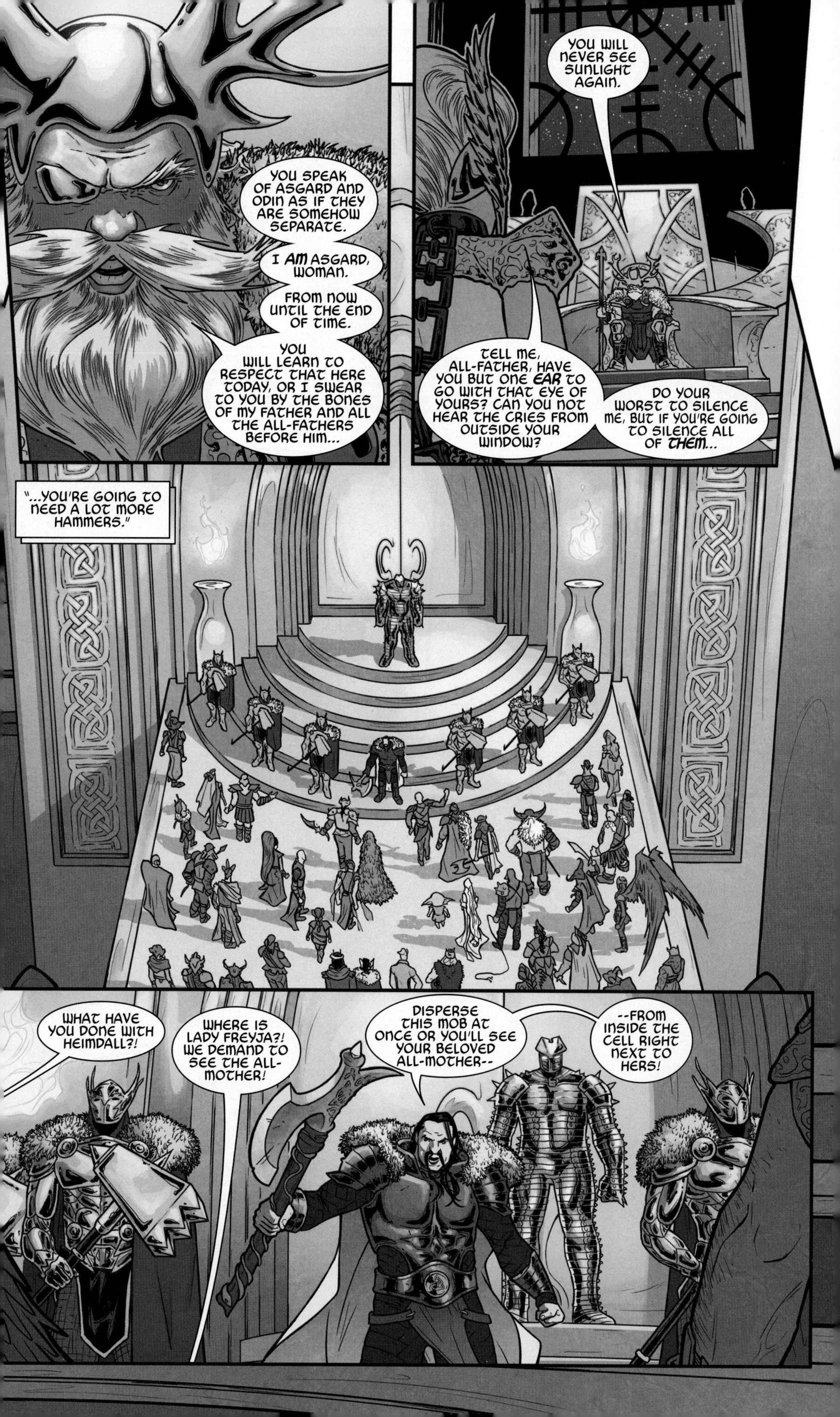
YOU SPEAK OF ASGARD AND ODIN AS IF THEY ARE SOMEHOW SEPARATE.
I *AM* ASGARD, WOMAN.
FROM NOW UNTIL THE END OF TIME.
YOU WILL LEARN TO RESPECT THAT HERE TODAY, OR I SWEAR TO YOU BY THE BONES OF MY FATHER AND ALL THE ALL-FATHERS BEFORE HIM...
YOU WILL NEVER SEE SUNLIGHT AGAIN.
TELL ME, ALL-FATHER, HAVE YOU BUT ONE *EAR* TO GO WITH THAT EYE OF YOURS? CAN YOU NOT HEAR THE CRIES FROM OUTSIDE YOUR WINDOW?
DO YOUR WORST TO SILENCE ME, BUT IF YOU'RE GOING TO SILENCE ALL OF *THEM*...
"...YOU'RE GOING TO NEED A LOT MORE HAMMERS."
WHAT HAVE YOU DONE WITH HEIMDALL?!
WHERE IS LADY FREYJA?! WE DEMAND TO SEE THE ALL-MOTHER!
DISPERSE THIS MOB AT ONCE OR YOU'LL SEE YOUR BELOVED ALL-MOTHER--
--FROM INSIDE THE CELL RIGHT NEXT TO HERS!

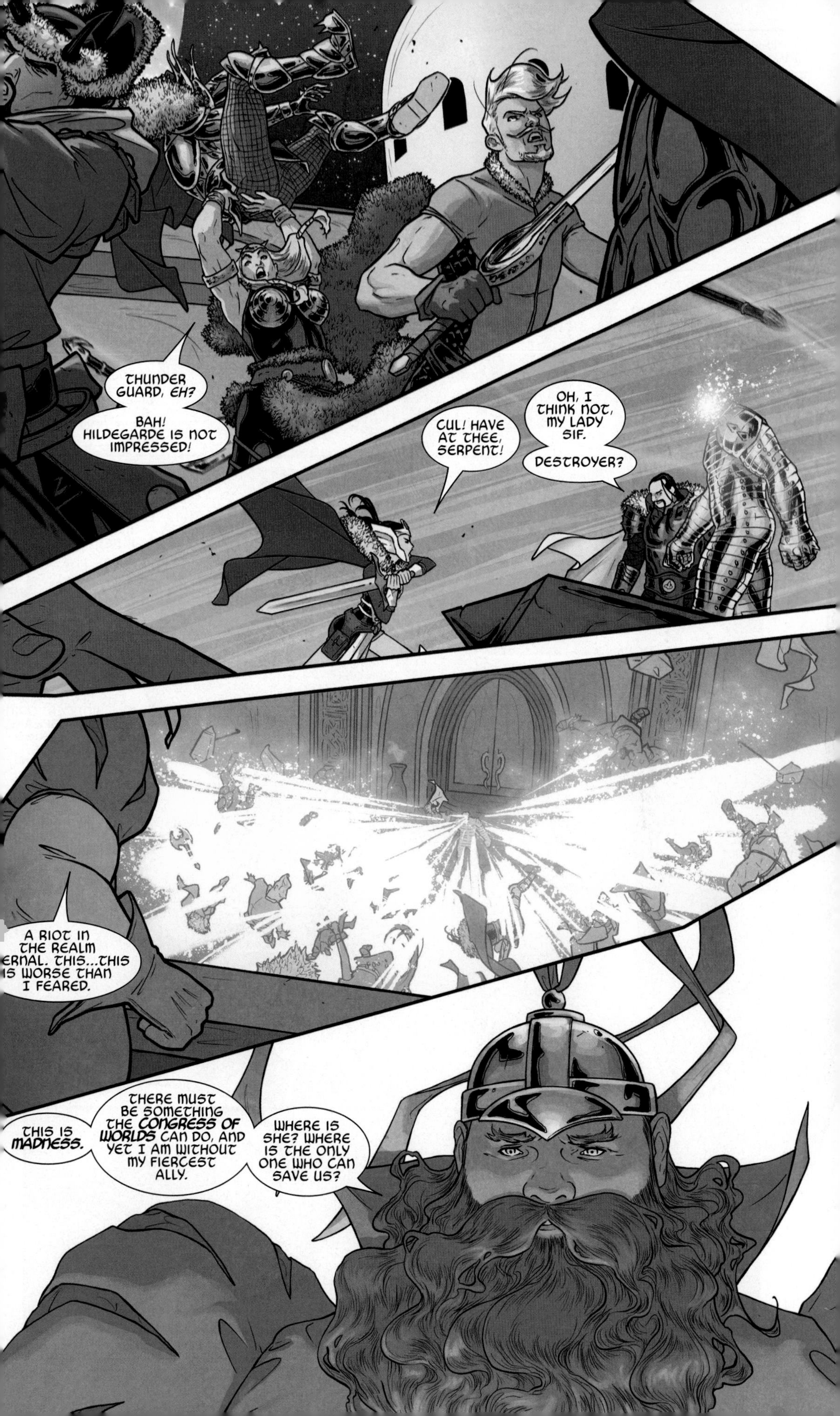
THUNDER GUARD, EH?
BAH! HILDEGARDE IS NOT IMPRESSED!
CUL! HAVE AT THEE, SERPENT!
OH, I THINK NOT, MY LADY SIF.
DESTROYER?
A RIOT IN THE REALM ERNAL. THIS...THIS IS WORSE THAN I FEARED.
THIS IS MADNESS.
THERE MUST BE SOMETHING THE CONGRESS OF WORLDS CAN DO, AND YET I AM WITHOUT MY FIERCEST ALLY.
WHERE IS SHE? WHERE IS THE ONLY ONE WHO CAN SAVE US?

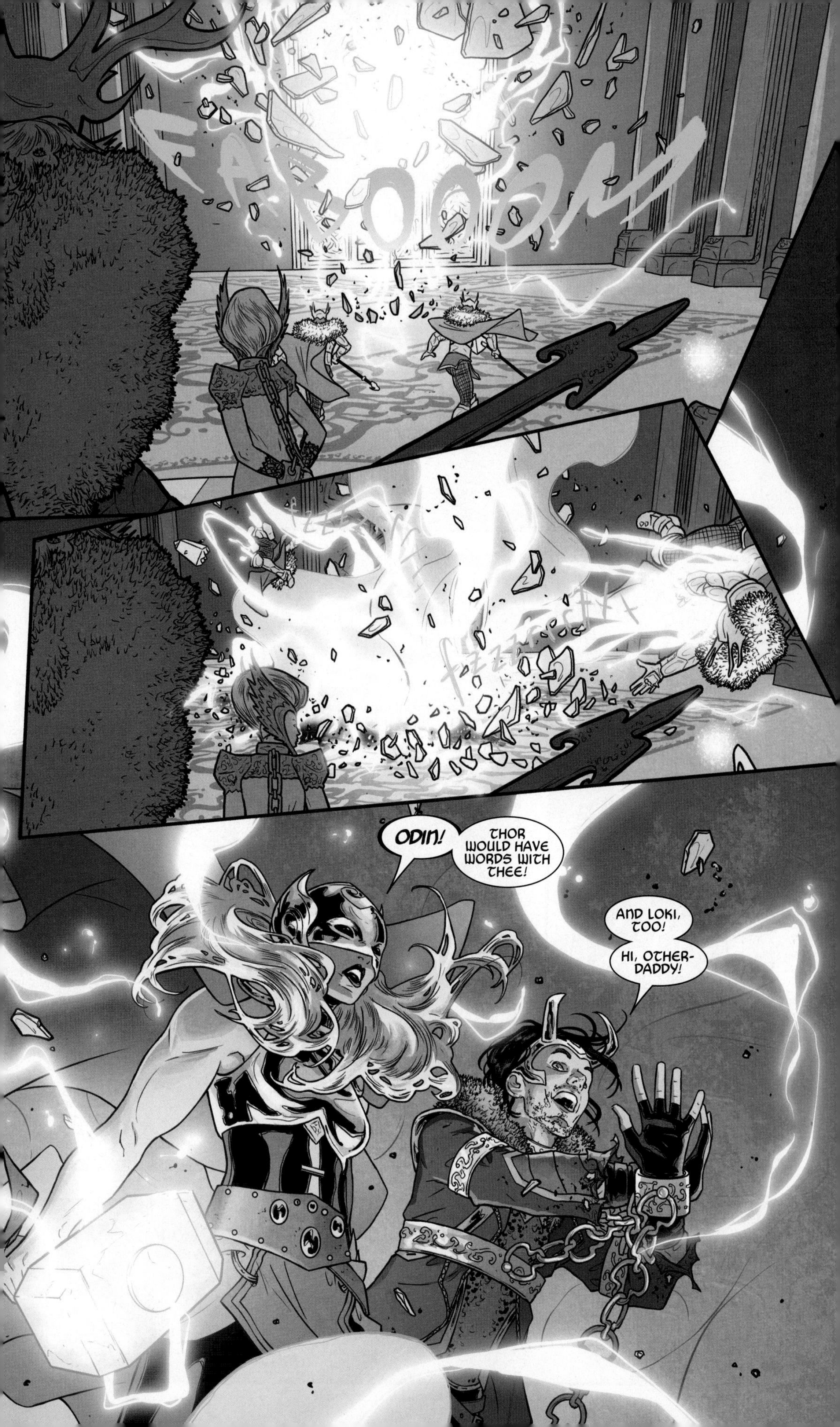

FABOOOM
fzzzt
fzzzzzzzt
ODIN!
THOR WOULD HAVE WORDS WITH THEE!
AND LOKI, TOO!
HI, OTHER-DADDY!

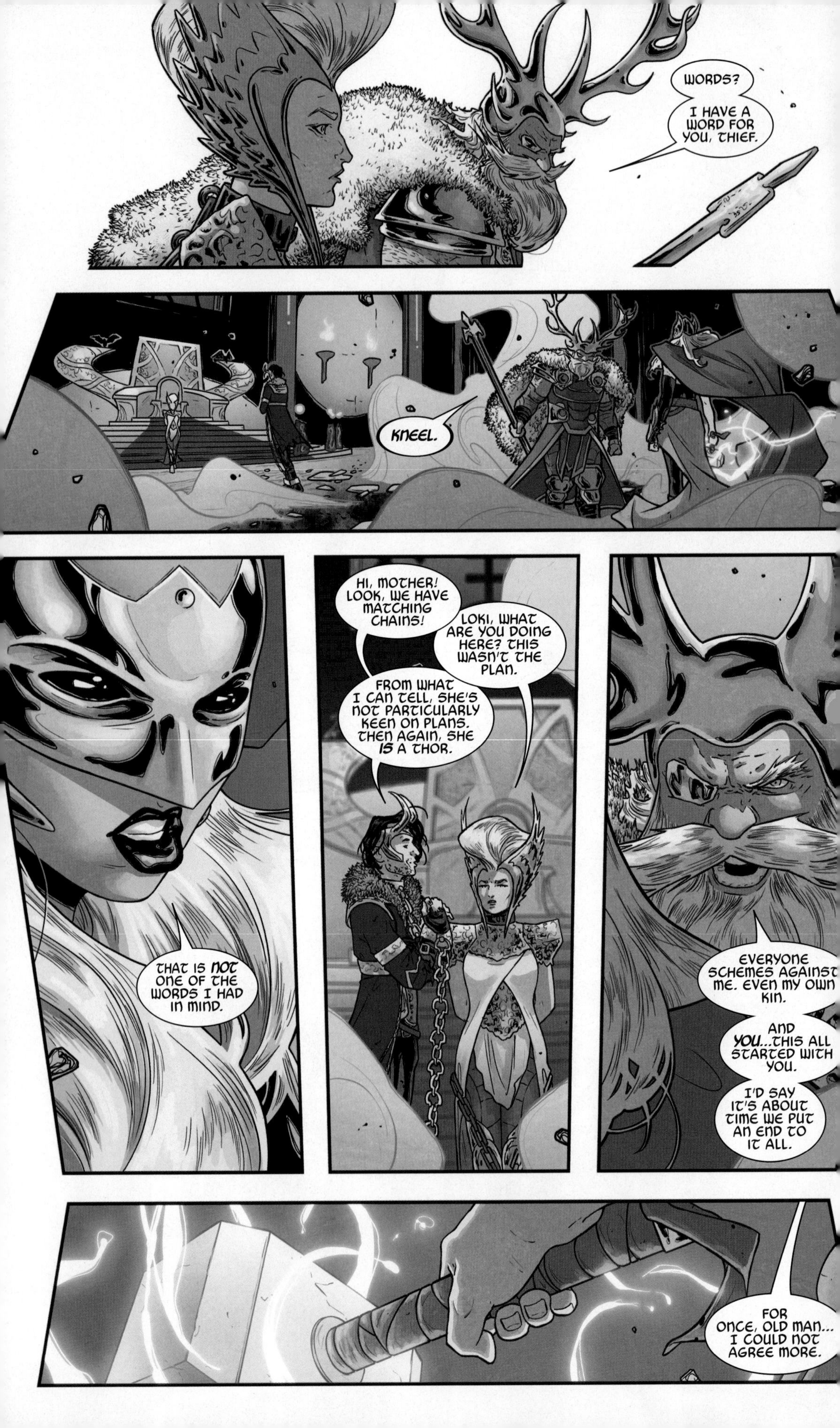
WORDS?
I HAVE A WORD FOR YOU, THIEF.
KNEEL.
THAT IS NOT ONE OF THE WORDS I HAD IN MIND.
HI, MOTHER! LOOK, WE HAVE MATCHING CHAINS!
LOKI, WHAT ARE YOU DOING HERE? THIS WASN'T THE PLAN.
FROM WHAT I CAN TELL, SHE'S NOT PARTICULARLY KEEN ON PLANS. THEN AGAIN, SHE IS A THOR.
EVERYONE SCHEMES AGAINST ME. EVEN MY OWN KIN.
AND YOU...THIS ALL STARTED WITH YOU.
I'D SAY IT'S ABOUT TIME WE PUT AN END TO IT ALL.
FOR ONCE, OLD MAN... I COULD NOT AGREE MORE.

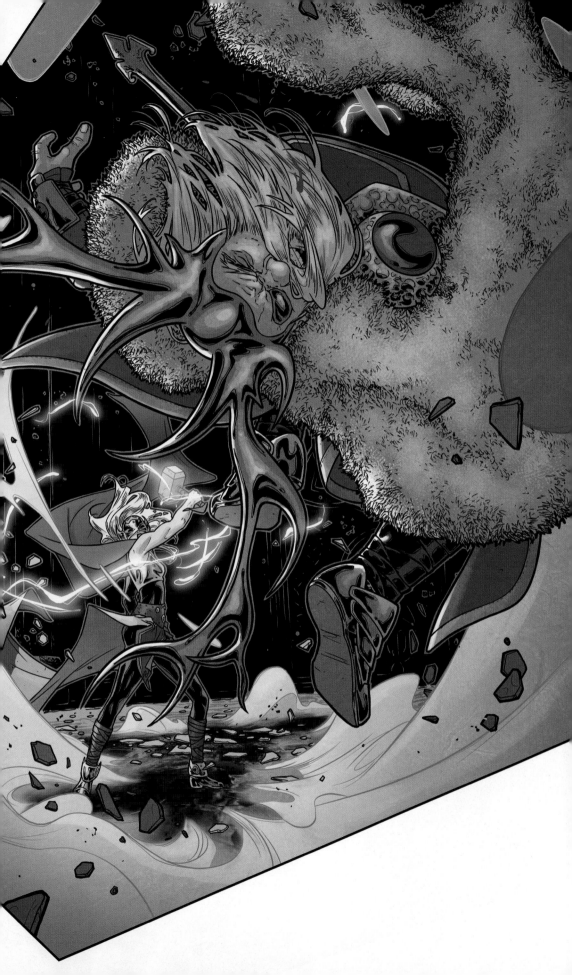

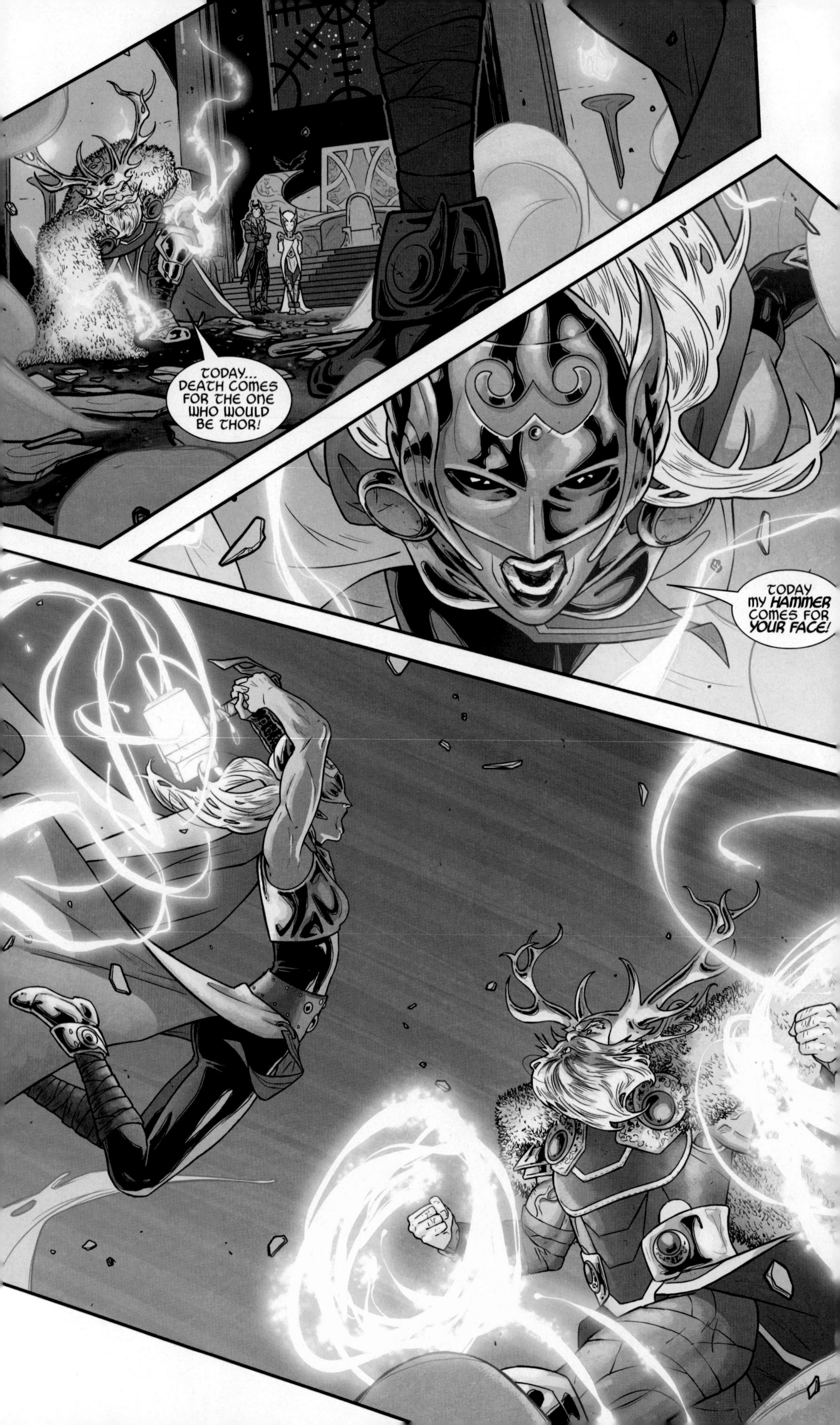
TODAY... DEATH COMES FOR THE ONE WHO WOULD BE THOR!
TODAY my HAMMER COMES FOR YOUR FACE!

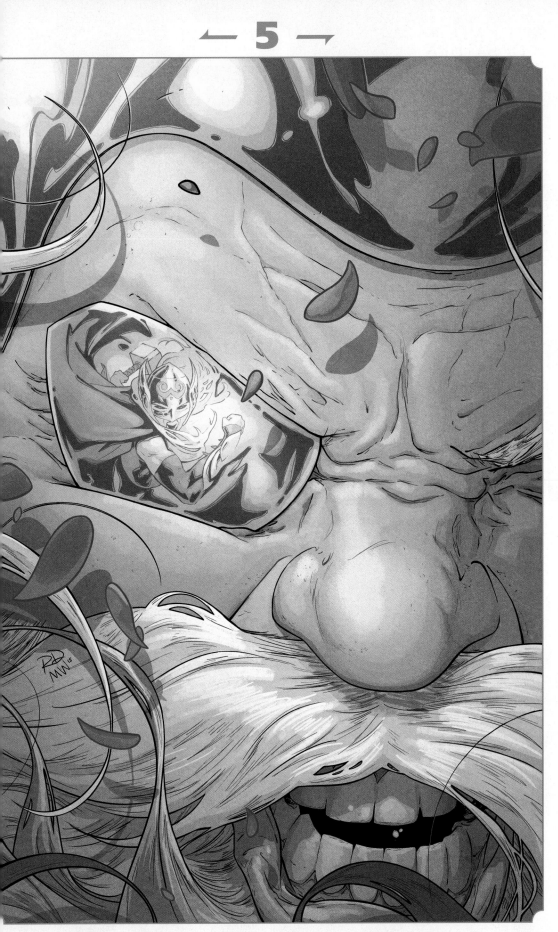

THE CIVIL WAR OF THE GODS

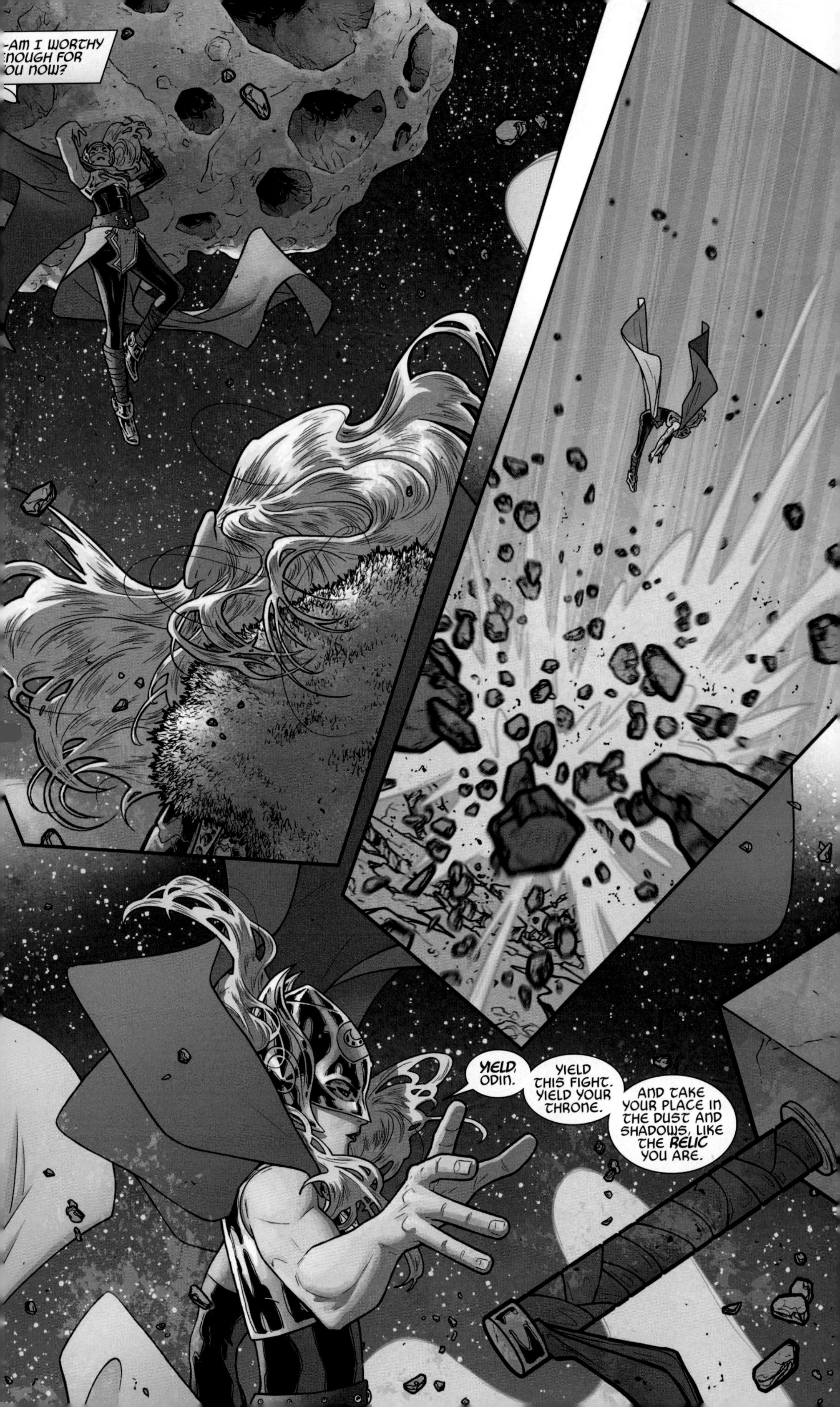
-AM I WORTHY ENOUGH FOR YOU NOW?
YIELD, ODIN.
YIELD THIS FIGHT. YIELD YOUR THRONE.
AND TAKE YOUR PLACE IN THE DUST AND SHADOWS, LIKE THE RELIC YOU ARE.

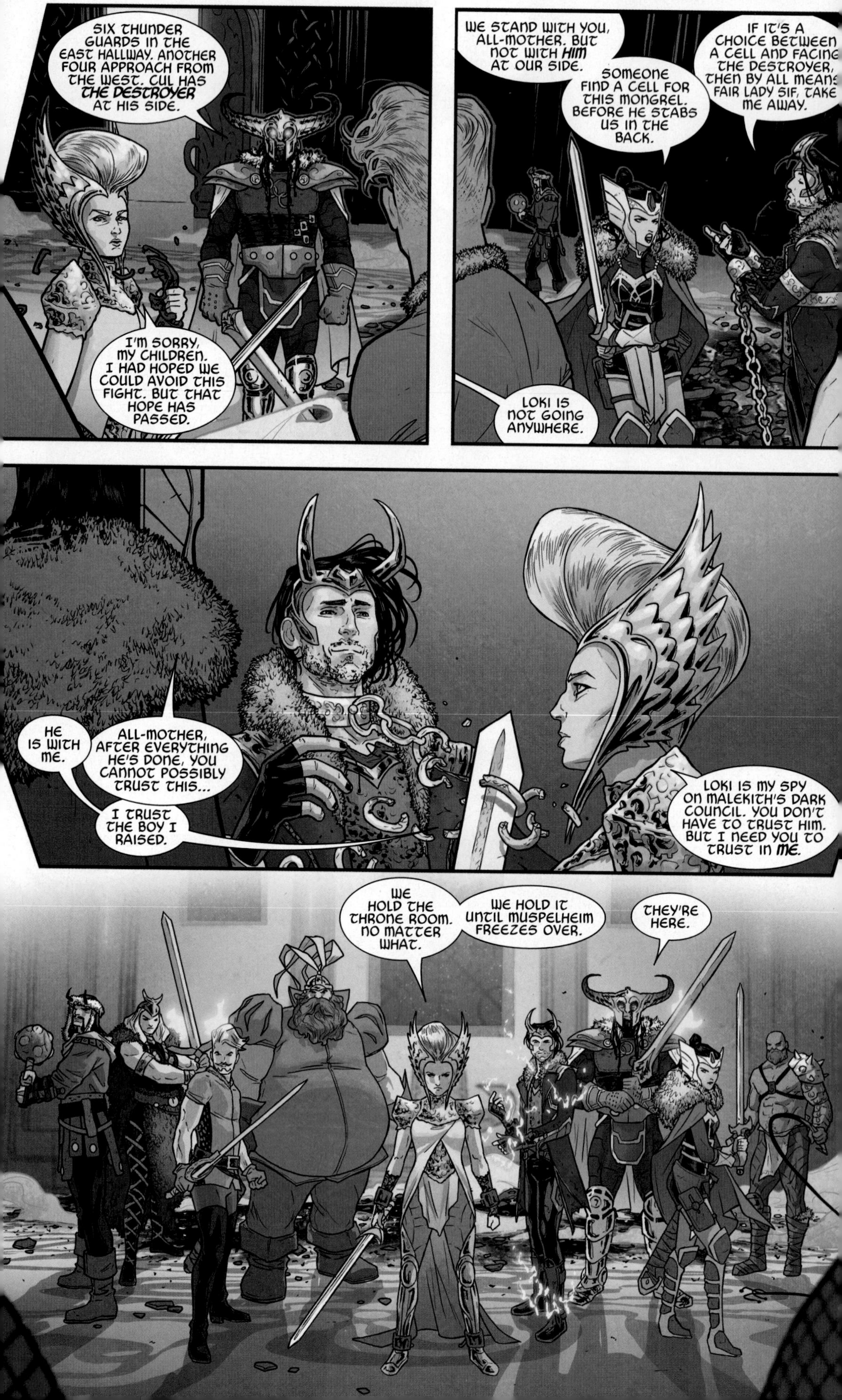
SIX THUNDER GUARDS IN THE EAST HALLWAY. ANOTHER FOUR APPROACH FROM THE WEST. CUL HAS THE DESTROYER AT HIS SIDE.
I'M SORRY, MY CHILDREN. I HAD HOPED WE COULD AVOID THIS FIGHT. BUT THAT HOPE HAS PASSED.
WE STAND WITH YOU, ALL-MOTHER. BUT NOT WITH HIM AT OUR SIDE.
SOMEONE FIND A CELL FOR THIS MONGREL. BEFORE HE STABS US IN THE BACK.
IF IT'S A CHOICE BETWEEN A CELL AND FACING THE DESTROYER, THEN BY ALL MEANS FAIR LADY SIF, TAKE ME AWAY.
LOKI IS NOT GOING ANYWHERE.
ALL-MOTHER, AFTER EVERYTHING HE'S DONE, YOU CANNOT POSSIBLY TRUST THIS...
HE IS WITH ME.
I TRUST THE BOY I RAISED.
LOKI IS MY SPY ON MALEKITH'S DARK COUNCIL. YOU DON'T HAVE TO TRUST HIM. BUT I NEED YOU TO TRUST IN ME.
WE HOLD THE THRONE ROOM. NO MATTER WHAT.
WE HOLD IT UNTIL MUSPELHEIM FREEZES OVER.
THEY'RE HERE.

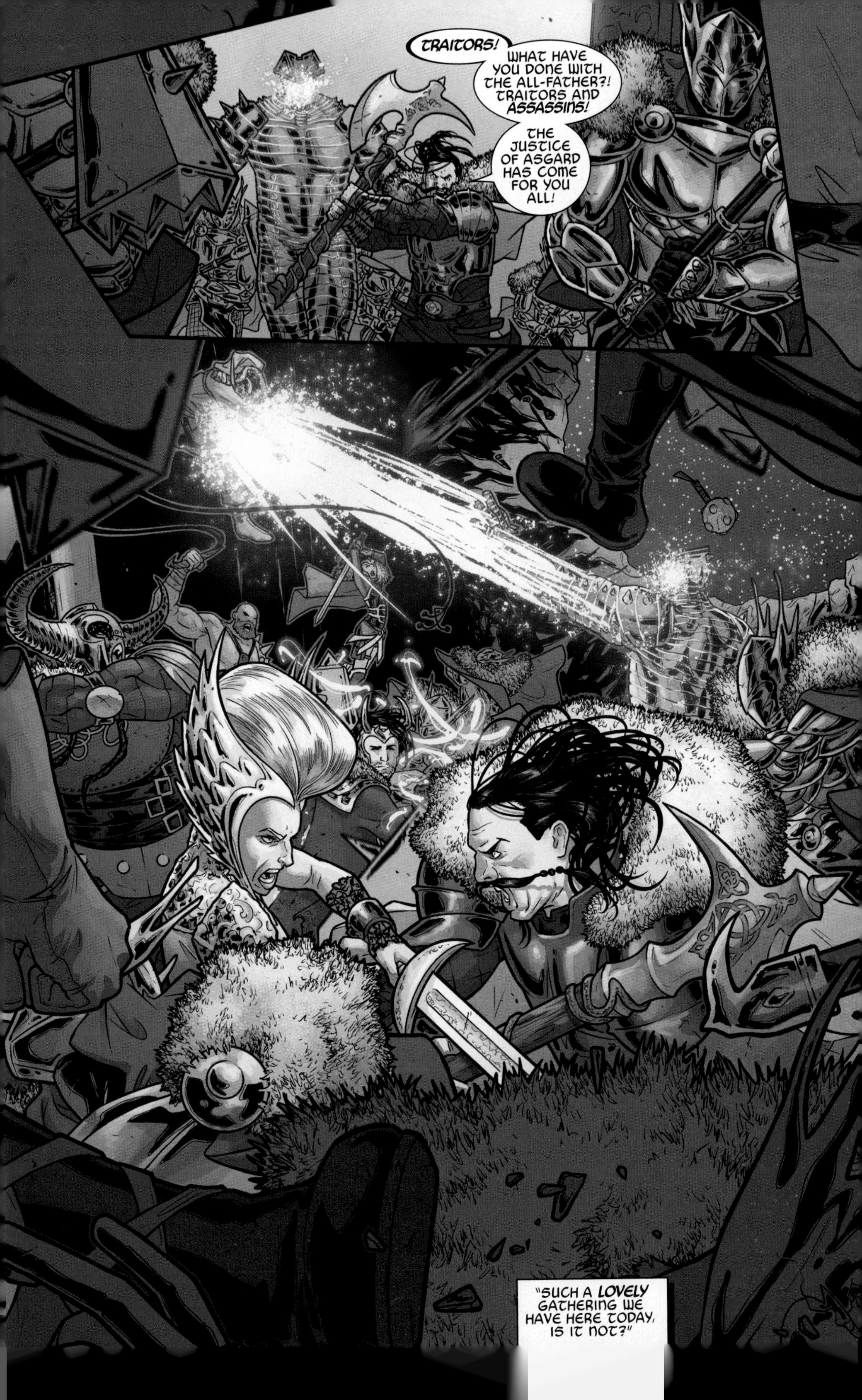
TRAITORS!
WHAT HAVE YOU DONE WITH THE ALL-FATHER?! TRAITORS AND ASSASSINS!
THE JUSTICE OF ASGARD HAS COME FOR YOU ALL!
"SUCH A LOVELY GATHERING WE HAVE HERE TODAY, IS IT NOT?"

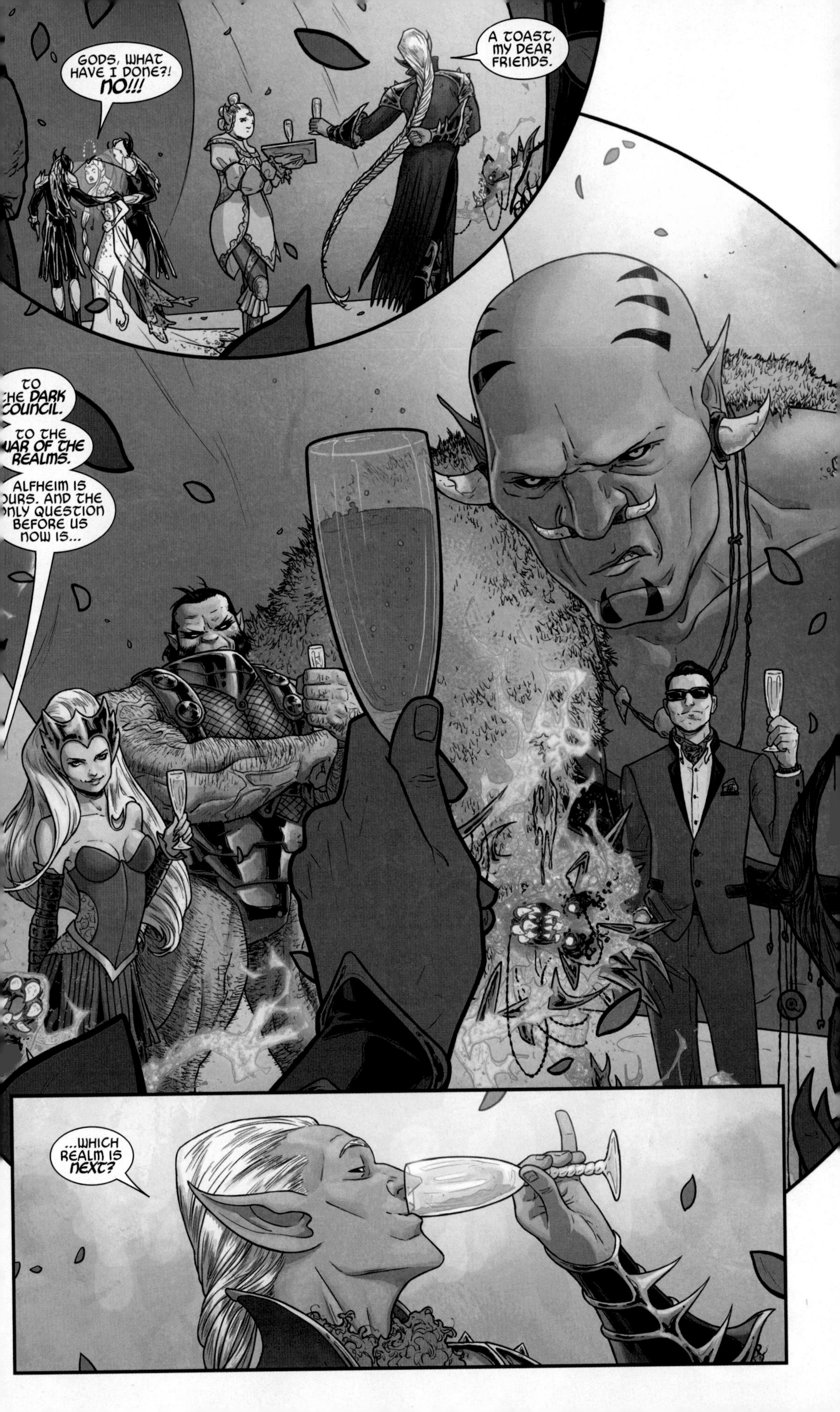
GODS, WHAT HAVE I DONE?! NO!!!
A TOAST, MY DEAR FRIENDS.
TO THE DARK COUNCIL.
TO THE WAR OF THE REALMS.
ALFHEIM IS OURS. AND THE ONLY QUESTION BEFORE US NOW IS...
...WHICH REALM IS NEXT?

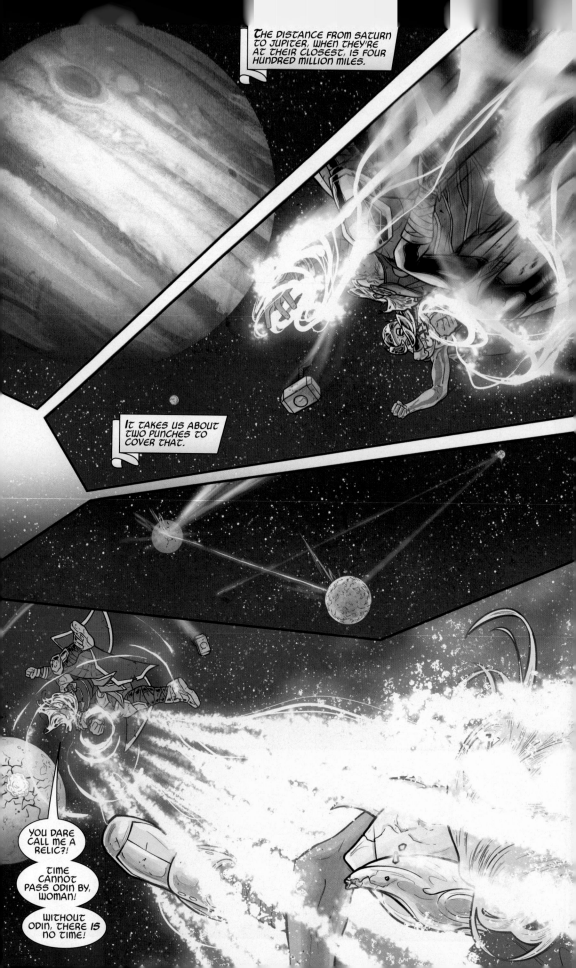

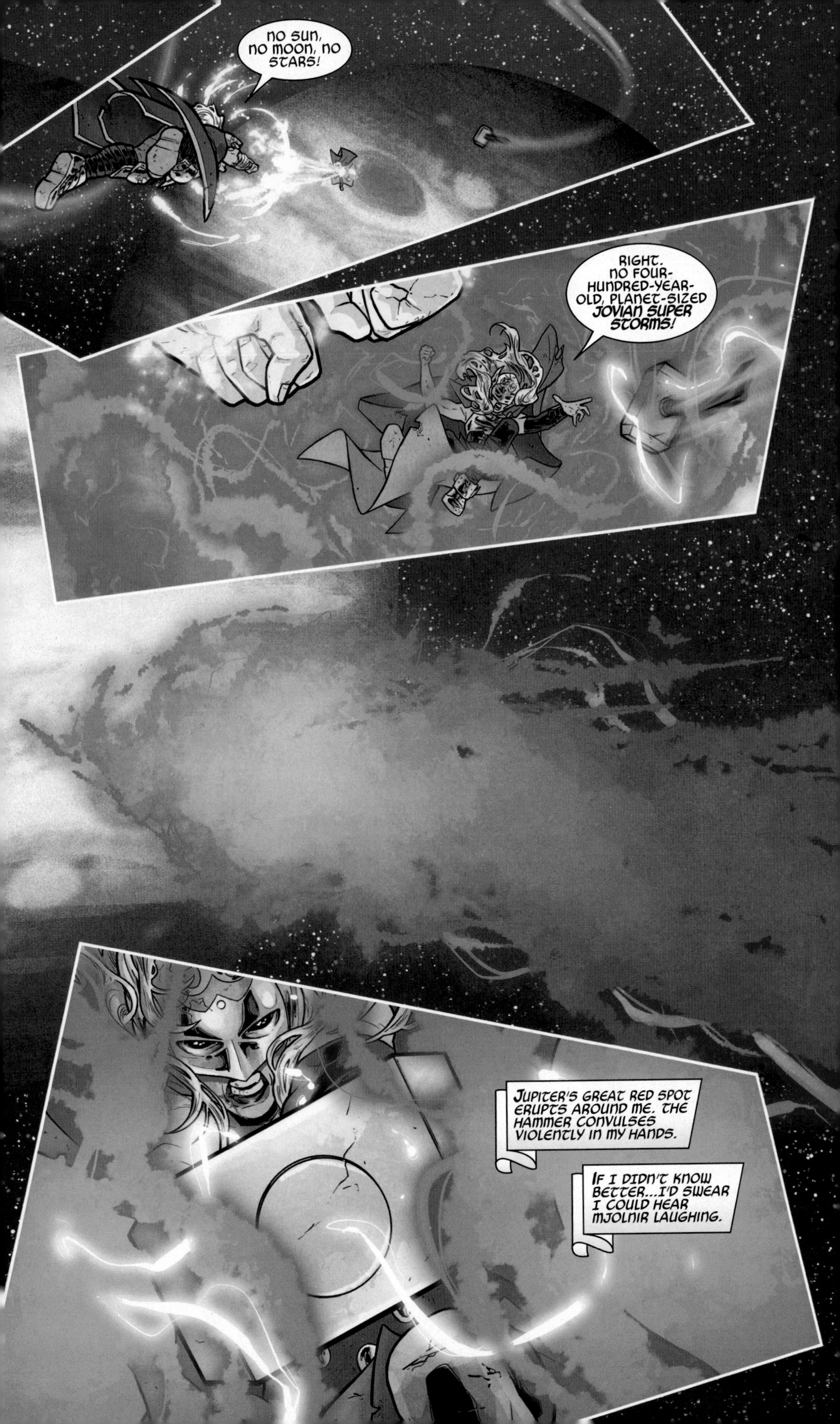
NO SUN, NO MOON, NO STARS!
RIGHT. NO FOUR-HUNDRED-YEAR-OLD, PLANET-SIZED JOVIAN SUPER STORMS!
JUPITER'S GREAT RED SPOT ERUPTS AROUND ME. THE HAMMER CONVULSES VIOLENTLY IN MY HANDS.
IF I DIDN'T KNOW BETTER...I'D SWEAR I COULD HEAR MJOLNIR LAUGHING.

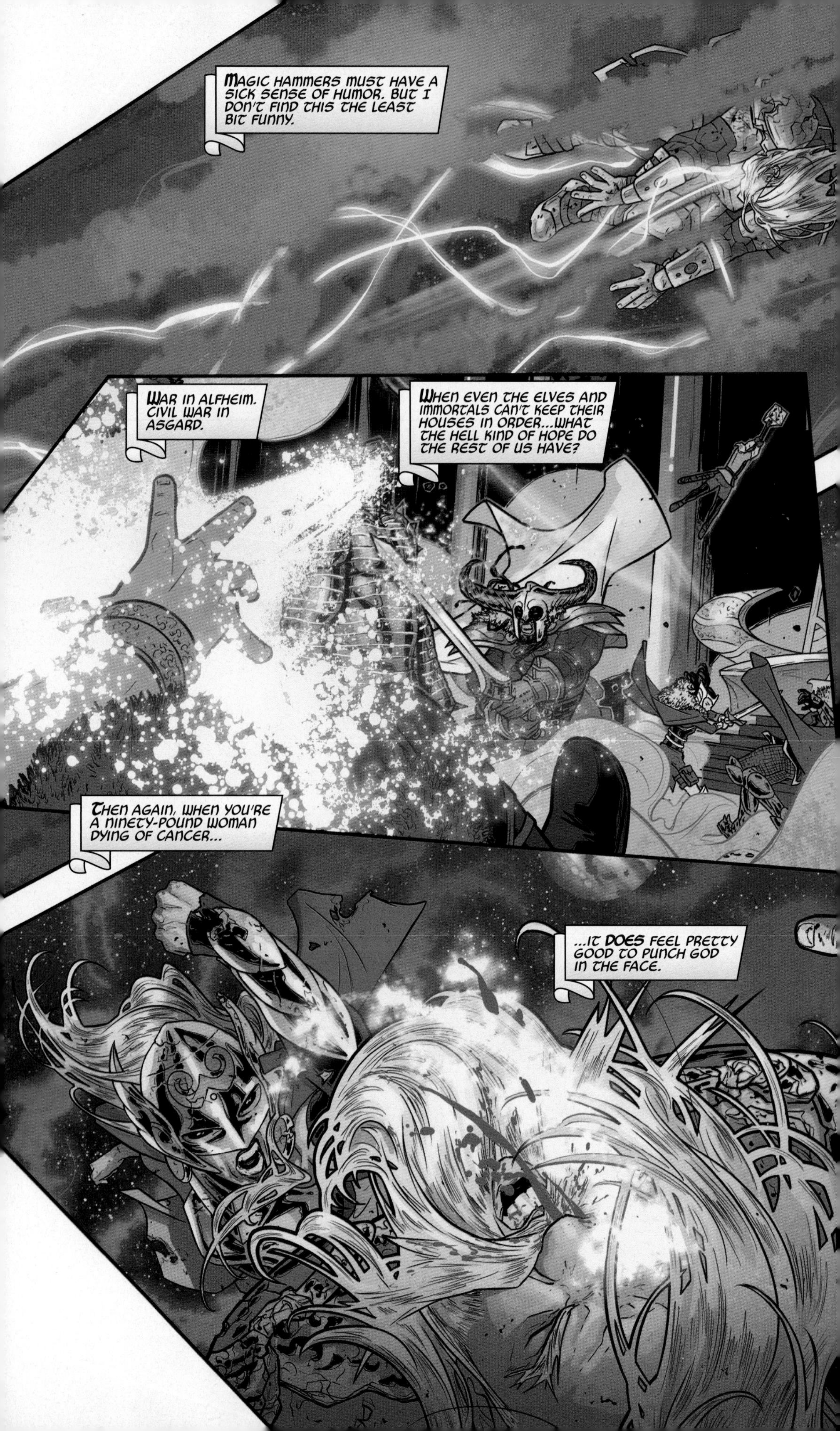

MAGIC HAMMERS MUST HAVE A SICK SENSE OF HUMOR. BUT I DON'T FIND THIS THE LEAST BIT FUNNY.
WAR IN ALFHEIM. CIVIL WAR IN ASGARD.
WHEN EVEN THE ELVES AND IMMORTALS CAN'T KEEP THEIR HOUSES IN ORDER...WHAT THE HELL KIND OF HOPE DO THE REST OF US HAVE?
THEN AGAIN, WHEN YOU'RE A NINETY-POUND WOMAN DYING OF CANCER...
...IT **DOES** FEEL PRETTY GOOD TO PUNCH GOD IN THE FACE.

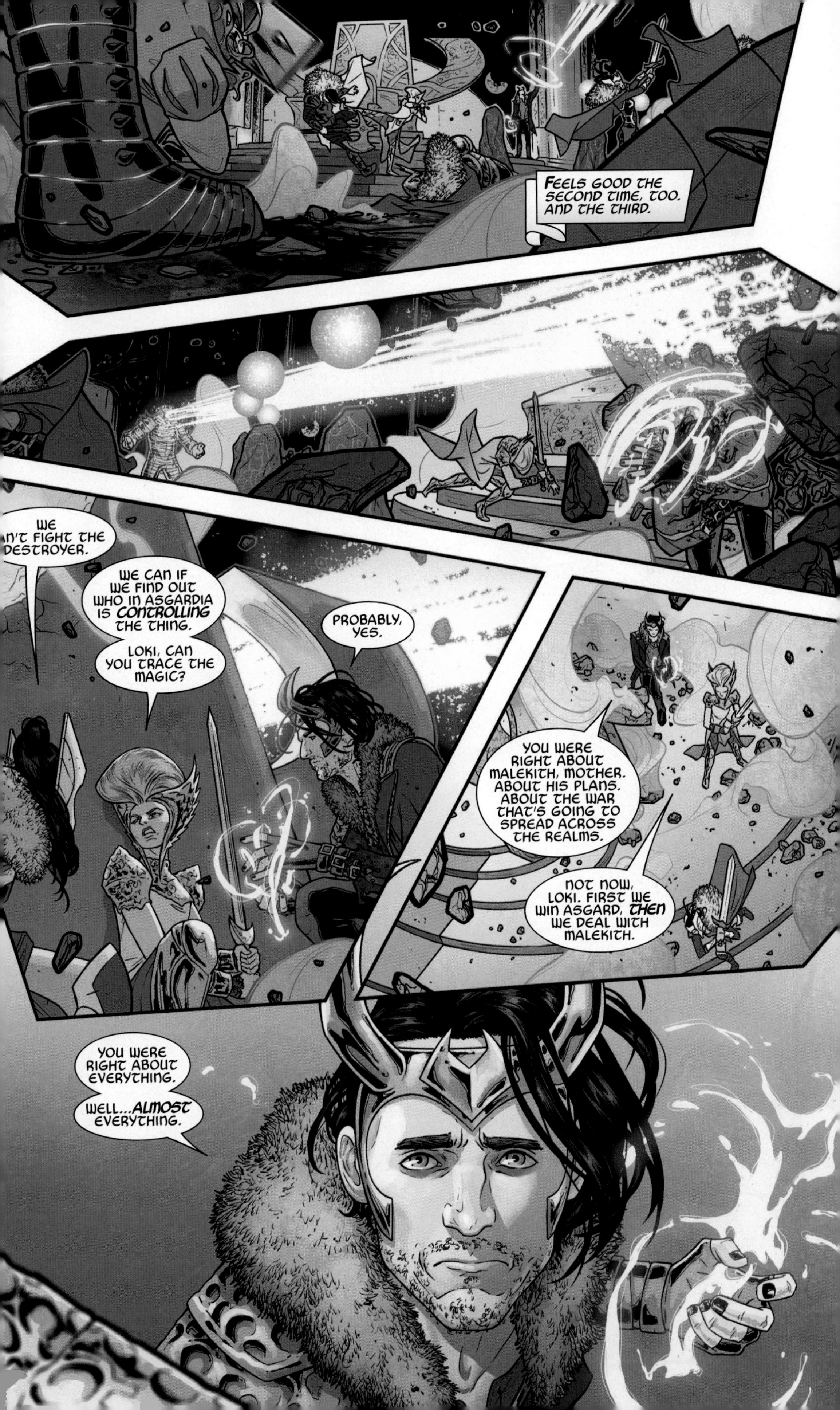

FEELS GOOD THE SECOND TIME, TOO. AND THE THIRD.
WE CAN'T FIGHT THE DESTROYER.
WE CAN IF WE FIND OUT WHO IN ASGARDIA IS CONTROLLING THE THING.
LOKI, CAN YOU TRACE THE MAGIC?
PROBABLY, YES.
YOU WERE RIGHT ABOUT MALEKITH, MOTHER. ABOUT HIS PLANS. ABOUT THE WAR THAT'S GOING TO SPREAD ACROSS THE REALMS.
NOT NOW, LOKI. FIRST WE WIN ASGARD, THEN WE DEAL WITH MALEKITH.
YOU WERE RIGHT ABOUT EVERYTHING.
WELL...ALMOST EVERYTHING.

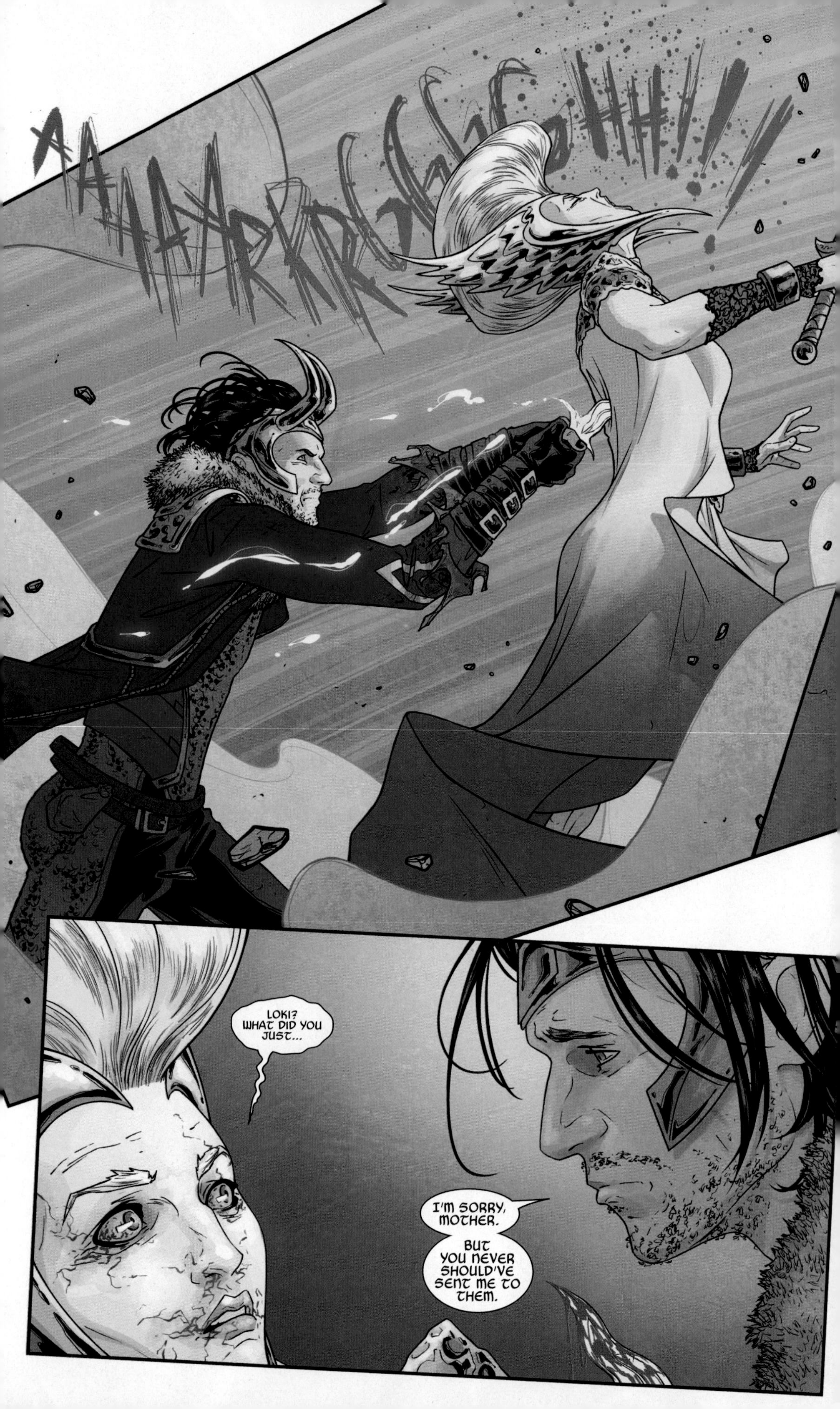
AAAARRRGGHH!!
LOKI? WHAT DID YOU JUST...
I'M SORRY, MOTHER.
BUT YOU NEVER SHOULD'VE SENT ME TO THEM.

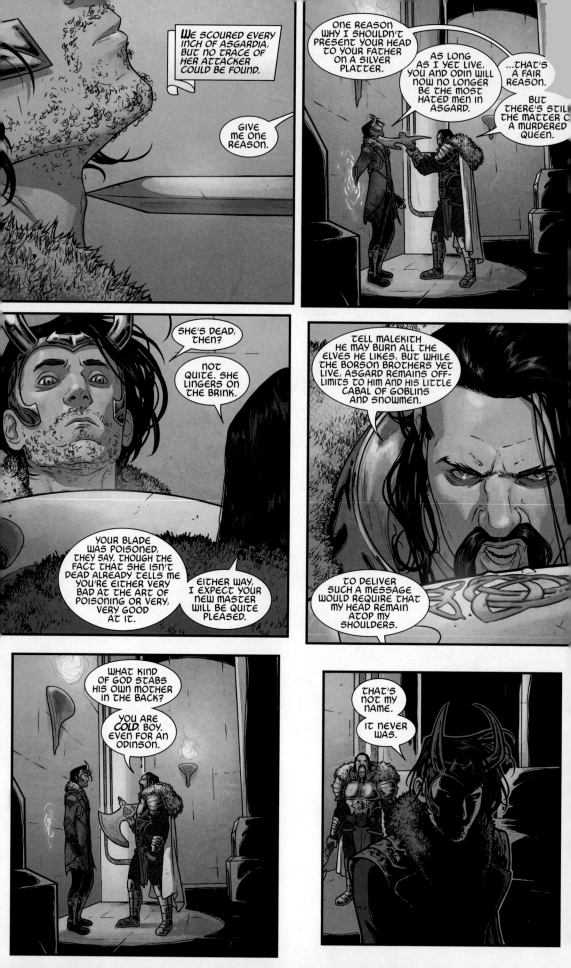

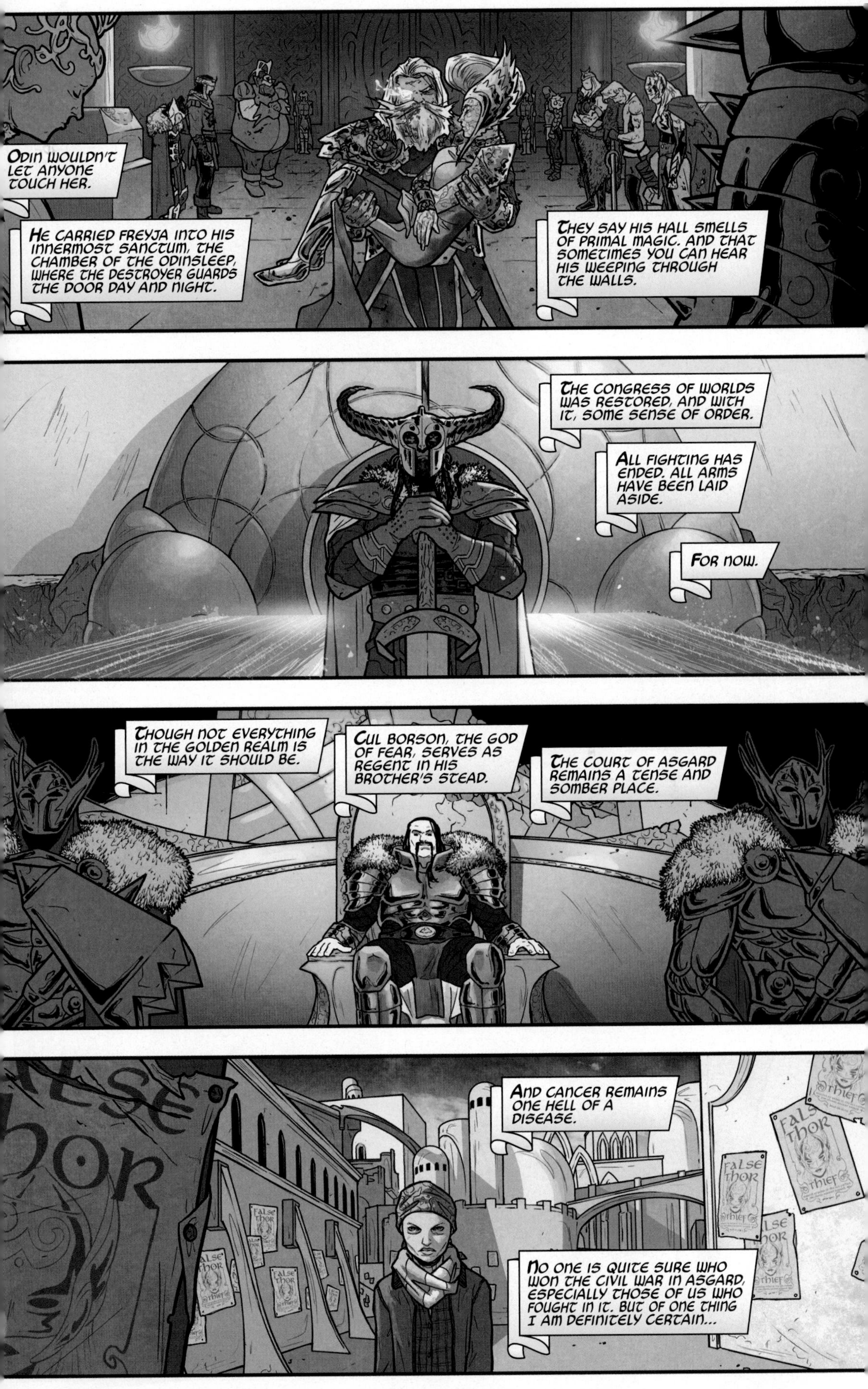

ODIN WOULDN'T LET ANYONE TOUCH HER.
HE CARRIED FREYJA INTO HIS INNERMOST SANCTUM, THE CHAMBER OF THE ODINSLEEP, WHERE THE DESTROYER GUARDS THE DOOR DAY AND NIGHT.
THEY SAY HIS HALL SMELLS OF PRIMAL MAGIC. AND THAT SOMETIMES YOU CAN HEAR HIS WEEPING THROUGH THE WALLS.
THE CONGRESS OF WORLDS WAS RESTORED, AND WITH IT, SOME SENSE OF ORDER.
ALL FIGHTING HAS ENDED. ALL ARMS HAVE BEEN LAID ASIDE.
FOR NOW.
THOUGH NOT EVERYTHING IN THE GOLDEN REALM IS THE WAY IT SHOULD BE.
CUL BORSON, THE GOD OF FEAR, SERVES AS REGENT IN HIS BROTHER'S STEAD.
THE COURT OF ASGARD REMAINS A TENSE AND SOMBER PLACE.
AND CANCER REMAINS ONE HELL OF A DISEASE.
FALSE THOR
NO ONE IS QUITE SURE WHO WON THE CIVIL WAR IN ASGARD, ESPECIALLY THOSE OF US WHO FOUGHT IN IT. BUT OF ONE THING I AM DEFINITELY CERTAIN...

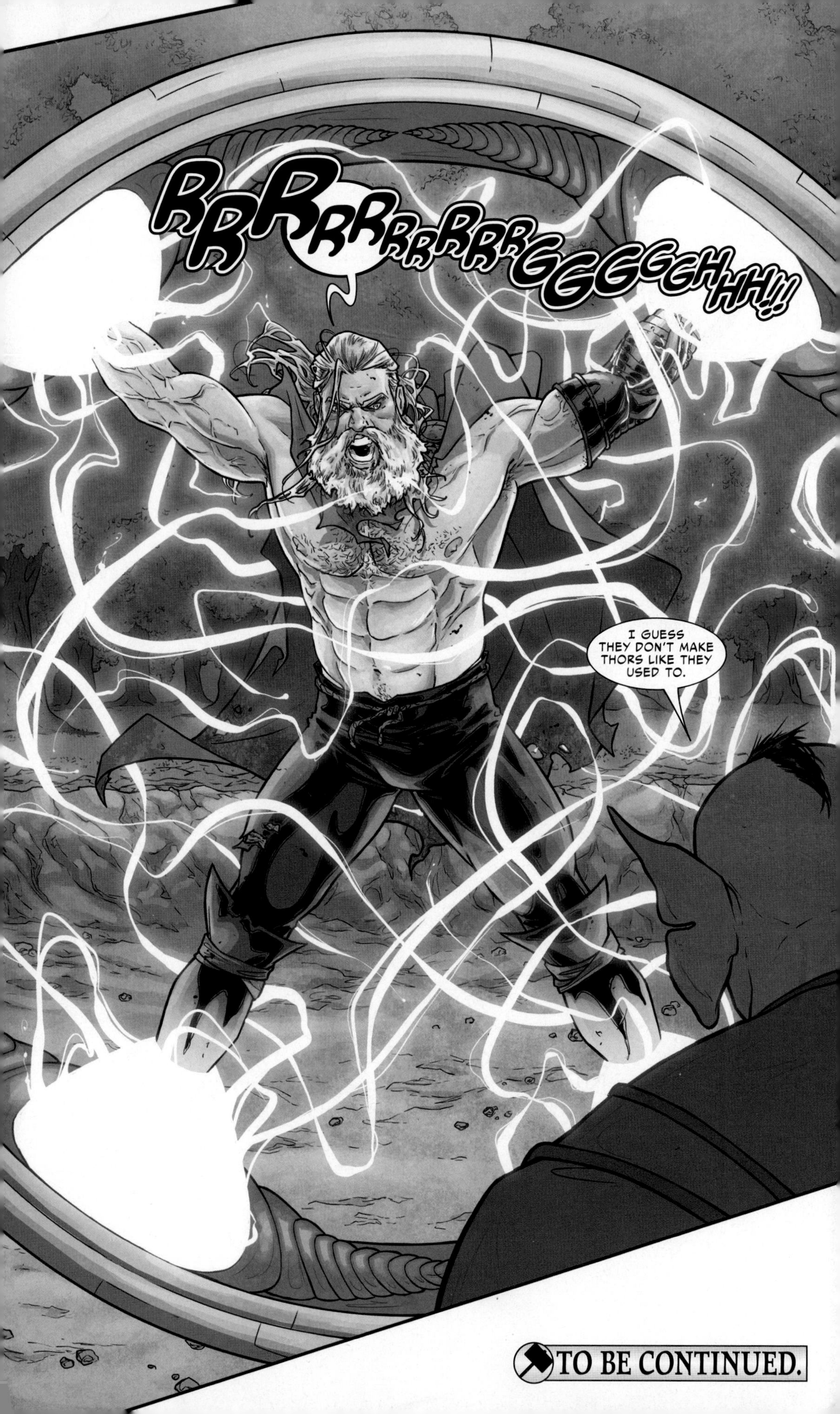
RRRRRRRRRRRGGGGGHHH!!!
I GUESS THEY DON'T MAKE THORS LIKE THEY USED TO.
TO BE CONTINUED.

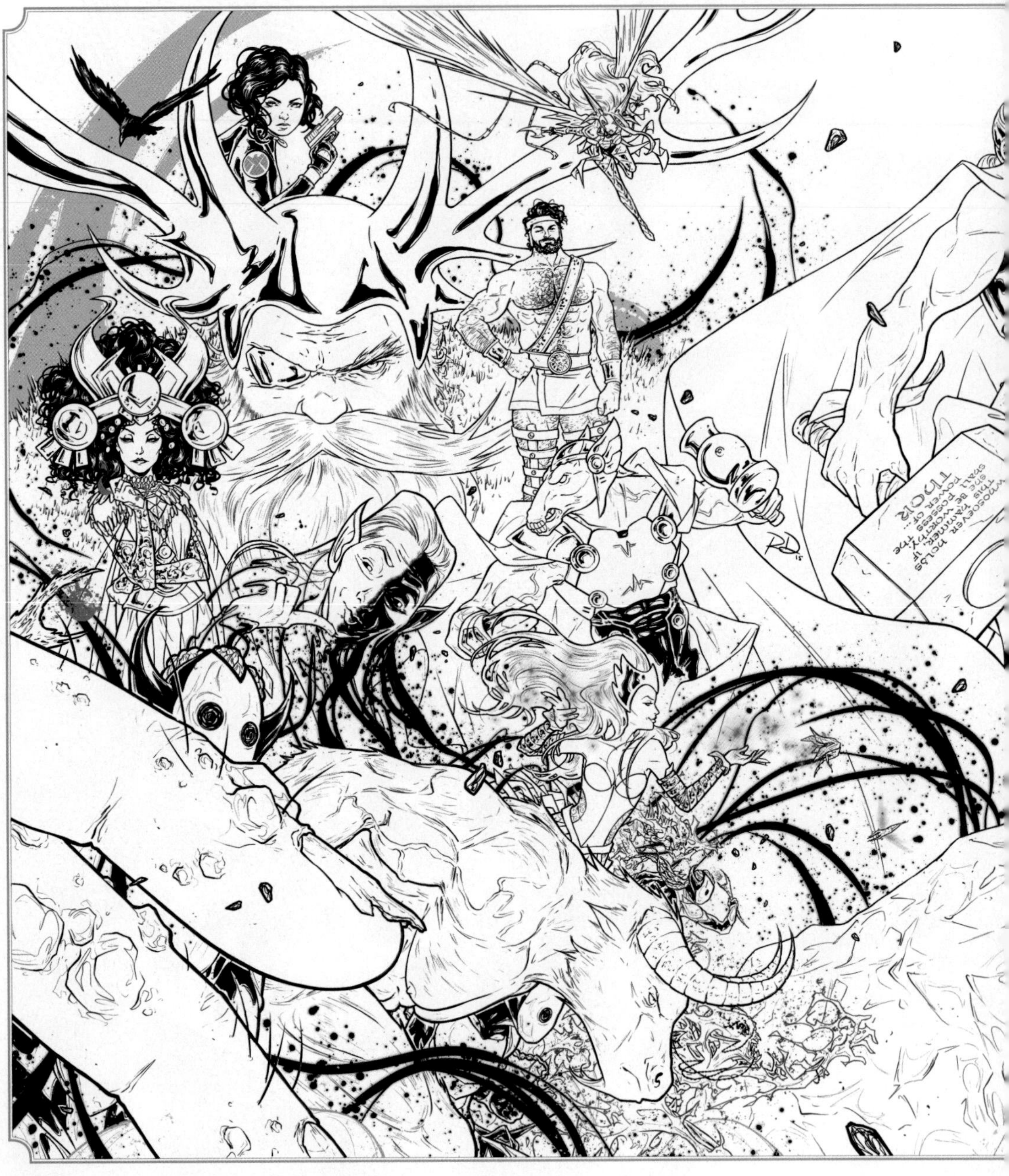
whosoever holds this hammer, if she be worthy, shall possess the power of... THOR

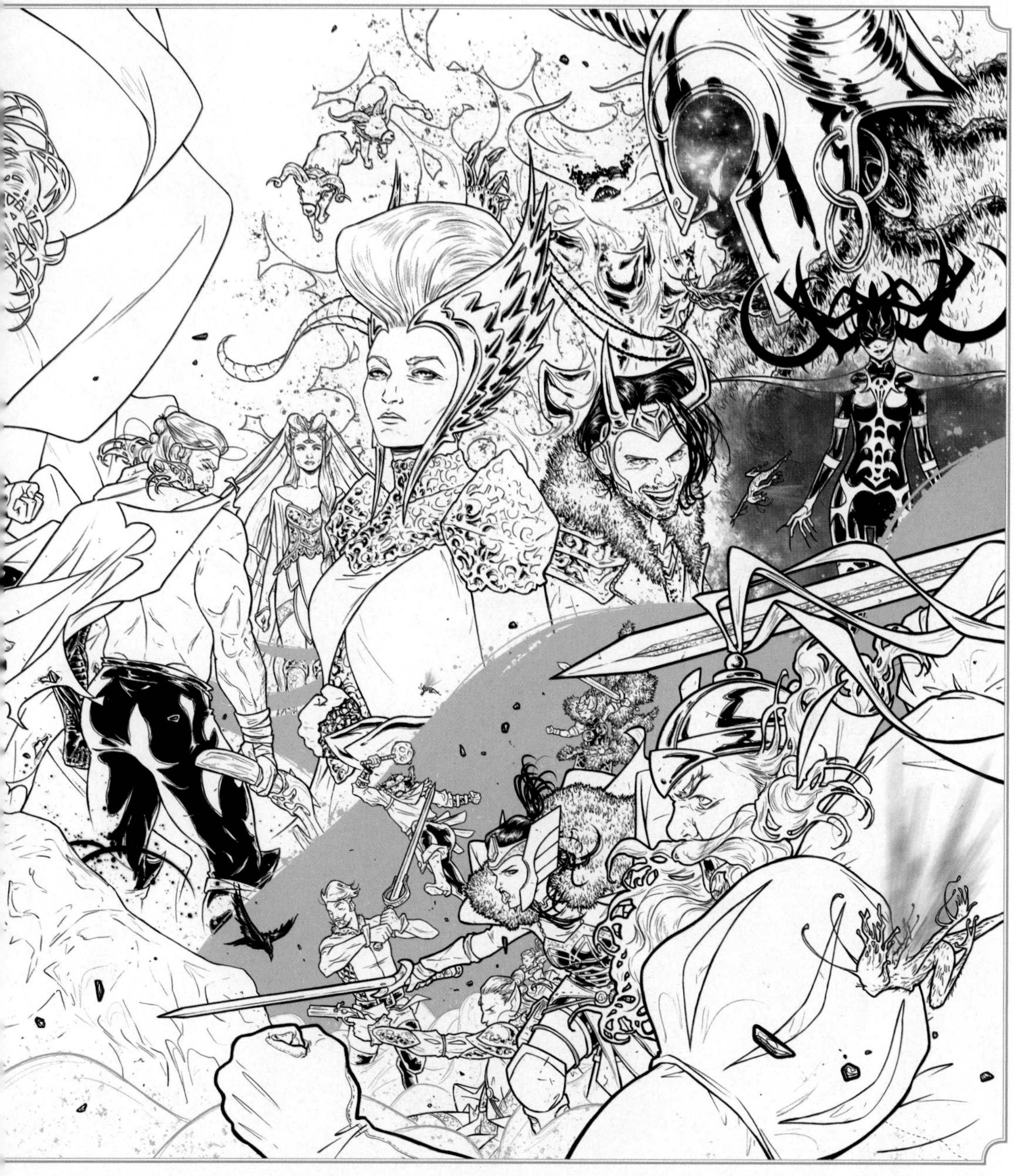

MIGHTY THOR # 1 COVER INKS
BY **RUSSELL DAUTERMAN**

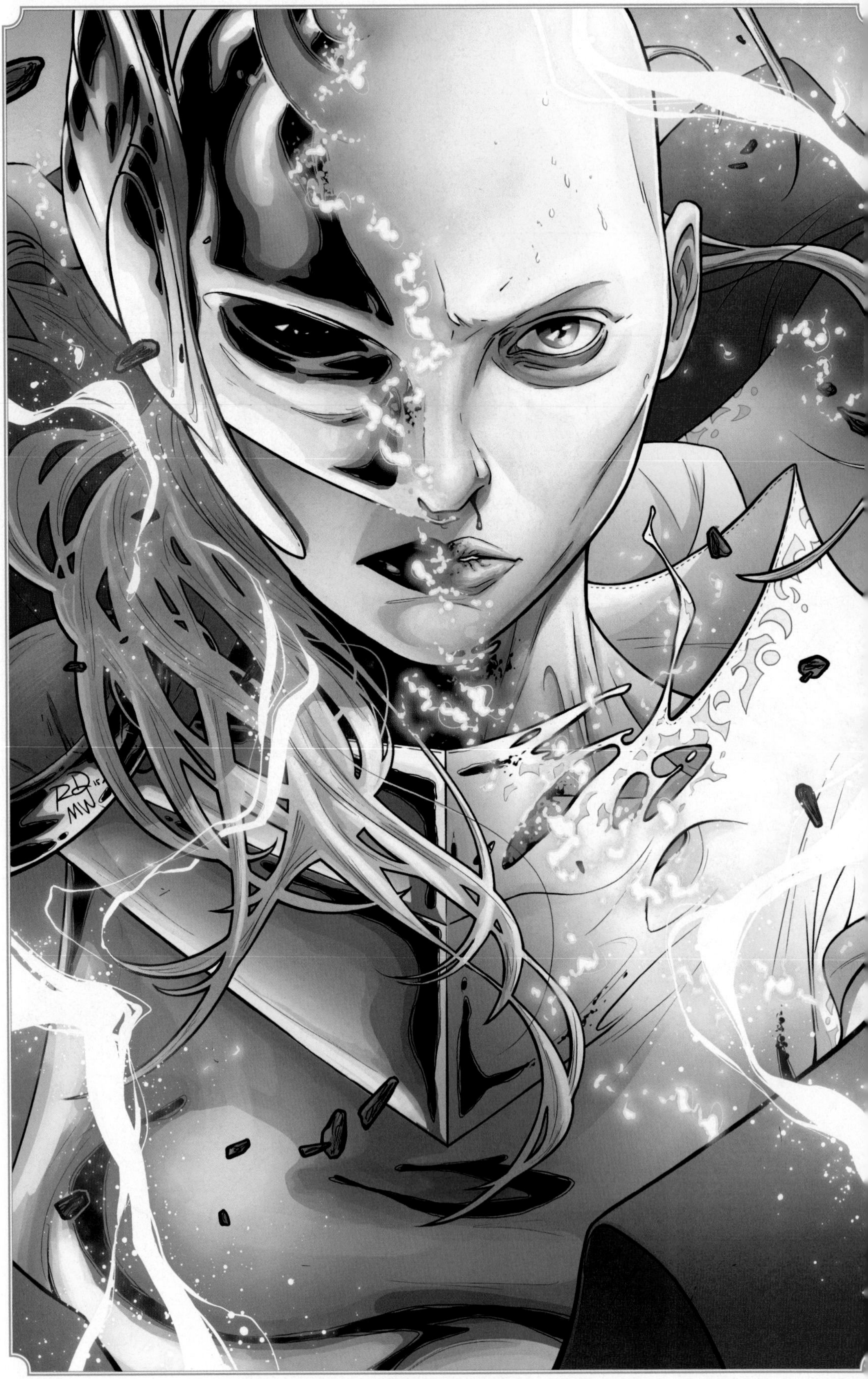

MIGHTY THOR # 1 VARIANT
BY **RUSSELL DAUTERMAN**

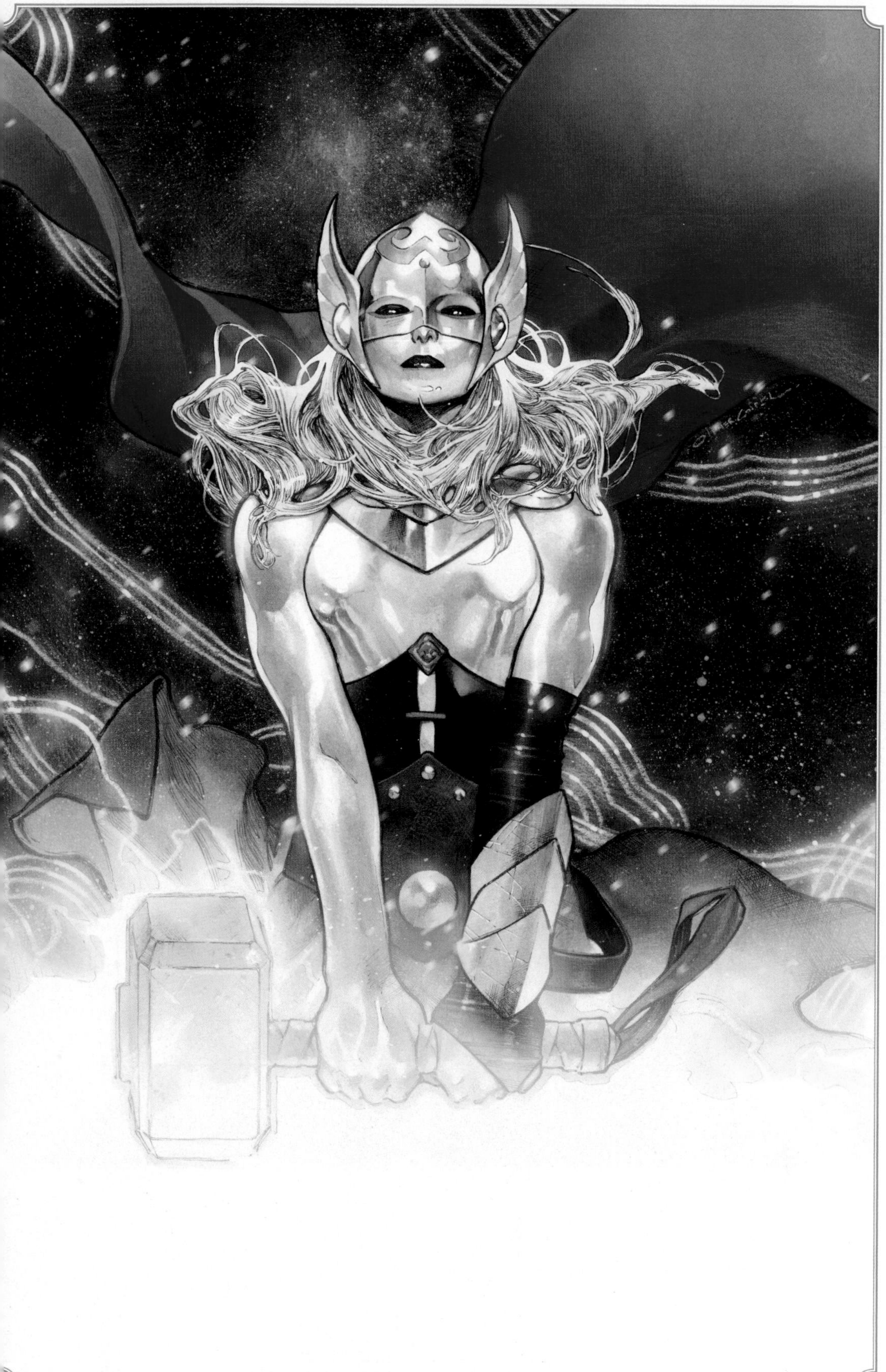

MIGHTY THOR # 1 VARIANT
BY **OLIVIER COIPEL**

MIGHTY THOR # I HIP-HOP VARIANT
BY **MIKE DEODATO**

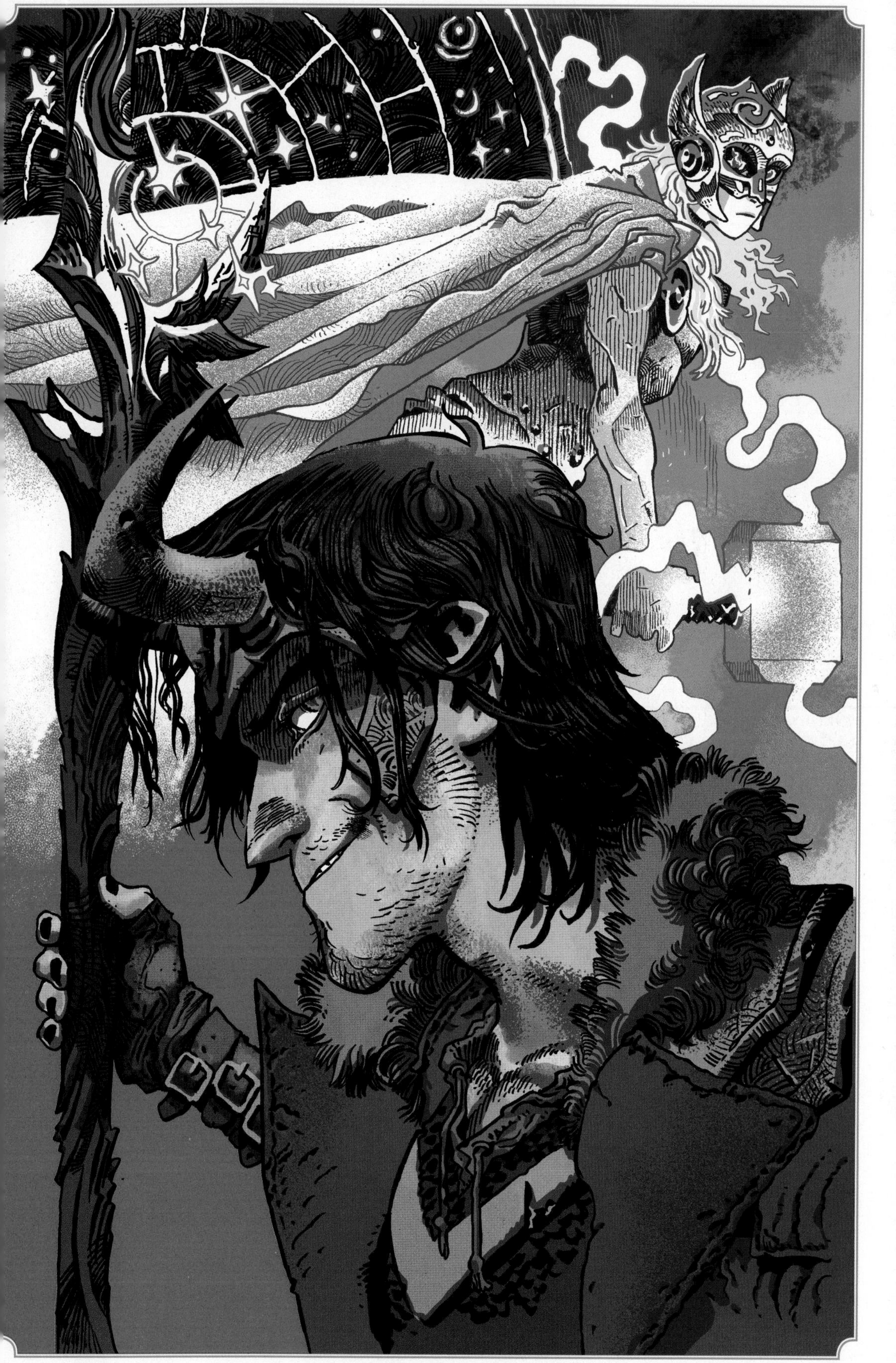

MIGHTY THOR # 2 VARIANT
BY **ARTYOM TRAKHANOV**

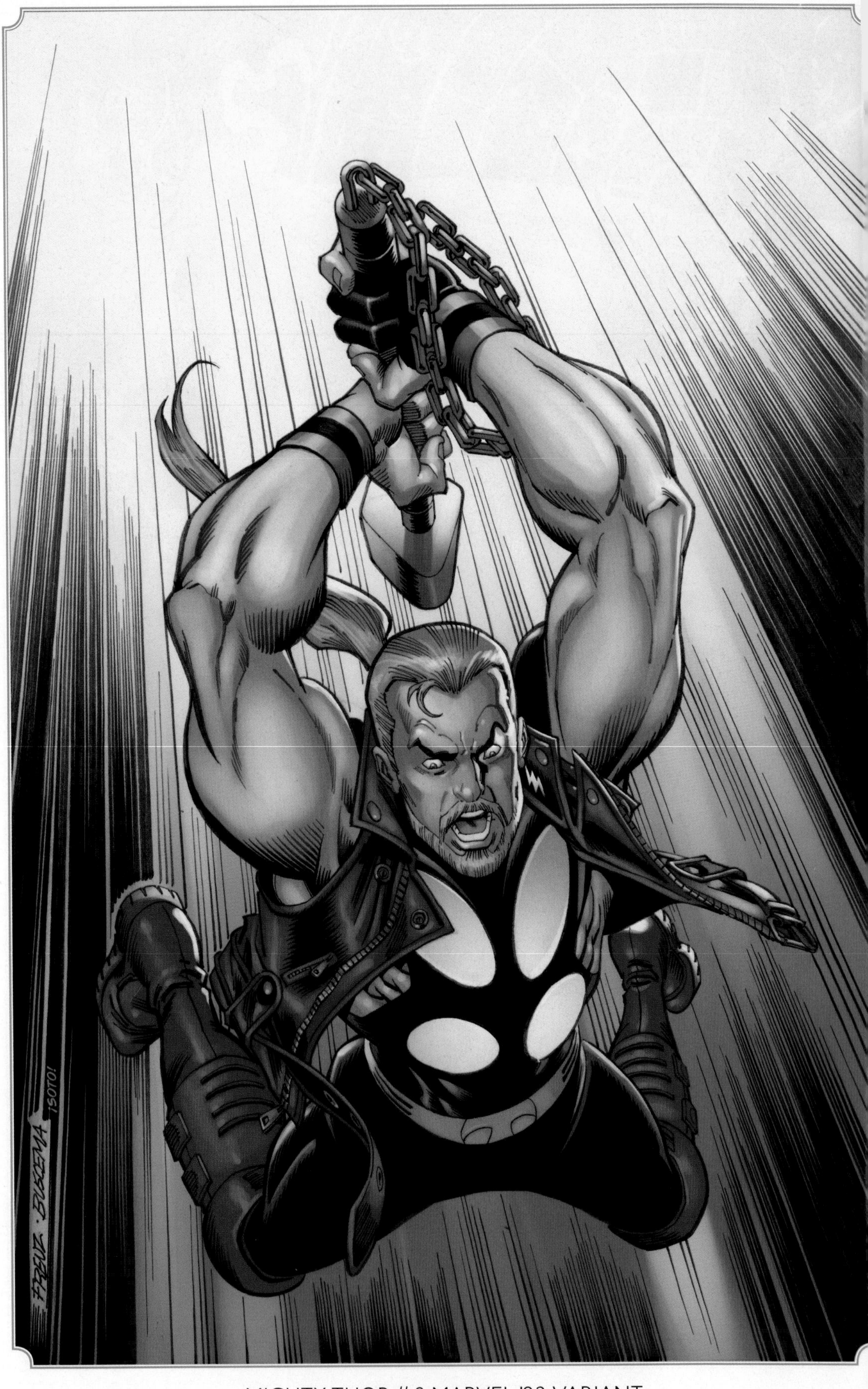
FRENZ · BUSCEMA
¡SOTO!

MIGHTY THOR # 2 MARVEL '92 VARIANT
BY **RON FRENZ**, **SAL BUSCEMA** & **CHRIS SOTOMAYOR**

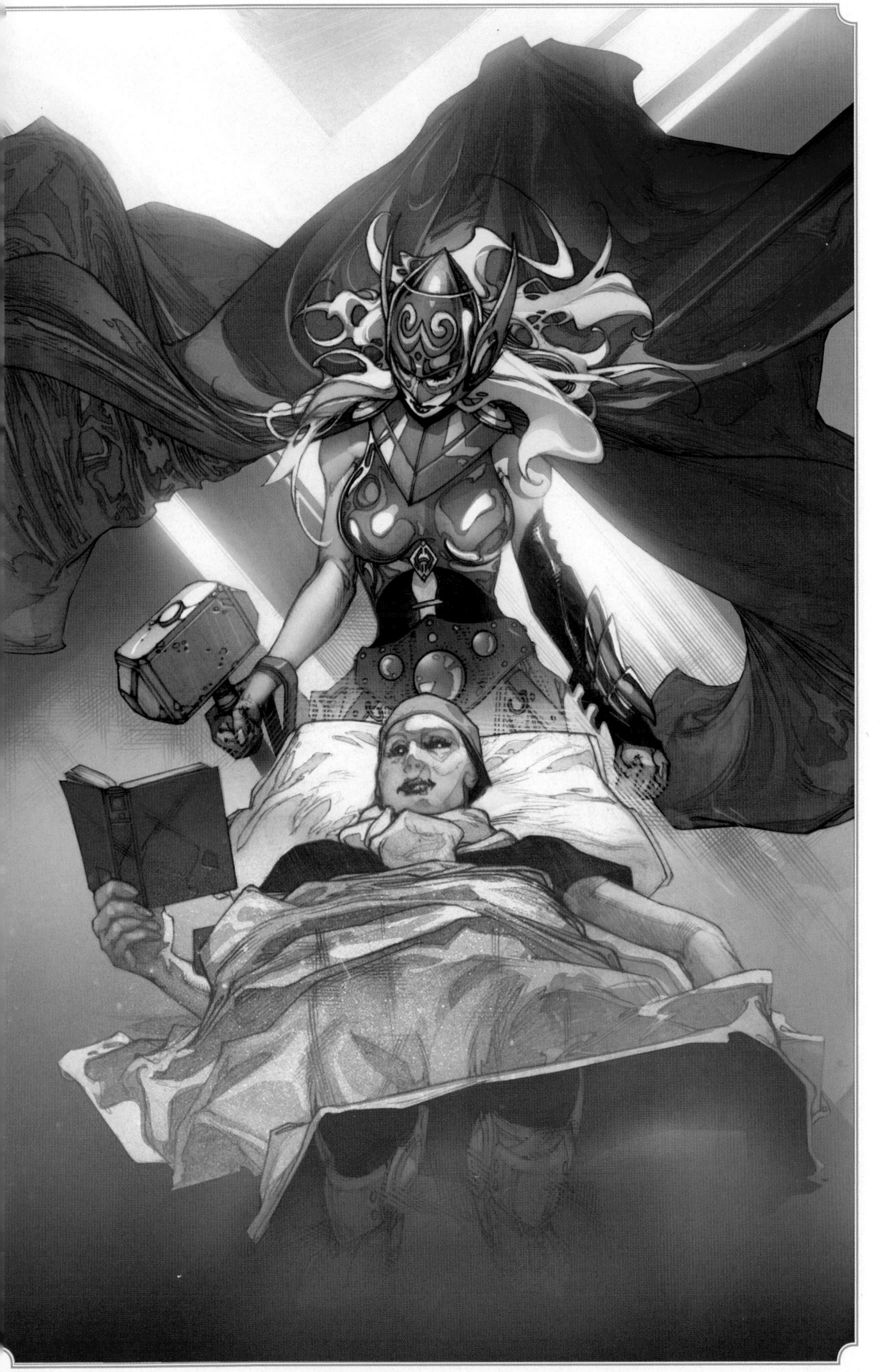

MIGHTY THOR # 3 VARIANT
BY **SIMONE BIANCHI** & **DAVID CURIEL**

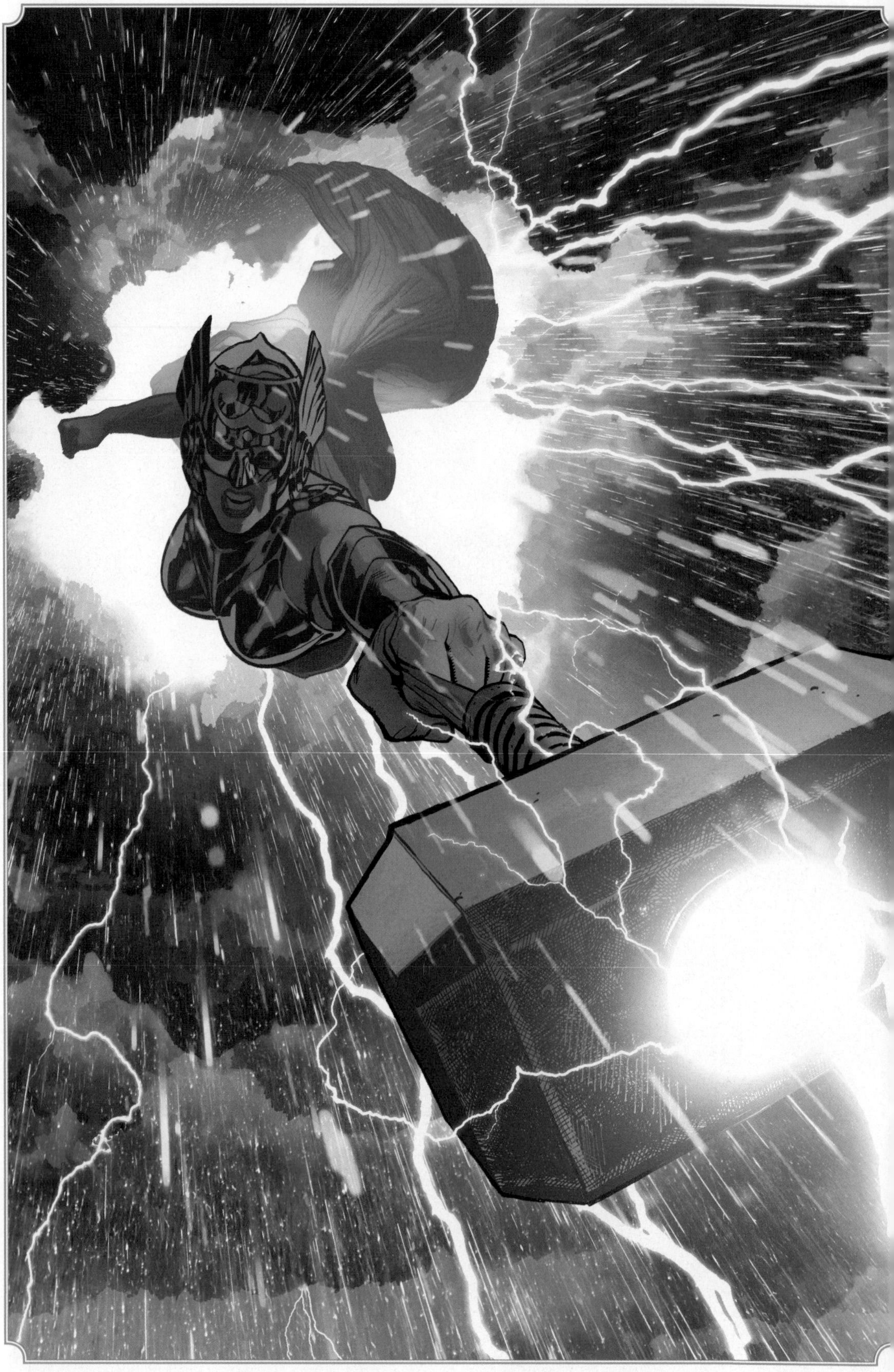

MIGHTY THOR # 4 VARIANT
BY **ADAM HUGHES**

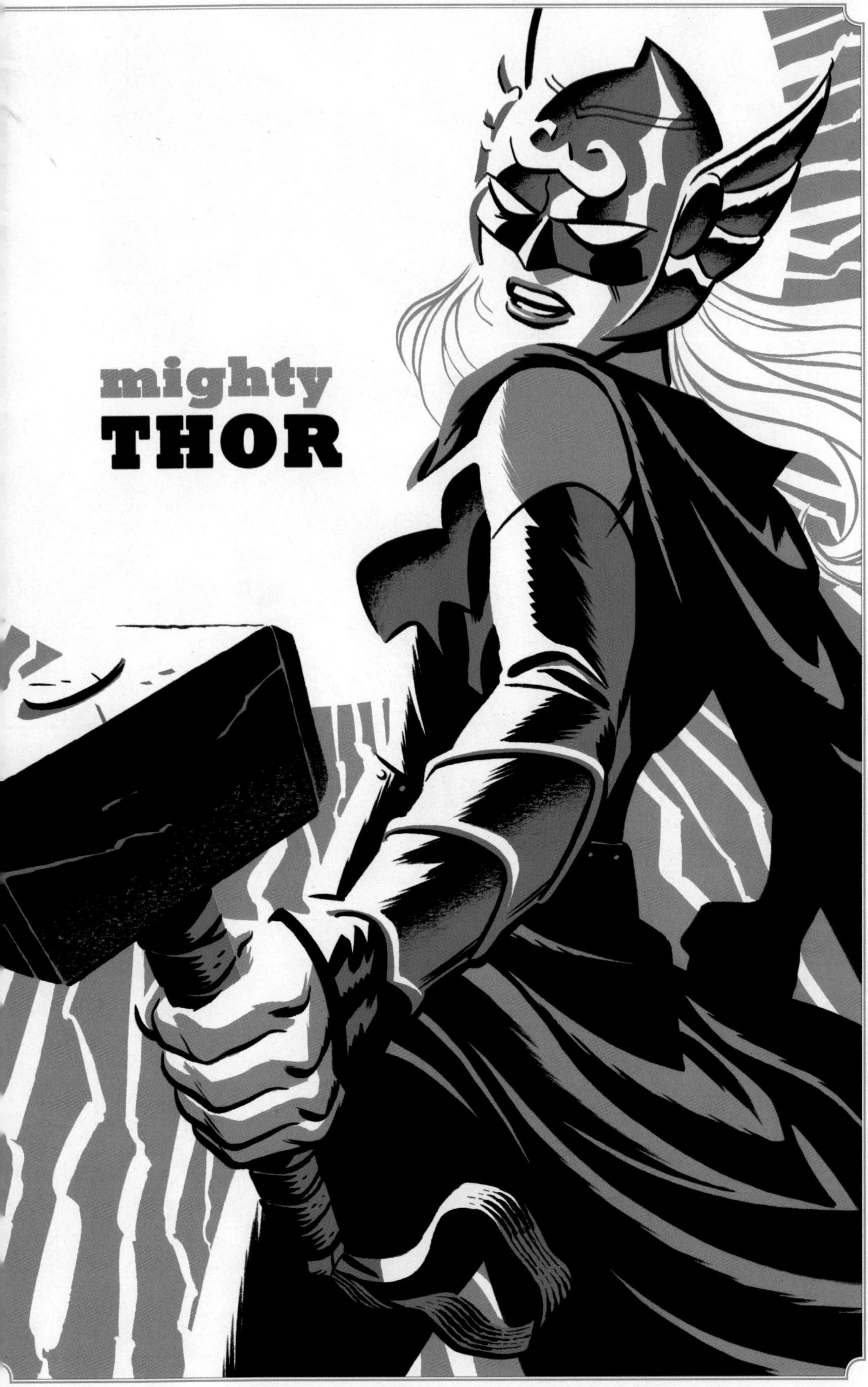
mighty
THOR

MIGHTY THOR # 4 VARIANT
BY **MICHAEL CHO**

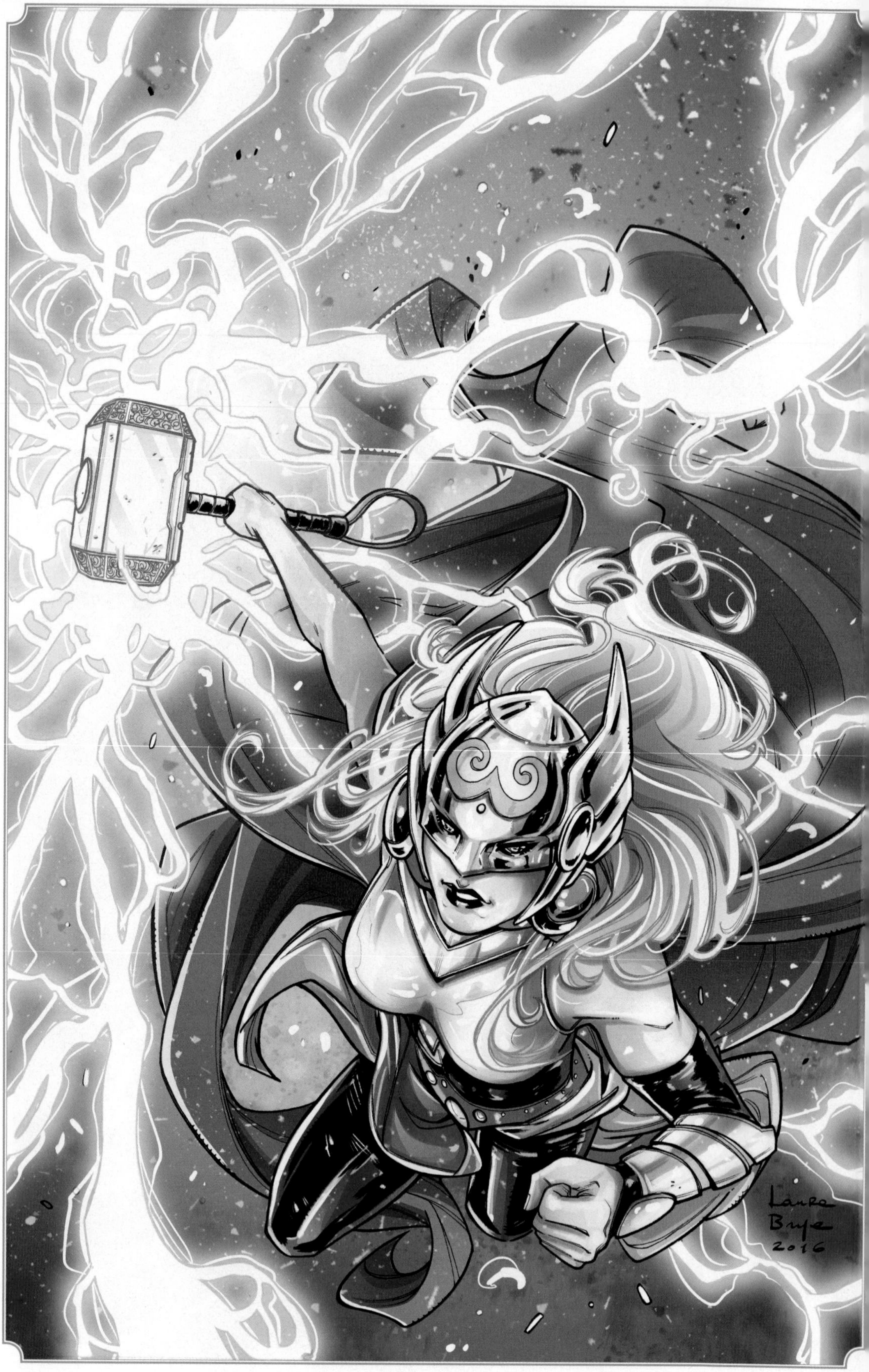

MIGHTY THOR # 5 WOMEN OF POWER VARIANT
BY **LAURA BRAGA**

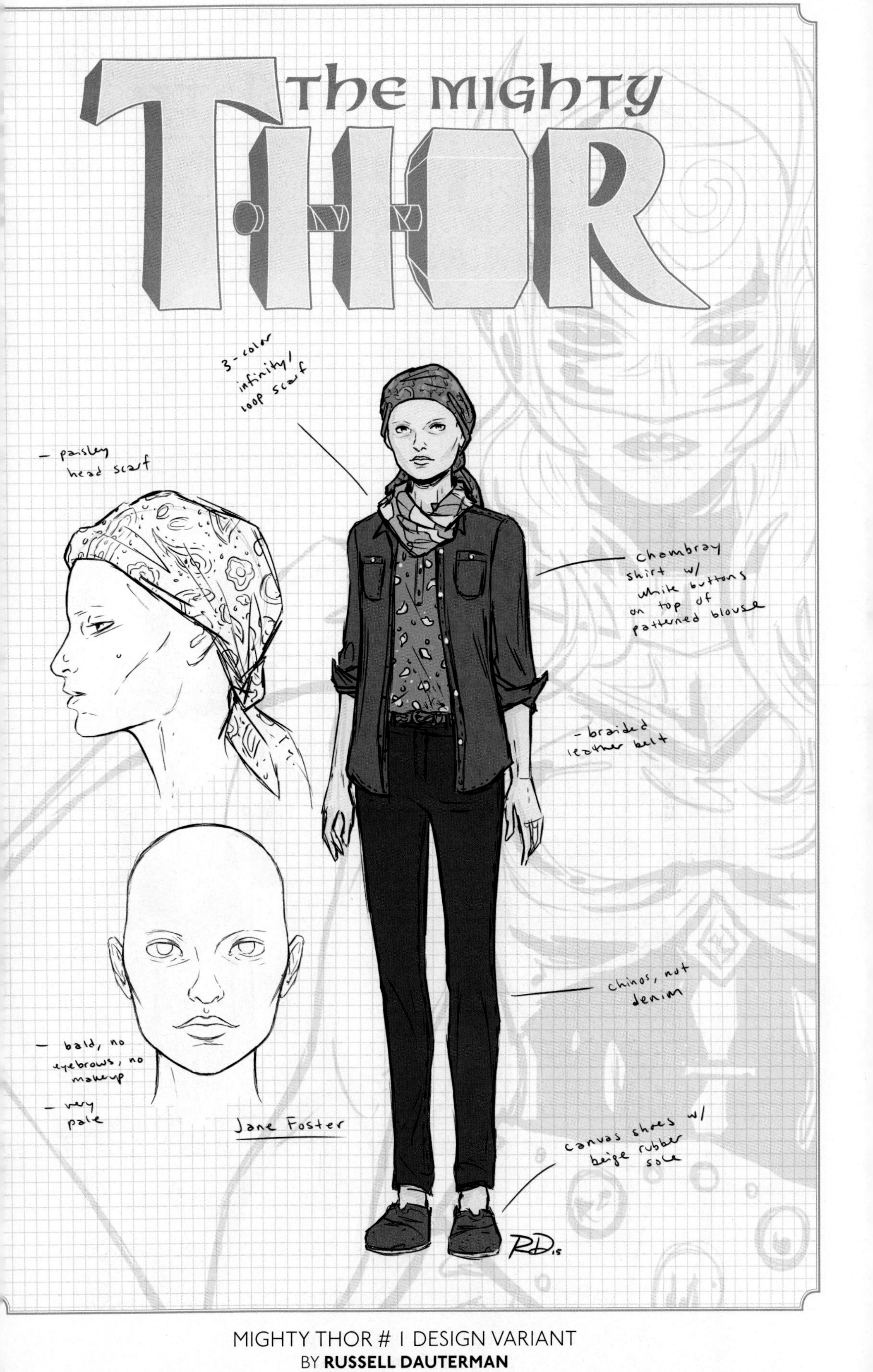
THE MIGHTY
THOR
3-color infinity/loop scarf
- paisley head scarf
chambray shirt w/ white buttons on top of patterned blouse
- braided leather belt
chinos, not denim
- bald, no eyebrows, no makeup
- very pale
Jane Foster
canvas shoes w/ beige rubber sole

MIGHTY THOR # 1 DESIGN VARIANT
BY **RUSSELL DAUTERMAN**

MIGHT THOR # 2 DESIGN VARIANT
BY **RUSSELL DAUTERMAN**

THE MIGHTY THOR

Hela

"cape" made of transparent smoke coming out from the underside of her shoulder spikes

- slight greenish tint to skin
- Purple lips

lots of curly hair

- line of makeup under eye

metal

strings

lime green magic

Karnilla

Queen of Cinders

- bronze body suit, mostly covered by flames
- spikey bits poke through fire

MIGHTY THOR # 3 DESIGN VARIANT
BY **RUSSELL DAUTERMAN**

FREE
DIGITAL COPY

TO REDEEM YOUR CODE FOR A FREE DIGITAL COPY:

1. GO TO MARVEL.COM/REDEEM. OFFER EXPIRES ON 5/18/18.

2. FOLLOW THE ON-SCREEN INSTRUCTIONS TO REDEEM YOUR DIGITAL COPY.

3. LAUNCH THE MARVEL COMICS APP TO READ YOUR COMIC NOW.

4. YOUR DIGITAL COPY WILL BE FOUND UNDER THE 'MY COMICS' TAB.

5. READ AND ENJOY.

YOUR FREE DIGITAL COPY WILL BE AVAILABLE ON:
MARVEL COMICS APP FOR APPLE IOS® DEVICES
MARVEL COMICS APP FOR ANDROID™ DEVICES

MARVEL
FREE DIGITAL
COPY OFFER

PEEL HERE TO REVEAL CODE ➡